All About
DERIVATIVES

FULLY REVISED SECOND EDITION

All About
DERIVATIVES

MICHAEL DURBIN

New York   Chicago   San Francisco   Athens   London   Madrid
Mexico City   Milan   New Delhi   Singapore   Sydney   Toronto

4 5 6 7 8 9 10 11 12 13 14 15 16   FGR/FGR   1 0 9 8 7 6 5 4

ISBN   978-0-07-174351-8
MHID   0-07-174351-0

e-ISBN   978-0-07-174352-5
e-MHID   0-07-174352-9

This publication is designed to provide accurate and authoritative information in regard to the subject matter covered. It is sold with the understanding that neither the author nor the publisher is engaged in rendering legal, accounting, securities trading, or other professional services. If legal advice or other expert assistance is required, the services of a competent professional person should be sought.
    —*From a Declaration of Principles Jointly Adopted by a Committee of the American Bar Association and a Committee of Publishers and Associations*

Library of Congress Cataloging-in-Publication Data

Durbin, Michael.
        All about derivatives / Michael Durbin—2nd ed.
            p.   cm.
        ISBN-13: 978-0-07-174351-8 (pbk : acid free paper)
        1. Derivative securities.   I. Title.

    HG6024.A3D87   2011
    332.64'57—dc22   2010029969

McGraw-Hill Education products are available at special quantity discounts to use as premiums and sales promotions or for use in corporate training programs. To contact a representative, please e-mail us at bulksales@mcgraw-hill.com.

This book is printed on acid-free paper.

To the splendor of Mom and the memory of Dad

CONTENTS

Chapter 11

Chapter 12

PREFACE

The public perception of financial derivatives has certainly changed since the publication of the first edition of *All About Derivatives*. More people are curious about them, asking questions about them, and wanting to know more than ever just what these seemingly bizarre financial instruments are all about.

Nearly everyone, it seems, knows that derivatives played a role in the 2008 global financial crisis—even if they can't begin to say *how*. What many people don't know is that the derivatives that got us into all that trouble were credit derivatives, a relatively new type of derivative bearing almost no resemblance to the traditional stock, interest rate, and currency derivatives that have been used extensively for many decades. And they were traded in the over-the-counter (OTC) market, a free-for-all venue that lacked—at the time—the trade standardization and clearing features of the listed or exchange markets where derivatives have historically traded. Traditional derivatives are price guarantees used to protect against (or wager on) future price changes. Credit derivatives guarantee not the price of something, but rather the ability of borrowers of money—say, holders of mortgages—to repay their loans. Those are very different things.

Alas, they are all considered "derivatives," and there's not much we can do about that. We can, however, make a modest effort to understand the distinction. An entirely new chapter, Chapter 12, "Derivatives and the 2008 Financial Meltdown," is devoted to explaining the role of the credit default swap (CDS) during that painful economic period. This chapter also explains the much-publicized collateralized debt obligation (CDO), which is technically not a derivative security but can be—and was—created synthetically using credit default swaps.

In addition, every bit of the first edition was reviewed to make sure it is still relevant to what's going on today with derivatives, and to clean up a few errors (some rather embarrassing) the author failed to catch the first time around. Any errors that might have slipped into this one will be noted at www.michaelpdurbin.com.

ACKNOWLEDGMENTS

I once had a college professor who would mark papers with *BGO!* wherever he caught a student wasting the reader's time on a "blinding glimpse of the obvious." He would certainly mark this page as such, because it is indeed obvious how indebted I am to the many readers who took the time to e-mail me with comments, suggestions, and errors after reading the first edition of *All About Derivatives*, or to post reader comments on various book sites such as Amazon. For this most valuable feedback, I especially thank Steve Alpher, Calvin Chan, David Cheung, Joe Cheung, Ms. Cooke, Sushrut Damle, M. Henry De Feraudy, Robert Gerovski, Fe Ike, Charles Kangai, Mike Kuzmiak, Jeremy McCurdy, Eric Paradis, B. Patel, Mike Pensinger, Mehul Rangwala, Santo Ricciardi, Shahid Shuja, Inkyu Son, S. Sweeney, John Williamson, David Wilusz, and Tao Zhou.

For ushering this second edition into existence, I must thank the forever resourceful, inventive, and persistent Morgan Ertel, my editor at McGraw-Hill. And for turning Zip files full of punctuationally dubious Word documents into a finished product that looks like an actual book, terabytes of thanks go to the fine McGraw-Hill production team, especially Julia Anderson Bauer, Marisa L'Heureux, and Susan Moore.

INTRODUCTION

If you are new to the world of financial derivatives, it might seem a vast and beastly place, fraught with disaster and maddening in complexity. And I must inform you now, before you turn even one page more, that it is, indeed, all of those nasty things. But don't run off just yet, for I can also tell you this: at the center of this world lies a stable and accessible core of ideas. Rest assured that there is a relatively undisputed foundation of facts and formulas upon which everything else is built around here, a body of knowledge that fits easily between the covers of a cheap paperback. Like this one.

This slender tome tries to explain the wily financial instruments known as derivatives. We've tried to make it the book anyone would want when first learning about any new subject—complete, readable, and all about fundamentals. So while it does not explain all the fancy stuff, it does explain the basic contracts—forwards, futures, swaps, and options—from which nearly every derivative is derived. It certainly doesn't explain every way one can use derivatives, but it does provide numerous examples in simple language illustrating how derivatives are used every day by scads of individuals and organizations around the globe. Also, this modest book doesn't waste ink on things like "technical trading" strategies (they're mostly bunk anyway) and other surefire miracles for making money, but it does explain things like what it means to be "long a put" or "short a call." And it explains a raft of terms like *volatility, arbitrage, forward rate,* and *delta.* And how to price the darn things. And where they are traded and by whom. And—well, that's about it.

Is this book for you? Do you want to learn the basics in a hurry without suffering too much math? Then it's for you. Of course there is math, but we've done our best to tuck it away so that you needn't bother with it if you don't want to. Students will certainly want to know all this stuff, math and all. But our book can be handy too if you don't really work with derivatives but occasionally need to understand them. We're thinking about accountants, lawyers, nonfinancial managers, human resource professionals, software developers, government workers, bus drivers (you never know), and folks like that. And if you do work with derivatives but come across some tidbit in your work you don't recognize, and would prefer not to reveal your ignorance by asking, then just flip to one of these pages, and nobody will know.

Is this book for the individual investor? Sure it is. Just don't make any investment based on what you read in this book. Ever. Want to get some idea of how derivatives fit into the larger world of investments? Then read and learn. Want ideas for where to invest your money? Go somewhere else, dear reader, anywhere but here. While the principles in here apply to your world in concept, they don't always apply in practice. Bottom line, what's between the covers of this modest book is not investment advice, so please do us all a favor and don't get any ideas.

Back to the math: Is a lot of it required in learning about derivatives? Only if you need to delve into the details of how they are valued. You can understand more than you might think about derivatives with no more math than what you learned in high school. We'll barely talk about math until the second half of the book, and then we'll explain all the math before we use it or direct you to an appendix. To absorb the content herein, all you really need is a healthy curiosity and modicum of patience.

It's easier than you might think to get what derivatives are all about. And once you do, you'll be well equipped to venture further into this vast and beastly world—or to decide not to.

CHAPTER 1

Derivatives in a Nutshell

When you first learned about trees as a child, someone no doubt pointed to one and said "Tree!" and not "Norway Maple!" and certainly not *"Acer platanoides!"* Only later did you learn there are many types of trees, alike in some ways and different in others. This method of learning employs the concept of abstraction, and our brains are indeed wired for it. We can learn about derivatives the same way. What then is a derivative in the abstract? A derivative is a price guarantee.

Nearly every derivative out there is just an agreement between a future buyer and future seller, or *counterparties*. Every derivative specifies a future price at which some item can or must be sold. This item, known as the *underlier*, might be some physical commodity, such as corn or natural gas, or some financial security, such as stock or a government bond, or something more abstract, such as a price index (we'll explain those in just a bit). Every derivative also specifies a future date on or before which the transaction must occur. These are the common elements of all derivatives: buyer and seller, underlier, future price, and future date.

Just as a shrub is much like a tree but not exactly like a tree, some derivatives guarantee something other than a price. Chief among these are credit derivatives, which are performance guarantees, not price guarantees (we'll cover them in Chapter 6, "Credit Derivatives"). Another variation is weather derivatives, which guarantee weather conditions like temperature or rainfall. Still, the vast, vast majority of derivatives are price guarantees, so it's plenty safe to think of them that way for now.

FOUR BASIC DERIVATIVES

As do trees, derivatives come in various shapes and sizes (but not nearly as many). Some derivatives are so simple they are known as "vanillas" and are employed nowadays with no more fanfare than when a plumber uses a wrench. Other derivatives are known as "exotics" and are so complex that the counterparties themselves may not truly understand them (which can lead to quite a bit of trouble).

But no matter how exotic, all derivatives are variations or combinations of just four basic types:

1. A *forward* is a contract wherein a buyer agrees to purchase the underlier from the seller at a specified price on a specified future date.
2. A *futures* is a standardized forward contract executed at an exchange, a forum that brings buyers and sellers together and guarantees that both parties will fulfill their obligations.
3. A *swap* is an agreement to exchange future cash flows. Typically, one cash flow is based on a variable or floating price, and the other on a fixed one.
4. An *option* grants its holder the right, but not the obligation, to buy or sell something at a specified price, on or before a specified future date. Most are executed at an exchange.

The chapters that follow delve into the fundamental characteristics of, and differences among, these four related contracts. We'll see, for example, that a forward contract is like a highly customizable futures contract. And a swap is essentially a bundle of related forwards. Forwards, futures, and swaps commit their parties to a future transaction, whereas the option conveys no such commitment to its buyer. The option, however, is the only one of the four with any inherent value upon inception. And because they are exchange-traded, futures and options tend to be more liquid (more of them are traded on a given day) and fungible (one is as good as another) than are forwards and swaps.

Despite such differences, forwards, futures, swaps, and options are all just variations of a price guarantee. And they are the pulleys and pistons with which virtually all derivative contraptions are built.

WHY ARE THEY CALLED DERIVATIVES?

A derivative is often defined as a financial instrument whose value derives from that of something else. It's a fair definition but slim. Let's dissect and expand it a bit to see what this "deriving" is all about. Oh, and remember the derivatives you learned about in calculus (if you ever took calculus)? Homonyms. These ain't them.

A *financial instrument* is just a standard type of agreement, or contract if you will, that bestows certain financial rights and/or responsibilities to its parties. For example, a mortgage is a type of financial instrument whereby in return for making monthly payments (your responsibility), you get to keep your house (your right). Stock is a common instrument that grants a right to some portion of a company's equity, or worth. Currency notes are instruments (Japanese yen, U.S. dollars, etc.) that grant a right to purchase. Term life insurance is another common instrument that pays out some cash should you expire before it does. And so on.

Quite importantly, instances of financial instruments have *value*. Shares of Microsoft may be selling or "trading" on the New York Stock Exchange for $30.82 each, whereas shares of IBM may go for $130.68. Those are their values or, loosely speaking, their *prices*. One British pound may trade for $1.55, and a 10-year U.S. Treasury note may trade for $979.69.

None of these qualify as derivatives, because their values do not depend directly on that of another instrument or commodity. Stock prices are determined by earnings expectations, supply and demand, and who knows what. Currency prices are determined by interest rates, confidence in the issuer's economic health, and so on.

Derivative financial instruments also have value. But unlike the values of nonderivative instruments, their values are tightly linked to the current market price of their underlier. Consider a tortilla maker that six months ago contracted with a farmer to buy 1,000 bushels of corn today for $25 per bushel (an example of a forward contract, by the way). Say the market price of a bushel of corn—known as its *spot price* (the price you can buy it for, "right here on the spot," for immediate delivery)—is now $28. What is the value of the tortilla maker's contract today? For each bushel of corn, the tortilla maker pays $3 less than it would have to pay on the spot market, so the contract must be worth 1,000 times $3, or $3,000. Were the spot price of corn not $28 but $30, the contract would be worth $5,000, using the same math. As you can see, the value of this contract depends quite a lot on the spot price of corn. Other factors affect the valuation of a forward contract, but the value of this or any derivative is principally derived (hence the name *derivative*) from the spot price of its underlier.

Intuitively, we might think of "value" as something positive. But with derivatives (and many nonderivative instruments), a value can just as easily be negative. It all depends on one's perspective. In the previous example, we examined the forward contract's value to the tortilla maker. What is that same contract's value to the farmer? With a spot price of $28 and contract price of $25, the farmer must sell those bushels to the tortilla maker for $3 per bushel less than the farmer could get in the spot market. So to the farmer, the contract must be worth 1,000 times –$3, or –$3,000. Whether a derivative's value is negative or positive depends chiefly on which side of the deal you are on. In this sense, many types of derivative are known as *zero-sum games*, because for every winner with a gain, there is a corresponding loser with an offsetting loss.

HOW DERIVATIVES ARE USED

You might think there are a zillion different reasons for using derivatives, but it turns out they are mostly used for just one of two basic functions: *hedging* and *speculation*. Hedgers use derivatives to manage uncertainty, and speculators use derivatives to wager on it.

Hedgers use derivatives to reduce financial risk, or the prospect that prices might "move against them." Consider our tortilla manufacturer, who knew six months ago that it would need to buy corn today. The company faced the prospect of corn prices rising excessively in the meantime and used a forward contract to mitigate that risk. It might also have used a futures contract or even an option. The key observation here is that financial risk occurs naturally, and derivatives can be applied to reduce, or hedge, that risk. Chapter 7, "Using Derivatives to Manage Risk," is all about hedging.

Speculators use derivatives not to reduce financial risk but to potentially profit from it. Doing so is known euphemistically as "taking a view" of future prices, because "taking a view" sounds more legitimate than "gambling." But speculating really is little more than gambling on an uncertain outcome. If one has a view that IBM's stock price will be higher in six months than it is today, one can buy options to buy IBM stock in six months at today's price.[1] If the prediction comes true, the buyer can profit handsomely. If not, he or she loses the amount paid for the option—100 percent of the investment. That's speculating.

It's worth noting that hedgers can hedge and speculators can speculate without derivatives. Many hedges and views can be executed by trading just the underlier. Then why use derivatives? Because derivatives use a powerful financial force known as *leverage*. Technically, leverage refers to doing something with borrowed money. And just as a nutcracker exploits leverage in the physical world, focusing mechanical energy so even a child can crack the hard shell of a nut, derivatives focus "financial energy" so hedgers and speculators can get more work done with less of an investment than would otherwise be required.

Consider our IBM speculator. Instead of buying options, this person could have simply bought up a bunch of stock and held it for six months, making the same basic "upside" when (and if) his prediction came true. By using options, the speculator makes the same basic play but lays out much less cash up front, as stock options are much less costly than the stock itself. But leverage does not come for free; to the speculator, its price is increased downside risk. When the IBM speculator using options was wrong, he lost 100 percent of the investment. Had the speculator purchased stock instead, he would have lost only some fraction of the investment—and would still have that stock, which could yet appreciate in the future.

Two other users of derivatives are *market makers* and *arbitrageurs*. Market makers are the merchants of derivatives. Not unlike fishmongers and fish, they buy derivative securities at one price and sell at a higher price, pocketing the difference as their profit. They might also eat one now and again (not always by choice), but mostly they act as sellers to want-to-be buyers and as buyers to want-to-be sellers, and they like to do so by taking on as little risk as possible. (We'll see how in Chapter 11, "Hedging a Derivatives Position.")

Arbitrageurs also avoid taking risks. They search for mispriced securities and attempt to profit from them—taking on no risk whatsoever if they do it right. If an arbitrageur sees the exact same option trading in one market for $5.00 and in another for $5.10, and can

---

[1] Such a speculator is known to be "bullish" on IBM. A "bearish" view is one that the stock will decline.

simultaneously buy at $5.00 and sell at $5.10, the arbitrageur makes a dime with virtually no risk. While arbitraging is harder and harder to do as markets become more efficient, the very fact they exist is a powerful driver of how all derivatives are valued. We'll see how later on. There are others with an interest in derivatives—regulators, accountants, systems developers, etc.—but hedgers, speculators, market makers, and arbitrageurs account for most of them.

And where do investors fit into the world of derivatives? Most investors—certainly most small investors—do not trade derivatives. These instruments simply aren't necessary to achieve their investment objectives. Some investors do use derivatives, however, as hedgers or speculators. Later on we'll learn about *protective puts* an investor can apply to stock positions to reduce the risk of loss in the event of a market downturn. And as we saw already in this chapter, the IBM investor used options to speculate on the future price of IBM stock.

DERIVATIVE MARKETS

Where do derivatives live? They live in the *markets* where they are traded. "Trading a derivative" just refers to a buyer and seller coming together and committing themselves to one of these price guarantees. A *trade*, then, is one of these transactions. These parties to a trade are known formally as *counterparties*. And just as there are markets for buying and selling nonderivative instruments such as stock (think New York Stock Exchange) and mortgages (think your bank), there are well-established markets for trading derivatives. And as with nonderivatives, there are two basic types of derivative markets: over-the-counter markets and exchange markets.

The *over-the-counter* (*OTC*) market is where two parties find each other and then work directly with each other—and nobody else—to formulate, execute, and enforce a derivative transaction. If I am an oil driller and you are a refinery, we might execute a forward contract for the sale of x barrels of crude oil at a price of y to be delivered z days from today. We can set x, y, and z however we like, as this is a completely private affair. This ability to tailor a contract to the exact needs of the counterparties is among the chief benefits of OTC derivatives. Forward contracts are by definition OTC instruments, and most swaps are traded OTC as well.

The *exchange* market (sometimes known as the *listed* market) is where a prospective buyer and seller can do a deal and not worry about finding each other. The exchange provides *market makers*, who act as sellers for those who wish to buy and buyers for those who wish to sell. It provides this feature, known as *liquidity*, by establishing and enforcing strict definitions for derivatives tradable on the exchange. So a buyer or seller gives up the ability to customize a deal, but in return, neither of them has to worry about finding a counterparty. Futures contracts are by definition exchange-traded instruments, and most options (not all) are traded on an exchange as well.

Another crucial distinction between OTC and exchange markets relates to guarantee of performance. With an OTC trade, the two parties have no fundamental assurance that the other side will hold up its end of the deal. When it comes time to execute a transaction, the seller may decide not to sell, or the buyer may decide not to buy. With an exchange trade, the exchange itself (actually a clearing organization associated with the exchange) guarantees that all counterparties will fulfill their responsibilities. It provides this assurance with margin accounts and daily marking to market, two mechanisms we will examine later on.

Beyond the exchange and OTC markets, there are also derivatives "markets" where the "traders" don't even know they are trading derivatives. Consider the typical mortgage that allows the borrower to pay off the balance early without penalty. The borrower has essentially executed an *embedded option* giving him or her the right, but not the obligation, to terminate the agreement. Another example is the *convertible bond* issued by many corporations, which gives bondholders an option to convert their position into company stock. (Arbitrageurs have a field day when the implied price of these embedded options diverges from the price of actual options.) We won't delve into these "stealth" markets in this book, but rest assured that the fundamentals of derivatives apply to those markets just as they do to the traditional exchange and OTC markets.

PRICING DERIVATIVES

A considerable amount of fuss and bother is spent on calculating the price, or value, of a derivative. Don't worry too much about the distinction between price and value. For most purposes, you can think of them as interchangeable terms for answering the question "What is one of these darn things worth?" Technically, *price* refers to an amount of money someone pays or receives, or is willing to pay or receive, in a transaction. A price typically includes some margin of profit or "edge" for one party or the other. *Value* is a price at which neither party would make any profit; for this reason, it is known more formally as a *fair market value* or sometimes *theoretical value*. Despite the technical difference, when people say "pricing," they are usually referring to calculating a value. Go figure! It's just one of those things to get used to around here, and we'll go with the crowd and generally use the term *pricing* in this book to refer to valuation.

It's worth knowing, by the way, that derivative prices are often expressed in the form of a *quote*. A quote is just a price at which someone is willing to buy or sell. A price at which one will buy is a *bid*. A price at which one will sell is an *ask* or *offer*. You'll often hear of a *bid-ask spread* for a given contract; that's just the difference between the bid and the ask. (A *quote with size* includes not just a bid or offer price, but also the number of contracts the quoter is willing to buy or sell at that price.) So at any moment during a trading day, when markets are behaving normally, a contract might have three basic monetary amounts associated with it: a bid price, a value greater than the bid price, and an offer price greater than value. These are illustrated in Figure 1-1.

Are bid prices always less than value? Are offers always greater? Theoretically, they should be, but in reality, they sometimes are not. Because derivative markets are so fast, vast, and complex, it does indeed happen that someone will bid above value or offer below it. But not for long. There's no shortage of arbitrageurs ready to "pick off" such bargains just as fast as they appear.

FIGURE 1-1

Typical Quote with Size

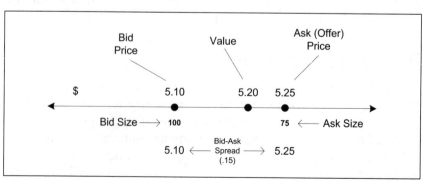

DERIVATIVE MATHEMATICS

You might have the notion that pricing a derivative requires a Nobel Prize in your back pocket, or at least an advanced degree in math. And it is indeed true that Wall Street hires a remarkable number of people with impressive sheepskins as *quantitative analysts* (or *quants*, as they are kindly known).[2] But fear not, many derivatives can be priced with little more than moderately advanced arithmetic.

Pricing a forward, futures, or swap is mathematically rather simple. The main task is the adjustment of values for time (between when the contract is executed and when the sale will occur) by calculating present values and future values. The formulas for present valuation and future valuation are rather intuitive, and we'll explain them fully before we actually use them. For understanding the math behind swap pricing, it helps to also understand the distinction between a *spot rate* and a *forward rate* and what a *yield curve* is all about. We'll explain all of that in the Appendix A, "All About Interest." The hard part in forward, futures, and swap pricing is not the math itself, but more practical challenges, such as which interest rate to use or which price to plug in for the underlier.

Understanding the intuition behind option valuation is easier than you might think. The basic idea is to construct an imaginary portfolio of non-option instruments (whose prices are comparatively easy to obtain) such that the portfolio payoff mimics or replicates that of the option. The price of such a portfolio gives you the price of the option, due to the so-called law of one price, which says two things with the same payoff must cost the same to prevent arbitrage. The one-step binomial tree, which you will find at the top of Chapter 10, "Pricing Options," illustrates this idea using very little math.

Understanding some of the mechanics behind option pricing can be challenging, as it involves nontrivial statistics and calculus. Actually pricing an option, thankfully, does not require much understanding of the math any more than operating a car requires you to understand the physics of internal combustion. For the mathematically curious, adventurous, or rusty, however, we will explain quite a lot of the math behind option pricing. It's pretty cool stuff.

---

[2] Interestingly enough, you'll often find more physicists than mathematicians at a typical derivatives shop. It turns out physicists have lots of practice with partial differential equations, which are used for option pricing.

The mathematically bashful can safely skip those sections of the book.

Another challenge when pricing derivatives is the sheer speed at which it must be performed. Some underlier spot prices change almost continuously. This means a derivative value calculated a moment ago can be dangerously obsolete. For example, when the price of an underlier changes, market makers often have only a few microseconds to recalculate the price of an option and respond accordingly.[3] If they don't, they can get picked off by the arbitrageurs and lose a pile of money. It's no wonder that firms in the derivatives business, especially market makers and arbitrageurs, spend vast sums of money on ever-faster computer systems for pricing and trading derivatives.

Mathematics comes into play not just in the pricing of derivatives but also in the area of financial risk management. This is especially true when hedging a derivatives position, when you need to know how the value of an existing derivatives position changes in response to changes in valuation factors—underlier price, time to expiration, interest rates, etc. If you recall anything from calculus, you'll remember that calculus is particularly suited for quantifying how values change, so you won't be surprised to learn there's a fair amount of calculus in this corner of the derivatives world.

COMMON UNDERLIERS

As noted before, a derivative's underlier is the thing that can or must be sold on or before some future date at a predetermined price. It is the thing bought and sold in a spot market whose value, which changes continuously and unpredictably, principally determines the value of a derivative. A simple underlier (we'll also talk about index and derivative underliers later on) can be a physical commodity such as a bushel of corn, or a financial security such as a share of stock. Now there are at least a zillion (perhaps two) types of things bought and sold in open markets, from rubber bands to skyscrapers. Which of these make good underliers to derivatives?

Theoretically, any traded item can be an underlier to a derivative. But things that become good derivative underliers tend to

---

[3] A microsecond is one-millionth of a second. In the land of derivatives, an entire second is a near eternity.

be both fungible and liquid. *Fungible* just means one is as good as another, as with barrels of oil and dollar bills, and *liquid* in this sense means there are large numbers of active buyers and sellers at any given time. It turns out that a couple hundred or so types of things on this planet meet these criteria. The vast majority of these fall into one of four categories: commodities, currency, money, and equities.

Commodities are physical goods, grown or manufactured and processed and shipped. They include grains such as corn and wheat, meats such as live hogs and pork bellies (dead hogs), and other foods such as coffee and sugar. Commodities also include metals such as gold and copper, and energy goods such as crude oil and natural gas. Commodities tend to be wholesale goods intended for manufacturers and service providers, rather than for consumers like you and me. Most commodity derivatives are exchange-traded at places like the Chicago Board of Trade and the New York Mercantile Exchange (NYMEX).

Currency meets the criteria for a good underlier. The currency market, also known as the *foreign-exchange* (*FX*) market, is in fact the world's largest spot market of any kind. On any given day, more than a trillion units of currency are bought and sold, with the price of each note changing almost continuously. Currency is a popular underlier for all sorts of derivatives, both OTC and exchange-traded.

Money is bought and sold (or "rented," if you will) when it is borrowed or lent in the form of loans, or bonds. When a government or corporation issues a bond, it is simply borrowing money. The price of money to an issuer is, of course, interest, which it pays to the bondholders (lenders) according to the terms of the bond. The market for this is known anachronistically as the *fixed-income* market from the days when all bonds paid a fixed rate of interest to their holders. There is a massive market for interest rate derivatives, the most common being interest rate swaps in the OTC market and a variety of futures in the exchange world.

An extremely popular derivative underlier is corporate *equity*, or stock. A share of stock represents a sliver of ownership in the company that issues it, and the stock market is, of course, a massive one. Options on stock trade heavily in both the OTC and exchange markets, at places like the International Securities Exchange and Chicago Board Options Exchange, and equity futures trade on numerous exchanges around the globe.

INDEXES AND CASH SETTLEMENT

Many derivatives have as their underlier not some simple item such as a share of stock or type of oil, but rather an *index*, or average price, of a broad group of related items. One of the best-known indexes of all is the Dow Jones Industrial Average in the United States. The "Dow" is a weighted average of 30 individual stock prices. It may not seem like an average stock price, being in the thousands of dollars when most stocks trade for under a hundred. It's so large because it is adjusted to account for corporate actions such as stock splits, where one share of stock is divided into two or more shares. Despite the mathematical legerdemain, the Dow is just an average stock price.

Now, you generally can't buy or sell on a spot market the "average" stock represented by an equity index. That's just a numerical abstraction. You can only buy or sell actual stock, whose price is probably not exactly the average.[4] And if a derivative is just a price guarantee for some future transaction, this begs an interesting question: How on earth can you have, say, a futures contract on something you cannot actually buy or sell spot? How can you commit to buy something tomorrow you can't buy today? We deal with this conundrum using *cash settlement*. This just means that when the time comes for the underlier to be sold (or even before), the parties don't actually buy and sell the underlier. Instead, they figure out the cash value of the derivative position and exchange the cash. Say, as a result of a forward agreement, I am obligated today to buy from you something for $3 that is currently selling for $2 on the spot market. If I were to actually buy that thing from you, you are $1 ahead (because you bought it for $2 and sold it to me for $3). I can settle that obligation by simply giving you $1. Cash settlement, by the way, can be employed for just about any derivative, and it must be employed for index derivatives.

And that's about enough for the nutshell.

---

[4] In some markets, you can trade a "tracking stock" or exchange-traded fund (ETF) such as "spiders" (SPDR) and "the Qs" (QQQQ). These pseudo-equities look like stock but take their value from an index. You can also trade options on ETFs.

CHAPTER 2

The Forward Contract

A forward contract is an agreement to buy something on a future date at a specified price. If you've ever purchased a car and agreed to buy it before the date you actually took delivery, you've already been "long a forward contract."

Here's another quick example involving a future purchase of foreign currency: The U.S.-based Gizmo Company agrees to purchase 100,000 circuit boards from a South Korean manufacturer in one year, at a per-unit price of 24 won (the currency of South Korea, abbreviated KRW). At the time, the won-dollar exchange rate is 1,200 KRW/USD, meaning $1 will buy 1,200 won (U.S. dollars are abbreviated USD). The total delivery price of 2,400,000 won, then, will be $2,000 at the current exchange rate. Should the won-dollar exchange rate decrease over the next year, the dollar price of the purchase will increase.

To fix the future price of the circuit boards in U.S. dollars, Gizmo executes a forward contract with a bank to purchase 2,400,000 won for $2,000 in one year's time. After one year, the dollar-won exchange rate decreases to 1,000 KRW/USD. Thus, 2,400,000 won would cost $2,400 on the spot market. Gizmo, however, executes its forward contract and spends only $2,000 for 2,400,000 won, which the company uses to pay for the circuit boards.

A SALES AGREEMENT IN ADVANCE

The forward contract is the simplest of all derivatives. This OTC derivative obligates one party to buy the underlying commodity or

13

security and the other party to sell it, for a set price on some certain date in the future. The party with an obligation to buy is known as the *long party*, as that party holds the *long position*. The party with an obligation to sell is the *short party*, as that party holds the *short position*. The guaranteed price is the *delivery price* or *contract price*, and the date on which the sale will transpire is the *delivery date*.

The key benefit of a forward is the mitigation of uncertainty; both buyer and seller lock in a price that does not change. On the flip side of this benefit, in nearly every case, is a virtual guarantee of loss by one party or the other come delivery. Unless the spot price equals the contract price, either the long party will pay more than spot, or the short party will receive less than spot. Consider again the forward purchase of a car. Say the day after you sign your purchase agreement, some celebrity talks up the car on his or her TV show, and it becomes wildly popular, driving up the price consumers are willing to pay. You still pay the contract price. Not only did you "trade a derivative," but you also pulled off a very effective hedge (much to the chagrin of the dealer, by the way, who is stuck selling at the contract price). More on hedging later.

We tackle forwards first because they provide a nice starting point for learning derivatives. Other derivatives behave much the way forwards do with some variations. A futures is just a forward traded on an exchange, and a swap is just a portfolio of forwards. Even an option is very much like a forward in some cases, when it is "deep in the money," a concept we'll get to later on. Because forwards provide a nice baseline for so many derivatives, in this chapter we'll spend a bit of extra time on concepts we'll return to again and again.

COMMON FORWARDS

Among the most common forwards are those on currency. Foreign-exchange forwards, or *FX forwards*, mitigate uncertainty around exchange rates. As we saw in the Gizmo example, a *foreign-exchange rate* gives the price of one unit of some currency (for example, U.S. dollars) in units of another (South Korean won). So an exchange rate is really just a price. Corporations regularly commit to advance sales or purchases in a currency different from their own, and FX forwards let them lock in the prices of those purchases in their own currency.

Forwards are also common in the energy commodity markets, where drillers, refineries, industrial consumers, and other participants often commit to large sales and purchases months or years in advance for commodities like oil and natural gas. The spot price of these commodities can fluctuate wildly over the course of time, so commodity forwards allow buyers and sellers to plan transactions at a guaranteed price.

Another common underlier is money itself. Borrowing money costs money, and interest rates change all the time. If a firm knows it will need to borrow money in the future, it can lock in the interest rate with a *forward rate agreement* (*FRA*, pronounced so it rhymes with "ahh"). Here the underlier is some fixed amount of money (say, $1 million), the delivery price is an interest rate (say, 3.5 percent), and the delivery date is some time in the future (say, six months). Using an FRA, the firm can be certain of its ability to borrow a million bucks in six months at 3.5 percent, no matter what the prevailing interest rate turns out to be. We'll get back to FRAs when we turn to swaps, which—as noted already in this chapter—are just like portfolios of FRAs.

FORWARDS AND OBLIGATION

A distinguishing characteristic of the forward is its bestowal of obligation. No matter what the spot price of the underlier come delivery date, the long party must buy, and the short party must sell—even if it hurts. If you are long at $30 and the market price on the delivery date is $25, you must buy at $30. Because you have to buy something for $5 more than it's worth, you lose $5. Conversely, if the market price on the delivery date is $35, then the short party is the loser.

The losing party in a forward deal can also default. Should the spot market move against the long party, he or she might simply refuse to buy. Likewise, a short party might refuse to sell. This possibility of default—an example of *credit risk*—is another distinguishing characteristic of a forward as an OTC instrument. In practice, forward counterparties can post collateral with each other in the form of cash or marketable securities, which the gaining party can keep, should the losing party walk away. (If you want to avoid the default risk inherent to a forward, you may be able to use a futures contract instead, but you will have to give up some flexibility and choose from a standard set of predefined contracts. Or you can use an option, but you'll need to pay a premium up front whether you exercise or not. More on these later.)

PAYOFF

A handy device for understanding any derivative is its *payoff* as illustrated by a *payoff diagram*. And what is payoff? It's essentially the value of the contract on its delivery date. And we know already that payoff (value) can be either negative or positive, depending on whether one is long or short. Recall how we valued the tortilla maker's forward contract on the date of delivery in Chapter 1 by taking the difference between the delivery price and spot price. That's just what a payoff diagram illustrates, only it does so for a whole range of spot prices all at once.

The payoff diagram is a visual representation of the not-so-visual *payoff function*. In mathematics, a function is just a formula into which you plug inputs to get some output. There are two payoff functions for any derivative, one for the long party and one for the short party. Remember why? One party's gain is equal and opposite to the other's pain. Here are the payoff functions for a forward:

$$P_{Fwd,Long} = S - K \qquad \text{(Formula 2.1)}$$

$$P_{Fwd,Short} = K - S \qquad \text{(Formula 2.2)}$$

Formulas 2.1 and 2.2 say the payoff for the long party ($P_{Fwd,Long}$) is spot (S) minus delivery price (K), and the payoff for the short party ($P_{Fwd,Short}$) is delivery price (K) minus spot (S).

To get a feel for these relationships, imagine a forward contract on gold with a delivery price of $400 per ounce. Now consider five possible spot prices come delivery date: $600, $500, $400, $300, and $200. If we plug these into the payoff function (for the long party), we get the results listed in Table 2-1.

The payoff table clearly illustrates why some payoffs are positive and some are negative. The long party is, of course, obligated to buy at the delivery price, K. If, on the delivery date, the spot price (S) is greater than the delivery price, the long party will buy something for less than market price and therefore make a gain, or positive payoff. If spot is below delivery price, the long party will buy something for more than market price and therefore have a

TABLE 2-1

Long Forward Payoff

S	K	$P_{Fwd,Long} = S - K$
600	400	200
500	400	100
400	400	0
300	400	−100
200	400	−200

loss, or negative payoff. So the long party's payoff is just spot minus delivery price in all cases.

Notice that for any value of S, there is only one possible value for P. This makes drawing a payoff diagram quite easy. The format for a payoff diagram is shown in Figure 2-1.

The vertical axis represents possible payoffs. (For our gold forward example, think of the numbers on both axes as multiples of $100.) Note that the payoff stretches endlessly up and down, with positive payoffs (gains) represented above 0, and negative payoffs (losses) represented below.

The horizontal axis represents all possible spot prices on delivery date. It stretches endlessly in a positive direction only, as under-

FIGURE 2-1

Payoff Diagram Format

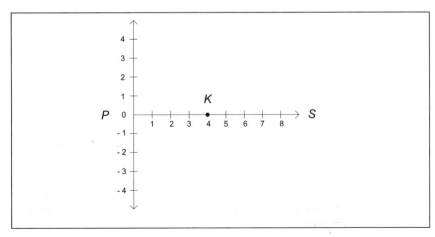

lier prices can go no lower than zero. (Remember, we're talking here about spot prices being lower-bounded by zero, not derivative payoffs or values, which can be either positive or negative.)

To illustrate the long party's payoff for our gold forward, we simply plot the payoffs from the payoff table at the various intersections of S and P. (Remember, K is just a fixed point on the horizontal axis—that is, one possible spot price.) Choose any S value, and use the payoff table or payoff function to determine the corresponding P value. If P is positive, place a point P units above the line at point S. If negative, place it P units below the line at point S. Now do this for a few more values of S to get something like Figure 2-2. Then connect the points, and you are done, as we see in Figure 2-3.

Notice that payoff is a straight line, so you really need only two points to make a complete payoff line. And now notice that the payoff line is at 45 degrees to the x-axis. This is true of all forward payoffs expressed on a payoff diagram, which means you need only one point and a line drawn at 45 degrees through that point to plot the payoff line.[1] And one point is always just K, so you really don't

FIGURE 2-2

Sample Payoff Points

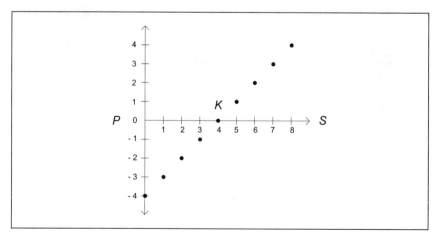

---

[1] This is just an application of the equation for a line, $y = mx + b$, which you might recall from algebra.

FIGURE 2-3

Long Forward Payoff Diagram

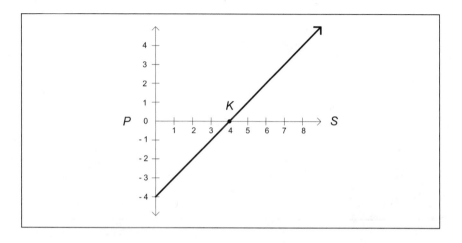

need to calculate any payoffs. Just draw a line intersecting the *x*-axis at *K* with an angle of 45 degrees.

What of the short party? We know already that this person's payoff is just the opposite of the long party's. Table 2-2 shows the payoff for both parties.

To draw the short party's payoff, you again choose values for *S*, plot payoff points, and connect the lines. Or, knowing that the short payoff is the opposite of the long payoff, you can just draw a second line intersecting the *x*-axis at point *K*, going 45 degrees in the other

TABLE 2-2

Long and Short Forward Payoff

S	*K*	$P_{Fwd,Long} = S - K$	$P_{Fwd,Short} = K - S$
600	400	200	−200
500	400	100	−100
400	400	0	0
300	400	−100	100
200	400	−200	200

FIGURE 2-4

Short Forward Payoff Diagram

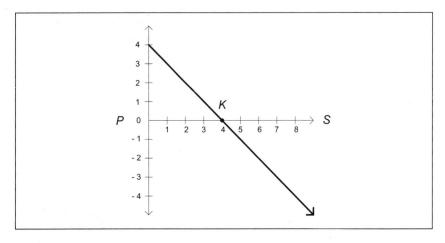

way. Either way, you will end up with a short party payoff diagram, as shown in Figure 2-4.

So payoffs illustrated on a payoff diagram are always straight lines, they always intersect the *x*-axis at *K* at 45 degrees, and the long payoff is always the opposite of the short payoff. What happens if we add these payoffs to determine the net payoff of a forward deal?

FIGURE 2-5

Net Forward Payoff Diagram

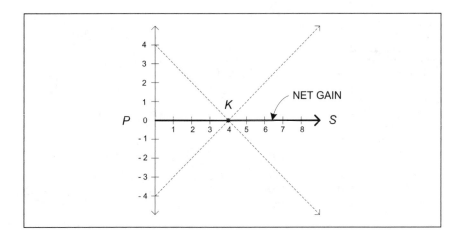

On a payoff diagram showing both long and short payoffs, this is trivial. Choose a few values for S, and find the vertical midpoint between the short and long payoff at S. Plot a few of those points, and then connect them with a line, as shown in Figure 2-5. The result, of course, is zero, because of the zero-sum game: one party's gains are perfectly offset by the other party's equal and opposite losses.

We'll see plenty more payoff diagrams in the chapters that follow. Although they aren't terribly intuitive at first blush, once you get a feel for these things, you'll find them quite handy.

CHAPTER 3

The Futures Contract

A *futures contract* is a highly standardized forward contract executed at an exchange. Here's a quick example: The Royal Mill buys wheat to make flour. Lots of it. Royal plans to buy 50,000 bushels of wheat in six months, and the company wants to lock in a price now. Royal executes 10 wheat futures contracts at the Minneapolis Grain Exchange with a delivery price of $3.00. Each contract guarantees the delivery of 5,000 bushels of wheat in six months for $3.00 per bushel. Royal can now expect to pay a net total price of $150,000 for its wheat. Six months later, the going price of wheat has risen by 50 cents to $3.50. The total value of Royal's futures position on 50,000 bushels, with an original delivery price of $3.00, has thus risen by $25,000. Royal buys 50,000 bushels from its regular supplier at $3.50, or $175,000 altogether. The net price of Royal's wheat purchase is $175,000 less the $25,000 futures gain, or $150,000 as desired.

AN EXCHANGE-TRADED FORWARD

A futures contract, often shortened to just "futures," is very much like a forward: A party agrees to either buy or sell an underlying commodity or security at a specified price on a specified date in the future. As with a forward, agreeing to buy is assuming a long position, and agreeing to sell is assuming a short position. The specified price in a futures contract is the *delivery price*. In later chapters, we'll see that a futures price is calculated in nearly the same way as a forward price. But unlike the over-the-counter (OTC) forward contract, a futures contract is traded on an *exchange*, a meeting place for buyers and sellers. As a result, a futures differs from a forward contract in three important ways:

1. **Anonymous counterparties:** Unlike parties to a forward, the buyer and seller of a futures contract typically don't know each other. The exchange generally takes care of matching up buyers and sellers, helping to provide an important market quality known as *liquidity*. (A liquid market is one where trading is more or less continuous, "flowing" like a liquid.) This can be a great advantage over the OTC forward, in which prospective counterparties must find each other.
2. **Standard contracts:** Exchanges also provide liquidity by strictly defining the terms of every contract executed. The type, quantity, and grade of underlier; its delivery price and date; and even the delivery location are spelled out in great detail. A prospective buyer or seller must choose from one of these predefined contracts. Parties to a forward, by contrast, are free to define the terms of their contract however they mutually agree to.
3. **Daily settlement:** This is the biggie. Whereas parties to a forward realize their payoff on delivery (or on some earlier date if they agree to cancel or unwind a contract), parties to a futures contract realize a payoff at the end of every trading day. This substantially reduces the risk of a party failing to meet its obligations—an inherent risk of an OTC contract like a forward. It also affects the value of a futures relative to an otherwise identical forward (more on this in just a bit).

The bottom line is that futures are generally more liquid than forwards and carry a smaller degree of default risk. Not all futures contracts are liquid, mind you, as exchanges from time to time offer contracts that just sit there, barely traded at all. But the more popular futures trade hundreds of thousands of contracts in a single day. (The term of art for number of contracts traded is *volume*.) And while an exchange guarantees the performance of contract counterparties (technically speaking, its clearing corporation usually provides the guarantee), it is possible that highly unusual market conditions could lead to widespread defaults on futures contract obligations—possible, but far less likely than forward contract default.

And here's an interesting fact about futures: 99 percent of all futures contracts are effectively canceled before any delivery actually occurs! Why? As we saw in the example at the beginning of this chapter, the real reason the Royal Mill contracted to purchase wheat on the exchange was not to secure the physical wheat, but to obtain protection against rising wheat prices—that is, to guarantee a price. Even though most commodities bought and sold on an exchange are never delivered, the fact they *can* be delivered—and *must* be delivered if the long party chooses—is one of the things that keep a futures price fair.

COMMON FUTURES

Hundreds of types of futures contracts are regularly traded on exchanges around the globe. Like forwards, futures have underliers that fall into two groups: *commodity underliers* are physical goods that can be (but need not be) physically delivered; *financial underliers* are securities such as a government bond or currency, or an index, as discussed in Chapter 1. When futures were invented more than 100 years ago (Did you imagine derivatives have been around so long?), all underliers were commodities. Financial futures did not come into prominence until about the 1970s, and today something like 80 percent of all futures are financials.

Futures contracts are traded on a dozen or so exchanges around the world. Each is not unlike a produce market where producers and consumers meet up to do business. Some contracts are traded exclusively on one exchange, and others are traded on multiple exchanges. Here are just a few:

- Chicago Mercantile Exchange (CME)
  Contract: E-Mini S&P 500 futures
  Underlier: Weighted average price of 500 stocks that make
      up the S&P 500 index
- New York Mercantile Exchange (NYMEX)
  Contract: Light, sweet crude oil futures
  Underlier: 1,000 barrels (42,000 U.S. gallons) of crude oil
      delivered at Cushing, Oklahoma
- Chicago Board of Trade (CBOT)
  Contract: 30-year U.S. Treasury bond futures
  Underlier: One 30-year U.S. Treasury bond with face value at
      maturity of $100,000

- Minneapolis Grain Exchange (MGEX)
  Contract: Hard red spring wheat futures
  Underlier: 5,000 bushels of No. 2 or better Northern Spring
           Wheat with at least 13.5 percent protein
- Hong Kong Exchange (HKEx)
  Contract: Hang Seng Index futures
  Underlier: Weighted average stock price of 33 stocks traded
           on the Stock Exchange of Hong Kong

As with any securities exchange, you don't just call a futures exchange directly and place an order. Rather, an exchange has clearing members entitled to actually execute trades. They can take orders from brokers, who take orders from commercial and retail folk like you and me.

DAILY SETTLEMENT

At the end of every trading day, all outstanding futures positions are valued or *marked to market* by the exchange. "Marking to market" is just another way of saying "calculating current value" based on a new futures price, the number of contracts in the position, and whether they are long or short. These "MTMs" or "marks" determine each party's payoff. Parties with a positive payoff (gain) get some money that same day. Those with a negative payoff (loss) get a bill. Losing parties don't always have to pay their entire bill. Instead, based on creditworthiness and other factors, they may be entitled to pay only some percentage of their obligation into a *margin* account. If their obligation should exceed a certain threshold, they receive a *margin call*. (The margining mechanism is not unique to futures; it is used for options and other exchange-traded securities as well.) A margin deposit for an exchange-traded contract is analogous to collateral that OTC counterparties typically demand of each other.

In a way, futures contracts are terminated at the end of every day and replaced automatically with new ones having identical terms. This means that at the start of a trading day, the value of every futures position is zero! Those values change throughout the day, of course, due to changes in futures prices based on spot price changes and other factors. At day's end, those value changes result in new MTMs, contract holders realize a gain or loss, and the whole thing starts over again the next day. This really simplifies the valuation of a futures contract, as we'll see later on.

This daily marking to market is also the key to mitigating credit risk. Because everyone settles up daily—realizing any profit or loss before they go home, as it were—no party's obligation is permitted to grow unbridled for more than one day. With a forward, one's exposure might be allowed to grow for the entire term of the contract, potentially resulting in a staggering debt for the losing party. Not so with futures contracts, which are nearly devoid of the extreme credit risk inherent to forwards.

Daily settlement also has a subtle effect on futures prices as compared with otherwise identical forward prices, and a dramatic affect on their comparative valuation. As mentioned earlier, a futures price—the guaranteed price at which the long party must buy and short party must sell—is intuitively the same as an otherwise identical forward price when a contract is executed. Income, storage, interest, and anything else reflected by a forward price are similarly reflected by a futures price. But because futures are settled daily, you need to consider the daily cash flow requirements and the present value of those settlements when calculating a futures price.

We won't delve further into this; the effect of daily settlement on the difference between a forward and futures price is comparatively modest. *After* the trade, however, the value of a futures position is different from the value of an otherwise identical forward in a big way. Why? Because the daily settlement is essentially the realization of any profit or loss. So at the start of any trading day, a futures contract has a zero value. The value at any time during the day is simply the value change since the opening bell. The value of a forward, in contrast, is the value change since its execution. In Chapter 8, "Pricing Forwards and Futures," we'll see an example intended to make this clear.

LIQUIDITY RISK

While an exchange provides liquidity by always having buyers for prospective sellers and vice versa, some contracts are more liquid than others. And the liquidity for a given contract can change over time. This leads to *liquidity risk*, which is simply the chance that you may not find a trading opportunity at a desirable price when you are ready to get out of a position. For example, when demand for long contracts is comparatively high, trading activity tends to increase, and so does the price as buyers "bid it up." Or when both supply and demand are comparatively low, trading activity decreases, *bids* (the price at which you can sell) tend to be low, and *offers* (the price at which you can buy, also known as an *ask*) tend to be high. This difference between the bid and ask at a given point in time is known as the *bid-ask spread*.

The point is, to get out of a position, you may have to buy at a price higher than you would like or sell for a price lower than you'd like, and you may even have trouble finding a bid or offer with the quantity (size) you need. That's liquidity risk.

CHAPTER 4

The Swap Contract

A swap contract is an agreement to exchange future cash flows. Swaps are used to exchange cash flows based on all sorts of things—stock returns, the price of electricity, etc.—but typically we're talking about cash flows stemming from interest payments. In most interest rate swaps, one cash flow is based on a variable or *floating rate* of interest, and the other on a *fixed rate*. Here's a quick example.

The Gondor Corporation has borrowed $10 million from a commercial bank. Under the terms of the loan, every three months for the next two years, Gondor will make an interest-only payment based on a floating rate of interest according to the London Inter-Bank Offered Rate (LIBOR) index (see Appendix A, "All About Interest," for more about LIBOR). Thus, Gondor does not know today how much interest it will pay for this loan. To reduce its exposure to changing interest rates, Gondor enters into a fixed-floating swap agreement with Marlow Securities. Under the terms of the swap, every three months, Gondor will make an interest-only payment on $10 million to Marlow based on a fixed rate of 3.75 percent. In return, Gondor will receive from Marlow an interest payment based on current LIBOR with which to make its payment to the bank. Using the swap, Gondor has effectively converted its floating-rate obligation to a fixed rate and mitigated its exposure to unpredictable interest rates.

AN EXCHANGE OF CASH FLOWS

The grandpappy of all swaps, and the one we'll focus on, is the *fixed-floating interest rate swap*. Owing to its ubiquity, this over-the-counter (OTC) instrument is often known as a "plain-vanilla swap," and once you understand this one, you'll basically understand them all. The plain vanilla is the most common of a whole breed of instruments known as *interest rate derivatives* or *fixed-income derivatives* (from the days when most bonds paid fixed rates of interest). Interest rate derivatives are derivatives whose underlier is money. The price of borrowing money is, of course, more money, or interest, hence the name.

We defined a swap as an exchange of cash flows. What is a "cash flow," and what does it have to do with buying and selling? How is this a price guarantee? Recall first that when we borrow money, we typically pay interest at regular intervals over the life of the loan—once a month for your mortgage, perhaps quarterly for a commercial loan, and so on. Each of these interest rate payments is a cash flow. The cash flows, of course, from the borrower to the lender.[1] So cash flows are just payments, and payments involve a price. When that price (interest rate) is specified and guaranteed up front, the loan is known as a *fixed-rate* loan, or debt, or obligation. When that price is not specified up front, but instead is subject to change for reasons we'll get to later on, the loan is known as a *floating-rate* loan. A fixed-floating swap is an agreement to exchange cash flows based on a fixed rate of interest with cash flows based on a floating rate of interest. Plain vanillas are most often used to effectively convert a fixed-rate loan to a floating-rate loan or vice versa.

In the Gondor-Marlow swap example from the first page of this chapter, one of the parties (Marlow Securities) is a swaps dealer or financial institution that makes a market in swaps—that is, provides them to parties who need them. This is true of most swaps, and a swaps dealer is, of course, just as likely to pay fixed as receive it. In this example, as the "seller of money" at a fixed price of 3.75 percent, Marlow has the short position. Gondor has the long position, as it is buying at that rate. It's not always easy to tell who is long and who

---

[1] The term *cash flow* is misleading, with its conjuring of a liquid substance moving continuously, not sporadically as it does really, with a number of discrete payments over time. "Cash squirt" would be more descriptive, but who could keep a straight face?

is short in a swap. Just think of it in terms of the fixed rate: the fixed payer is the long party; the fixed receiver is the short party.

The traditional method of teaching swaps involves two parties where neither is a dealer. Each has a preexisting liability—one a fixed-rate loan, and the other a floating-rate loan—and each desires the other's liability. The party with the fixed obligation would prefer floating, and the party with the floating obligation would prefer fixed.

To illustrate, imagine that entrepreneurs Boris and Chloe have each taken out separate $1 million loans on which they will make yearly interest payments for 10 years to their respective lenders, Aaron and Dimsdale. Say Boris has a floating-rate loan; he pays a variable rate of interest based on LIBOR. And say Chloe has a fixed-rate loan; she makes regular payments at a 6 percent interest rate, as depicted in Figure 4-1.

Imagine that Boris would prefer a fixed rate and Chloe would prefer a floater. Boris promises Chloe, "Every 12 months for the next 10 years, I will pay you 6 percent of a million bucks." That cash flow—$60,000 flowing once a year for 10 years—constitutes the fixed part of the swap, known as the *fixed leg*. And Chloe says to Boris, "Every 12 months for 10 years, I will pay you the current LIBOR rate of interest on a million bucks." That's the floating part, or *floating leg*. Boris and Chloe have now executed a swap, the proceeds from which they will use to pay their respective loans, effectively converting those loans between fixed and floating. It's as if Boris agrees to make Chloe's loan payments and Chloe agrees to make his, as in Figure 4-2.

The $1 million on which Boris and Chloe base their swap is known as the *notional* amount of the swap. In most swaps, it never actually exists—that is, there is no million dollars in some account or being wire-transferred from one party to another. (We're not talking about the original loans here, just the swap.) The notional

FIGURE 4-1

Floating-Rate and Fixed-Rate Borrowers

FIGURE 4-2

Floating-Rate and Fixed-Rate Borrowers with a Swap

amount is simply a number used when it comes time to calculate payments. It's worth understanding this distinction, because when you hear about a "$100 million swap," it's not at all the same thing as, say, a $100 million loan. About the only time a swap notional is realized is in the case of a cross-currency swap, in which one leg is in one currency and the other leg is in another; in that case, we do exchange notional amounts to remove the effect foreign-exchange rate changes would have on the swap.

Does Boris or Chloe pay anything for this swap? Does one pay the other a fee of some kind? No. The basic theoretical swap is defined such that neither party pays anything to the other at the outset of the deal. (The trick here is setting a fixed rate such that the fixed side of the swap has exactly the same net present value as the floating side. You'll learn more about that when we get into valuation in Chapter 9, "Pricing Swaps.") Payments are made only on the payment dates prescribed by the swap—in this case, every 12 months for 10 years.

Notice, too, that both parties have agreed to pay the other some money every 12 months. This isn't literally necessary. If I owe you $12 and you owe me $10, I can simply give you $2, and you keep your $10. It's the same with swap payments. If on some payment date, Boris owes Chloe $60,000 and Chloe owes Boris $48,000, then Boris simply pays Chloe $12,000, or the difference between the two. This practice is a form of *netting* and comes up all the time in finance.

In our example, payments occur once a year. This is known as the swap's *tenor* or *coupon frequency*. In practice, these tenors are often something less than a year. A common tenor is three months. So instead of swapping cash flows once a year, the parties do so four times per year, or quarterly. Other common tenors are six months and one month. The two legs of a swap need not have the same tenor. One common configuration is the semiquarterly swap, with a six-month fixed leg and three-month floating leg.

By entering into the swap with Chloe, Boris can count on receiving each period funds with which to pay his debt to Aaron. And he knows exactly what he must pay to Chloe in return: 6 percent of a million bucks, or $60,000. No longer is Boris at the mercy of the floating LIBOR. No matter where LIBOR ends up or "sets" each year, he knows he'll get just the right amount from Chloe for paying off Aaron. And his obligation to pay at 6 percent is fixed, so no more uncertainty. He is not free of all risk, however, as he still faces the possibility, say, that Chloe defaults on her end of the bargain and doesn't make her payments. This is an example of *credit risk* (more on this when we get to Chapter 6, "Credit Derivatives"). But he is free of the market risk he would otherwise face were it not for the swap.

SWAPS IN PRACTICE

In practice, swaps get quite a lot more complicated than our theoretical example with Boris and Chloe. First, one party is nearly always a big bank or derivatives dealer of some kind, not another debtor with an actual obligation. In addition, often the principal changes or *amortizes* over the life of the contract, the interest payments might compound or be based on an average rate, and we may handle holidays this way or that. We'll cover these and other variations in Appendix B, "Swap Conventions."

It might seem a painfully tedious job to specify dozens of variables when constructing a swap. Fortunately, before working out a particular trade, swap counterparties typically have already executed something called a *master agreement*. It's basically an agreement to terms that can apply to any trade the two parties might execute. Further, the master agreement itself almost always refers to a set of *ISDA* definitions (known as ISDAs, pronounced "IZ-duhs"), to be really sure both sides know what they're agreeing to. These definitions are named for the International Swaps and Derivatives Association, which so kindly takes care of this tedious aspect of the swaps business. ISDAs spell out in exacting detail, using orders of magnitude more words than we do here, what precisely is meant by terms such as "modified following" and "actual/360." And without ISDAs, I can assure you, the swaps business would be nothing but a headache. ISDAs are like the dictionary Scrabble players agree to consult before starting a game, just in case there's a debate over whether or not words like *qat* and *hmph* can be played.[2]

But behind all the bells and whistles are those swapped cash flows, each sometimes known as a *coupon*, another term borrowed from the old days of fixed income. And each coupon period, it turns out, is really just a forward contract in disguise. It's a forward with an underlier of money, with an interest rate for a delivery price, whose spot rate is given by an index. We can also view a swap as two bonds, one with a fixed coupon and the other floating, with the bond cash flows exchanged. This is, in fact, the simpler way to view a swap, and one we'll use ourselves when we price a swap later on.

OTHER INTEREST RATE DERIVATIVES

As with ice cream, not all interest rate derivatives are plain vanilla. There are variations, not as prevalent as the fixed-floating swap but certainly worth knowing about.

Basis Swap

The first of these is the *basis swap*, which is like a plain vanilla but with two floating legs and no fixed leg. So instead of swapping a fixed-rate payment for a floating-rate payment, we swap a payment based on one rate index for that on another index. Say we borrow money from Citibank at its prime rate but would prefer to pay at LIBOR. We can execute a pay-LIBOR, receive-prime swap with the same notional and payment schedule as our loan. Then every period, we effectively pay LIBOR on the swap and use the proceeds from the swap to pay our loan.

The term *basis* comes from the idea of basis risk. Basis risk here refers to the idea that two price streams—think two rate indexes, say prime and LIBOR—may or may not move in unison. A basis swap can mitigate such uncertainty.

Currency Swap

So far, we have only considered swaps where both legs are denominated in the same currency. A *cross-currency interest rate swap* or

---

[2] According to my dictionary, they most certainly can.

currency swap is one in which the legs are denominated in different currencies. Say we borrow Australian dollars (ASD) at a floating rate and really wish to pay a fixed rate in U.S. dollars (USD). An ASD-USD fixed-floating swap is all we need. Basis swaps can similarly have legs in different currencies.

The key practical difference between a currency swap and a noncurrency swap has to do with the notional. As noted before, in a single-currency swap, the notional amount, or principal, need not change hands. It's just a computational abstraction, really, because there is nothing to be gained from two parties exchanging the exact same thing. But in a currency swap, we need to think about foreign-exchange rates. Consider a currency swap with one leg denominated in Australian dollars and the other in U.S. dollars. If the ASD-USD exchange rate fluctuates over the life of the swap, one party or the other is going to pay a price, as this changes the value of a payment in terms of the other currency. By exchanging notional at both ends of the trade, we mitigate that risk.

We won't go into the details to see how this is so, but imagine I give you ASD$1 million and you give me USD$1 million, and then five years later, you give me back my ASD$1 million, and I give you back your USD$1 million. No matter what happens to the exchange rate in the meantime, we both end up with what we started with in terms of our local currency. So we exchange notionals to remove *exchange rate* uncertainty from the picture, because the purpose of a cross-currency interest rate swap is to remove *interest rate* uncertainty. To deal with exchange rate uncertainty, we can turn to all sorts of foreign-exchange (FX) derivatives—forwards, futures, options—but in this section we're talking only about interest rate derivatives. It's a subtle distinction but an important one.

Interest Rate Options

The family of basic interest rate derivative also includes the cap, floor, collar, and swaption. A *cap* is a guarantee that an interest rate will not rise above a certain level, a *floor* similarly guarantees a lower bound, and a *collar* identifies a range in which rates are guaranteed to fall. A *swaption* grants the right, but not the obligation, to enter into a swap in the future. We'll see an example of using a cap in Chapter 7, "Using Derivatives to Manage Risk." There are plenty of other variations as well, and all are types of options with an underlier of money. And speaking of options . . .

CHAPTER 5

The Option Contract

An *option* grants its holder the right, but not the obligation, to buy or sell something at a specified price, on or before a specified date. Here's a quick example. Greta is a small investor who likes to trade stocks and options in her spare time. She believes the stock of the ZED Corporation, currently trading at $60, is undervalued and will increase over the next several months. Rather than buy the shares and hold them, Greta buys six-month call options on ZED with a strike price of $60. The options give her the right, but not the obligation, to buy ZED for $60 at any time over the next six months. In six months, ZED is trading for $62. Greta exercises her option and buys ZED for $60, realizing a gross profit of $2 per share.

A CONDITIONAL SALES AGREEMENT

An option is a price guarantee that may or may not result in a future sale. The parties to an option are its seller (the short party, also called the *writer*) and its buyer (the long party, also known as the *holder*). Upon execution, the writer receives from the holder a *premium* based on the option's value. In return for the premium, the option holder obtains the right—but not the obligation—to buy the underlier from the writer if it's a *call option,* or to sell the underlier if it's a *put option,* on or before some specified date. Note how the value-based premium makes an option radically different from a forward, futures, or swap, all of which have no theoretical value upon execution.

It's easy to get tangled up in the buying and selling of the option versus the buying and selling of the underlier. To sort this out, see Figure 5-1, which shows what changes hands and when. When you buy a call option, you buy the right to buy the underlier (or "call it in" from the writer). When you buy a put option, you buy the right to sell the underlier (or "put it back" to the writer). In both cases you are buying the option, but later you might be buying or selling the underlier depending on what kind of option you bought.

The price at which a call holder may buy or a put holder may sell is known as the *strike price* or *exercise price*. Electing to buy or sell the underlier is known as *exercising* the option. With exchange-traded options, the flip side of exercise—the effect of exercise on the writer—is known as *assignment*.[1] All options specify an *expiration*

FIGURE 5-1

Buying and Selling of Options vs. Underliers

<hr />

[1] Most options are exchange-traded, so counterparties are not literally matched up with each other. When a holder exercises, however, the exchange must choose some writer to sell (or buy) the underlier. Choosing that writer is known as "assigning" the exercise.

date. The holder of an American option may exercise on or before expiration. The holder of a European option may exercise *only* on expiration. We'll say more about the American-European thing later in this section.

Consider another simple example. Say you buy an American call option on some company's stock. It expires in six months and has a strike price of $20. Six months later, the stock is trading at $25. You can buy for $20 what others must pay $25 to obtain. So you exercise the option and buy the stock for $20. Nice. Now turn back the clock, and imagine the same scenario, except you already own the stock and bought a put instead of a call. At expiration, you can exercise your option and sell the stock for $20, or you can sell it on the spot market for $25. Clearly, you are better off selling spot than exercising your option, so you let the option expire, worthless. Oh well.

A financial instrument closely related to the option is the *warrant*. A warrant for all intents and purposes is just like the options we'll discuss in this book except the writer of the contract and the underlying stock issuer are the same party. If IBM, say, writes a call option on its own stock, then it has really written a warrant. There are subtle pricing differences between warrants and call options. For example, when a warrant is exercised, the company issues new stock to the holder, which itself has an effect on the value of the stock, which in turn has a value of the option.

Price Paths and Moneyness

A *price path* is the course of an asset's actual price as it changes over time. Imagine that the price path in Figure 5-2 depicts the daily closing prices, or the last price at which it trades each day, of the imaginary stock ZED over the course of several months. In a minute, we'll make it an option underlier. For now, just notice that at time 0, ZED trades at $60, after which it meanders randomly up and down over time. At the three-month mark, it trades around $61 and climbs past $63. Then at five months, the price drops back to around $62, and so on. The price follows no predictable pattern whatsoever. In financial parlance, a price path like this is known as a *random walk*. In fact, one of the basic tenets in the land of derivatives is that *all* price paths are random walks.

FIGURE 5-2

Sample Stock Price Path

Imagine we are at time 0. Of course, we cannot know the future price path of ZED, because it's unpredictable. Now imagine three different European call options on ZED all expiring in six months and having three different strike prices: $60, $62, and $64. Call these options cZED60, cZED62, and cZED64. The lowercase *c* indicates these are European call options; later we'll use uppercase to indicate American. Figure 5-3 superimposes the option strikes atop the price path.

Notice that ZED is trading at $62 upon expiration (or "expiry," as it is sometimes known). Take a look at the options, and consider their payoff, or value at expiration. Remember, they are call options granting the right to buy ZED at the strike price. Now, cZED60 lets the holder buy for $60 what otherwise would cost $62, so it must be worth $2. An option that pays off upon exercise like this is said to be *in the money* (ITM). Our cZED64, in contrast, lets the holder buy for $64 what otherwise costs $62. It is, of course, worthless. An option that does not pay off upon exercise is said to be *out of the money* (OTM). And what of cZED62? It lets the holder buy for $62 what otherwise costs $62, so it, too, is worthless. An option like this, with a strike price equal to (or very close to) the underlier spot price, is said to be *at the money* (ATM). The "moneyness" of an option gives an intuitive sense of an option's value. Question for extra credit: What if these options

FIGURE 5-3

European Call Option Strike Points

were puts instead of calls? Does it change their moneyness?[2] The answer appears in the footnote.

An option whose strike price is way off spot is known as "deep in the money" (e.g., a put with a strike of $60 when the stock is trading at $15) or "deep out of the money" (e.g., a call with a strike of $60 when the stock is trading at $15). A position in a deep option is nearly identical to a position in a forward. The idea here is that the deeper the option, the more likely it is to expire in the money. So holding a really deep ITM call is like holding a long forward position in the stock: you can pretty much count on owning the underlier, especially if expiration is approaching. Holding a really deep ITM put is like holding a short forward position: the underlier is good as sold.

Americans Versus Europeans

Now let's turn back to the whole European-versus-American thing. *European-style options* may be exercised only on their expiration

---

[2] It changes the moneyness of the 60-strike and 64-strike options. A 60-strike put expires out of the money when the underlier trades at $62, as it does no good to sell for $60 what you can otherwise sell for $62. The 64-strike put expires in the money. The 62-strike remains at the money whether it is a call or a put.

date. *American-style options* may be exercised at any time up to and including their expiration date. These labels, by the way, have nothing to do with geography; European options trade all the time in the States, and Americans trade all the time in the Old Country.

Let's turn our cZED62 into an American option and rename it slightly to CZED62. The uppercase C indicates American-style. Figure 5-4 shows how we might represent this option on the price path. This illustration shows the strike price and stock price at the end of each day until expiration. Unlike the European version, this American option can be exercised at any time up to and including the expiration date. And while it still expires at the money, ergo worthless, it goes in and out of the money a number of times between execution and expiration. Its holder could theoretically exercise at one of the times it is in the money and therefore make some money.

This example illustrates how American-style options are always more valuable than otherwise identical European-style options. With Europeans, you can only exercise on expiration, so it doesn't matter whether or not the option goes in the money before then. (Incidentally, this convention of using lowercase letters to signify Europeans and uppercase to signify Americans reinforces this idea that American options are more valuable than European

FIGURE 5-4

American Call Option Strike Line

FIGURE 5-5

Moneyness of a Sample Call Option

options. Lowercase equals less valuable; uppercase equals more valuable.)

It's easy to spot the moneyness of an option on a price path illustration with a superimposed strike line. A call is in the money when the stock price is above the strike line. It's out of the money when the stock price is below strike, and it's at the money whenever the stock price crosses the strike line. (A put is just the reverse: ITM when the stock price is below strike and OTM when above.) Figure 5-5 depicts the changing moneyness of CZED62 against our imaginary price path.

TYPES OF OPTION UNDERLIERS

As with most derivatives, there are different ways to answer the seemingly simple question "What kind of options are there?" The difficulty derives from the fact there are different ways to slice and dice the universe of options—that is, to organize it. There are at least three reasonable ways.

The first is by structure, and here we think of calls versus puts, Americans versus European, as covered already in this chapter. Think of these as the terms of the deal—the rights and obligations of each party.

The second way is by market—the places where options happen. There are basically two kinds of markets: exchange markets and over-the-counter (OTC) markets. Options are traded on both.

A third way we can organize the universe of options is by underlier. Along this dimension, the universe is vast. There are all sorts of things on which you can buy or sell options. Chapter 1 covered the range of possible "things"—commodities, securities, and so on—and this is no different really from derivatives in general. But when it comes to option underliers, we can also organize them structurally. Thankfully, almost any option underlier can be plunked into one of three buckets, which we will label "simple," "index," and "derivative."

Simple Underliers

If you are new to options, most options you've probably encountered have had simple underliers. A simple underlier is some individual commodity or financial security. Options on simple underliers grant the holder the right to buy or sell some "thing." If the thing is a commodity, it might be bushels of corn, barrels of crude oil, megawatts of electricity, or some other physical good. If the thing is a security, it might be a stock, a currency, a government bond, or something else along those lines. These options can be settled physically or for cash.

An example of a simple underlier option is the Microsoft stock option contract traded on the International Securities Exchange (ISE) and elsewhere. One contract allows the holder to buy or sell 100 shares of Microsoft on or before the third Saturday of the expiration month, at one of several different strike prices.

Index Underliers

An index underlier is a price index. Options on these underliers grant the holder the right, but not the obligation, to buy or sell some units of an index. Recall that an index is just an average, such as the Dow Jones Industrial Average. In finance, an index is often thought of as a "basket" of a variety of goods, like a sampler basket from an apple grower—you get a McIntosh in there, a Golden Delicious, a Granny Smith, and maybe some others. Index options are virtually always cash settled. You cannot easily buy or sell the index per se, but you can use index derivatives to make or lose money as if you could.

An example is the SPX option contract. The underlier of the SPX is 100 times the Standard & Poor's S&P 500 stock price index, which is an average price from 500 sample stocks. We'll see an example of using the SPX in Chapter 7, "Using Derivatives to Manage Risk."

Derivative Underliers

Derivative underliers are themselves derivatives. That sounds remarkably weird until you notice we've been talking about "buying and selling" forwards and futures and swaps and whatnot all along. And as I noted before, if you can buy or sell it and it's fungible and liquid, you can probably use it as a derivative underlier. The most common derivative underliers for options are futures: futures on a simple underlier or futures on an index. For example, at the Chicago Mercantile Exchange, one can trade the S&P 500 Futures Option contract, an option whose underlier is one S&P 500 Futures contract (whose own underlier is $250 times the S&P 500 stock price index).

It all might seem rather confusing . . . and here's a diagram to prove it! Figure 5-6 uses just one technical term—"thing"—to represent any commodity or security traded on a spot market, be it stock, barrels of oil, currency, whatever.

FIGURE 5-6

Types of Option Underliers

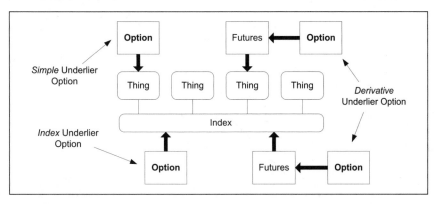

OPTION PAYOFF

The payoff diagram is a very handy tool for understanding options. For a forward, you'll recall, a payoff diagram gives a snapshot of possible contract values upon delivery. It's just a visual representation of the payoff function with a zero payoff indicated by delivery price. Figure 5-7 shows the long forward payoff from Chapter 2, "The Forward Contract."

Payoff diagrams work the same way with options, using just slightly different terms: they give a snapshot of possible contract values upon exercise, with a zero payoff indicated by strike price. Formula 5.1 shows the payoff function for a long call, and Figure 5-8 shows a corresponding diagram:

$$P_{Call,Long} = \max(0, S - K) \qquad \text{(Formula 5.1)}$$

(For the smarties: We're ignoring for now the effect of premium.)

You can see right away the big difference between a forward and an option payoff. The long forward payoff can go negative, but the long call option payoff cannot. And this makes sense, right? A call option holder has the right but not the obligation to buy; the holder will not buy at the strike price if he or she can buy at a better price on the spot market. (If you have a coupon to buy milk at $2.00 per gallon, and milk is selling for $1.80 at the market, will

FIGURE 5-7

Long Forward Payoff Function and Diagram

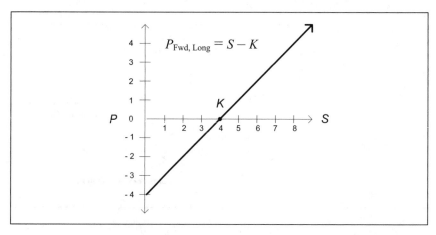

FIGURE 5-8

Payoff Diagram for a Long Call Option

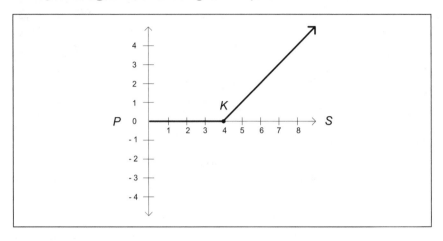

TABLE 5-1

Payoff Table for Long Call Option

S	K	$P_{Call,Long}$ = max(0, S − K)
$30	$40	0
$50	$40	$10
$60	$40	$20

you use the coupon?) This fact is illustrated in the payoff function by "max(. . .)," which is a function that returns the greater of its arguments—in this case, 0 and $S - K$. Stated in words, the long call option payoff is the greater of zero and the difference between strike price and spot price. (Note that the closely related "min[. . .]" function, which we'll use below, returns the lesser of its arguments.)

Say we have a call option with a strike price of $40. Consider three possible spot prices on exercise: $30, $50, and $60. Table 5-1 gives the payoffs under each of the three scenarios, and Figure 5-9 depicts the three scenarios on the payoff diagram. Notice how each is just one point on the payoff line?

And what of the writer, the short party to a call option? What is that party's payoff? It's just the opposite of the long party's payoff. Formula 5.2 gives the payoff function for the short call:

FIGURE 5-9

Payoff Diagram with Payoff Points for Long Call Option

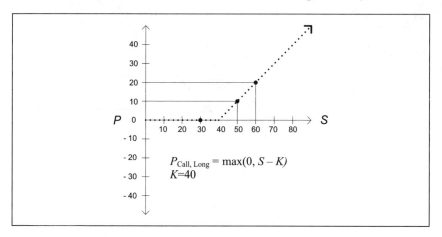

$$P_{\text{Call,Short}} = \min(0, K - S) \qquad \text{(Formula 5.2)}$$

If the long party gains $10, the short party must lose $10. Their payoffs are shown in Table 5-2 and Figure 5-10.

Because the short payoff is the exact opposite of that of the long, the sum of both payoffs is always zero. Disregarding option premiums, it's a zero-sum game. We can combine the diagrams and see a nice illustration of this idea, as in Figure 5-11.

Payoffs for put options are just the reverse of call option payoffs. With calls, there is no payoff for either party when spot is below strike. With puts, there is a payoff *only* when spot is below strike. For a pair of examples, take a look at Table 5-3 and Figure 5-12, on page 50, for a long put option, and at Table 5-4 (page 50) and Figure 5-13 (page 51) for a short put option.

TABLE 5-2

Payoff Table for Short Call Option

S	K	$P_{Call,short}$ = min(0, K − S)
$30	$40	0
$50	$40	−$10
$60	$40	−$20

FIGURE 5-10

Payoff Diagram with Payoff Points for Short Call Option

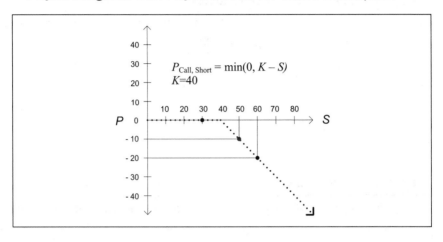

FIGURE 5-11

Net Call Option Payoff Diagram

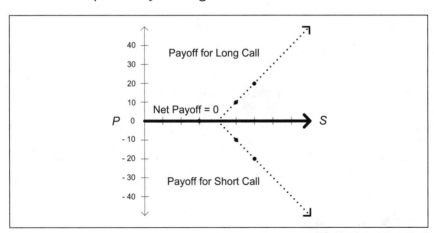

While we're here, let's step off the bus for just a minute. What happens if we plot the combined payoff of the long call position and short put position on the same diagram? We get the net payoff shown in Figure 5-14 (page 51). Does the diagonal line look like something we've seen before? Yes! It's just the payoff of a long *forward* contract. This illustrates how the payoff of a long forward position is the same as the combined payoff of a long call and short put position.

TABLE 5-3

Payoff Table for Long Put Option

S	K	$P_{Put,Long}$ = max(0, K − S)
$30	$40	$10
$50	$40	0
$60	$40	0

FIGURE 5-12

Payoff Diagram with Payoff Points for Long Put Option

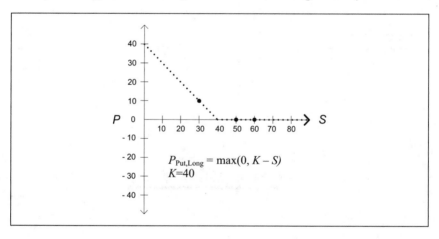

$$P_{Put,Long} = \max(0, K - S)$$
$$K = 40$$

TABLE 5-4

Payoff Table for a Short Put Option

S	K	$P_{Put,Short}$ = min(0, S − K)
$30	$40	−$10
$50	$40	0
$60	$40	0

FIGURE 5-13

Payoff Diagram with Payoff Points for Short Put Option

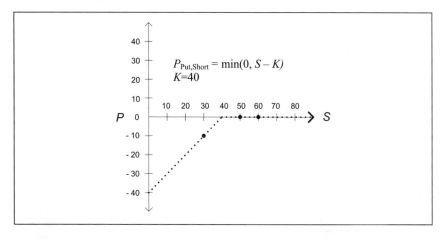

$$P_{Put,Short} = \min(0, S - K)$$
$$K = 40$$

FIGURE 5-14

Forward Payoff Synthesized with Options

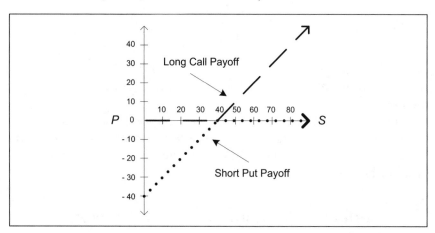

This example is a great illustration of *replication*. We can replicate, or synthesize, one position by constructing a position using different instruments that, when combined, give the same payoff. And by the law of no arbitrage, two positions with the same payoff must have the same value. This powerful notion of position replication is everywhere in the world of derivative pricing and is

FIGURE 5-15

Option Payoff Patterns

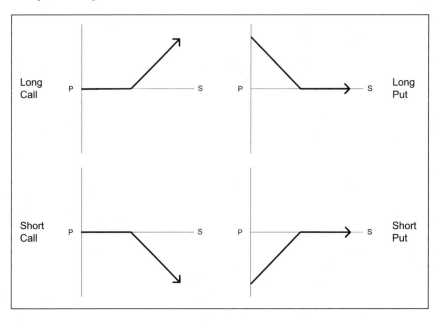

indeed like the glue that holds it all together. We'll get back to this when we arrive at option pricing, so keep it in mind. Now back on the bus.

Figure 5-15 illustrates the four basic option positions and their respective payoffs. If you plan to work with options, it's worth learning these so-called "hockey stick" patterns till they pop into your head without too much thought.

Effect of Premium on Option Payoff

So far we've ignored the effect of an option's premium on its payoff. The premium is money paid up front by the long party to the short party, so naturally it affects the net payoff of both parties. It decreases the payoff to the long party and increases the payoff to the short party. This is indicated on the payoff diagram by a slight shift down, in the amount of the premium, for the long payoff and up for the short payoff. Returning to this chapter's example of options with a strike price of $40, imagine that they have a $5 premium. Their true payoffs, net of premium, are shown in Figure 5-16.

FIGURE 5-16

Option Payoffs Net of Premium

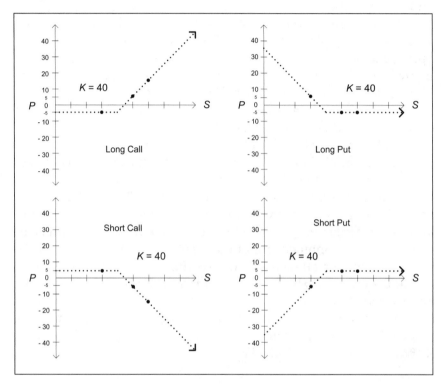

The payoff to the long party can actually go negative by the amount of the premium. In other words, the long party is out the premium whether he or she exercises the option or not. And if the long party does exercise, his or her payoff is decreased by the amount of the premium. To the short party, the premium is money he or she gets to keep, no matter what. The short party still can lose money, of course, as soon as the spot price increases sufficiently over strike. But the money the short party loses is offset by the premium.

OPTION STRATEGIES

Before we put away the hockey sticks, let's use them to illustrate common positions involving multiple instruments, often known as option *strategies* or *spreads*. The instruments in a strategy might be two or more of the same calls or puts at different strike prices or expiration dates, or an option plus a stock or bond position, or calls and puts together.

To get a feel for these, first consider the speculator who is convinced a stock price will increase. This trader can buy a simple call option and sit back and wait (perhaps nervously, depending on how many he or she bought). Figure 5-17 shows the payoff of a call with strike price K, an instrument we'll refer to as $c(K)$.

Now consider the speculator who expects a stock price will change in one direction or the other but isn't sure which direction. This trader can buy both a call and a put, both with the same strike price and expiration and different premiums, resulting in a net payoff that looks roughly like Figure 5-18.

This simple strategy is known as a *straddle*. The long party here will profit whether the price of the underlier goes up or down, as long as it goes up or down by more than an amount sufficient to recoup the combined premiums. If it does not, the long party will lose some or all of his or her premium. The short party to a straddle, by the way, has the same but opposite payoff. It looks like an inverted V.

A variation of the straddle is the *strangle*. A long strangle is made of a long put and long call at different strike prices, K_1 and K_2. Its payoff looks roughly like Figure 5-19.

FIGURE 5-17

Payoff Diagram, Net of Premium, for Long Call Option

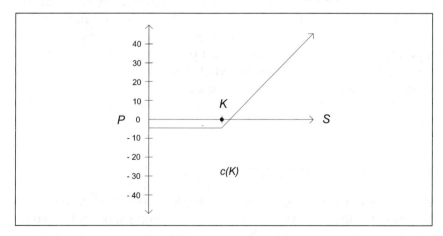

FIGURE 5-18

Long Straddle Payoff

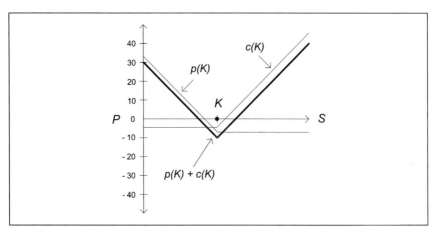

FIGURE 5-19

Long Strangle Payoff

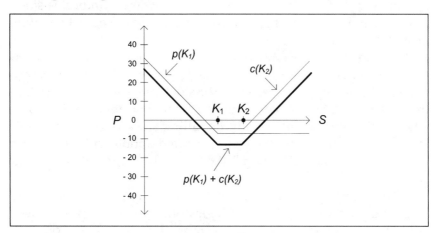

A *covered call* position consists of a written call $c(K)$—in the diagram, we attach a negative sign to denote that it is a short position—and long stock S purchased for S_0. As the option writer, you're protected should the stock price skyrocket and the call go deep into the money. You just hand over the stock you already own, covering

FIGURE 5-20

Covered Call Payoff

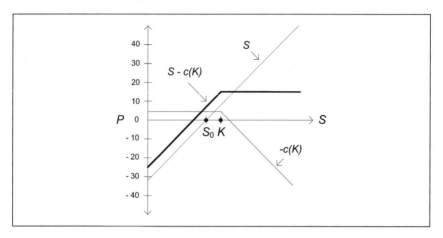

your, um, downside on the option contract. This strategy is also known as a "buy-write," as you are buying stock and writing an option. Its payoff is shown in Figure 5-20, where S indicates stock price at the time of payoff, S_0 is the initial stock price, and payoff is given by $S - c(K)$.

The idea of a covered put is the same but in reverse. When you write a put, you face a substantial loss should the option expire deep in the money—that is, when the stock price declines far below the strike price. So you cover it with a short position in the stock, whose value will increase with the falling stock price, compensating you for your loss on the put. A written option without a cover is known as a "naked option." Writing naked options is rarely a good idea.

Those strategies are just some examples to give you the basic idea. The number of option strategies one can cook up is limited only by one's imagination and tolerance for risk. Other common strategies include "bear spreads," "buggy whips," "bull combos," and "butterflies." (Okay, I made one of those up. Guess which one?)[3] Each combines two or more instruments to cook up some particular payoff to suit one's needs.

---

[3] Buggy whips.

It's tempting to think one can cook up some brand new strategy to crank out money like a machine, no matter where prices go, but all strategies are bound by the laws of arbitrage. And there are plenty of well-heeled trading firms, with plenty of money to spend on impressive computer systems, allowing them to take advantage of mispriced securities at nearly the speed of light.

CHAPTER 6

Credit Derivatives

The derivatives we have covered thus far deal with the *market risk* associated with the price of some underlying security or commodity. Credit derivatives deal with the *credit risk* associated with the performance of a party in fulfilling a financial obligation. In 2007–2008, over-the-counter (OTC) credit derivatives played a significant role in the global financial crisis that originated in U.S. mortgage markets. For much more about that, see Chapter 12, "Derivatives and the 2008 Financial Meltdown."

Here's a quick example of the most common credit derivative of them all, the *credit default swap:* An investor buys $10 million worth of five-year corporate bonds issued by a large manufacturer, in essence lending the manufacturer $10 million in exchange for periodic interest payments and return of the principal in five years. Over the life of the bond, changes in the creditworthiness of the issuer affect the value of the bond. For example, if the manufacturer declares bankruptcy, casting doubt on its ability to fulfill its payment obligations, the value of the bonds may drop to something well below $10 million.

To protect against the possibility of such a drop in bond value, the investor enters into a credit default swap with an insurance company. Under the terms of the swap, the investor pays an annual premium of 150 basis points (1.5 percent) on $10 million, or $150,000 per year for five years. If the manufacturer declares bankruptcy over the course of that time, the insurance company agrees to buy the bonds from the investor for $10 million, no matter what their

value. The investor house has thus rid itself of the credit risk of owning these bonds.

PERFORMANCE GUARANTEES

Just as we viewed forwards, futures, swaps, and options as variations on a price guarantee, you can think of credit derivatives as
variations on a *performance* guarantee. These instruments deal with
the possibility of some party not fulfilling its financial obligation.
Like other derivatives, they have counterparties and underliers.
And their value derives in part from the value of the underlier—but
only as that value is affected by a "credit event" such as bankruptcy.

In the preceding example, if the value of the bonds were to
decline due to changes in market interest rates (the chief factor in
bond valuation changes), the credit default swap would not compensate the investor. Only if the bond value declines as a result of
bankruptcy, in this case, does the credit default swap pay off for the
investor. And this illustrates one of the prime attractions of credit
derivatives: they enable the decomposition or "unbundling" of
overall risk into different types of risk, each of which can be dealt
with on its own. For example, a lender can use a fixed-floating swap
to hedge away its exposure to changes in interest rates on a fixed-
rate loan it writes, so it need not lose sleep should market rates go
through the roof. But that swap won't help the lender if the debtor
defaults. So the lender adds a credit default swap to the mix and
sleeps even better.

Credit risk exists with all sorts of financial instruments, but
most credit derivatives are concerned with debt securities, for example, bonds issued by corporations or sovereign states. Now, lenders
for years have used a variety of mechanisms for mitigating default
risk. They use loan syndication to spread risk across multiple lenders, borrower diversification (lending to multiple borrowers across
multiple economic sectors so as not to keep all eggs in one basket),
third-party loan guarantees, letters of credit, and other such devices.
Then what's so special about credit derivatives? They make possible
a *market* in credit risk.

While credit derivatives certainly cater to the inherent needs
of lenders, they also afford participation in the credit market by
parties with no preexisting exposure to a credit default. This makes
them much more than "just" default protection. Credit derivatives
are available to speculators, arbitrageurs, and market makers, just

as they are to lenders with a direct exposure to a borrower skipping town. A speculator who is confident a bond issuer will not default, for example, can sell a credit default swap just to collect the premium.[1] Just like the options arbitrageur or market maker, a sharp credit derivative arbitrageur or market maker can earn the spread between the market price of a credit derivative and a price at which he or she can confidently synthesize it.

What is the ultimate value of such marketization of credit risk? It's hard to say for certain, but a few things come to mind. In theory, anything that makes credit protection more accessible should encourage more lending by reducing a lender's exposure to default risk. But whether the data support such an assertion is difficult to say. It should also facilitate the fair pricing of credit protection, because arbitrageurs stand by to snatch up profits from any "bad" pricing of credit. And if nothing else, a liquid market in credit protection certainly makes credit protection more accessible.

The most common credit derivative is the *credit default swap*. Other credit contracts include the *total return swap* and *credit-linked note*. Most other credit derivatives are variations or extensions of one of these, and we'll touch on some of them later on.

Credit derivatives are generally traded on the OTC market in a market structure not unlike that of interest rate swaps and foreign-exchange (FX) forwards. Market makers publish "indicative prices" on some electronic forum or another, helping the prospective buyer or seller of protection to find a counterparty. But indicative prices are inherently nonbinding, and a firm trade price is set only after the two interested parties find each other. The exact price and other terms of the trade are typically documented in a master agreement or confirmation letter following guidelines published by the International Swaps and Derivatives Association (ISDA).

CREDIT DEFAULT SWAPS

The *credit default swap* (*CDS*), or *credit swap*, is the plain vanilla of credit derivatives. There are two primary parties to a CDS: the

---

[1] This begs a question, of course: How can a protection buyer be assured the protection seller won't default? It's a fine question, but it was only an academic question until 2008, when widespread default on credit contracts contributed to the global financial crisis. Much more on this in Chapter 12, "Derivatives and the 2008 Financial Meltdown."

protection buyer and *protection seller*. The protection buyer pays a *premium* or *CDS spread* to the protection seller. The premium is typically expressed in some number of basis points payable annually.[2] There is a third party, the reference entity, which issues some debt security (i.e., borrows some money). The reference entity's creditworthiness determines the value and payoff of the CDS, but this entity is not a direct party to the CDS. Should the reference entity experience one or more credit events over the term of the swap, the protection seller agrees to compensate the protection buyer for any loss incurred as a result of the credit event—for example, by purchasing the bond at face value, after which the buyer no longer pays the premium. The fundamental structure of a CDS is shown in Figure 6-1.

Incidentally, this type of CDS is known as a *single-name CDS*, as it relates to a debt security issued by a single reference entity. The entity is typically a large corporation but can also be a sovereign state that issues government debt. There are also *portfolio CDS* instruments whose payoff can be triggered by a credit event by more than one reference entity (more on these later in this chapter). As you might imagine, the primary buyers of single-name credit default swaps are commercial lenders and corporate bondhold-

FIGURE 6-1

Credit Default Swap

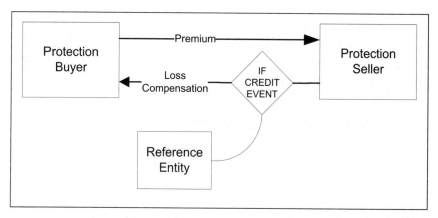

---

[2] A basis point is 0.01 percent, so 150 basis points, for example, would be equal to 1.5 percent.

ers. The primary sellers tend to be insurance companies and large financial institutions.

Now, calling these things "swaps" may seem a bit of a stretch. The swapping is not as obvious as with an interest rate swap, but you might view the premium payments as a stream of fixed payments and the potential payment of loss compensation as a single floating payment. Whatever. Credit default swaps are much more like a traditional insurance policy: if you replace "credit event" with "a tornado wrecks your house," these things are mostly indistinguishable from a homeowner's policy. If it helps, just think of one of these instruments as a tradable loan insurance policy.[3]

Credit swaps can be cash settled or physically settled. This basically determines how loss compensation works. In the case of cash settlement, the protection seller pays the net loss incurred by the protection buyer as a result of a credit event. If the buyer's $10 million bond portfolio devalues to $2 million, the buyer receives a check for $8 million. Physical settlement can apply when the subject of the swap is a publicly traded corporate security, such as a bond. If the terms of a swap call for physical settlement and the buyer's $10 million bond portfolio devalues as a result of a credit event, the buyer transfers ownership of the portfolio to the seller and receives a check for $10 million in return. The net effect is the same.

The credit event that triggers settlement can be anything the two parties agree to but is typically one or more of five credit events defined by ISDA: bankruptcy, failure to pay, obligation default, obligation acceleration, or restructuring. *Bankruptcy* involves seeking court protection against creditors when a company can't pay its bills. *Failure to pay* is essentially like missing a payment on a car loan. *Obligation default* occurs when the lender declares the borrower in violation of payment terms and demands return of the principal. *Obligation acceleration* happens when the terms of a debt call for immediate payment of some or all of a debt "ahead of schedule" as a result of some issue. And *restructuring* is a broad event that includes things like debt consolidation.

The CDS premium is often known as a *CDS spread*, although there is no explicit "spread" per se. The term is borrowed from the

---

[3] Indeed, if we're to continue calling these loan insurance policies "swaps," I say let's call car insurance "automotive mishap swaps" and homeowner's insurance "residential calamity swaps."

portion of a corporate bond yield attributable to the credit risk, a portion known as a *credit spread*. If you subtract from a corporate bond yield the risk-free rate, you are left with the compensation that investors receive for taking on the risk of the bond issuer defaulting. This "spread over Treasuries," as it is sometimes known, is often used as a measure of the probability of default by the issuer. (Treasury securities—"Treasuries"—are generally considered free of default risk.) And in theory, a reference entity's CDS spread should be equivalent to the credit spread on its debt securities trading at *par*, or time-adjusted face value. In practice, that's not always the case, for all sorts of reasons. Bottom line, the CDS premium is known as a spread for its close relationship to a corporate bond's credit spread.

Speaking of premium, it's a fine term for what the protection buyer pays for a credit default swap, because it really is an option premium—a put option premium, in fact. How so? Just think of the CDS notional (face value) as the strike price on a company's bond, and the market value of the bond as its spot price. If a credit event occurs, the CDS-as-put-option goes in the money by an amount given by strike minus spot, just as any put option would. When it comes to calculating payoff, a CDS is very much like a put option. It is quite different, however, when it comes to whether or not the payoff occurs. With a real put option, the holder is entitled to a payoff simply if the strike price is above spot price on or before some expiration date. With a CDS-as-put-option, the holder may get no payoff when the spot price is far below the strike. This is the case, for example, when the spot price is below strike due to changing interest rates. The CDS goes in the money, remember, only if a credit event occurs. Otherwise, it's just a put. Remember how, in Chapter 1, I said nearly any derivative can be seen as a variation on one of the four basic types? Right here we have a primo example.

TOTAL RETURN SWAPS

A total return swap (TRS), also known as a *total rate of return swap*, is a credit derivative and more. Here the protection seller makes a stream of regular payments—say, LIBOR plus 30 basis points, to the protection buyer. Now, this might seem backward at first, with the protection "seller" making payments, but stay with me. In exchange for those payments, the protection buyer transfers to the seller all income (think coupon payments) and capital changes (think changes in market valuation) with respect to a reference asset—i.e., the "total" return—but continues to own that asset for accounting purposes. The bidirectional payments are generally lined up to occur at the same time, so this really is a "swap" in the terms of a promised exchange of future cash flows. The TRS thus allows the seller to enjoy (or suffer) the economic consequences of owning an asset without actually owning it. In accounting terminology, the asset remains "off the balance sheet" as the seller essentially "rents" another's balance sheet for the duration of the agreement.[4] The TRS is illustrated in Figure 6-2.

And where does credit risk protection fit into this picture? If the asset is a debt security and its value decreases due to the creditworthiness of the issuer, the protection seller compensates the buyer, much as the seller does in a credit swap. Unlike the terms of a credit swap, however, the seller compensates the buyer for value loss due to any reason, not just credit events. And the asset of a TRS need not be a debt security at all. It can just as well be an equity, a stock index, or pretty much anything else on a balance sheet. As such, the TRS is indeed much more than just a credit derivative.

FIGURE 6-2

Total Return Swap

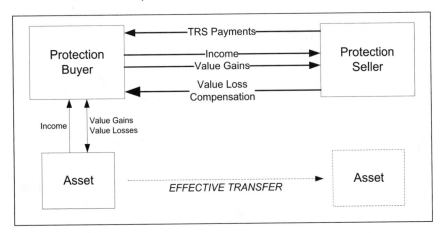

---

[4] The idea of off-balance-sheet accounting is not universally accepted as a good idea.

CREDIT-LINKED NOTES

A credit-linked note (CLN) is a vehicle for raising capital in which invested funds are held in reserve in case they are needed to compensate a protection buyer in the event of a credit loss. The overall structure, in fact, is very similar to a credit default swap: a protection buyer pays a premium in return for compensation should a credit event occur with respect to a reference entity. The protection seller, however, raises capital for the express purpose of credit protection by issuing CLNs to investors. Should a credit event occur, the capital is used to compensate the protection buyer for his or her loss. Otherwise, the capital is returned to the investor at the maturity of the note. In return for this possible loss of some (or all) of the investment, the investor is compensated with receipt of the protection buyer premium, less a spread to compensate the protection seller, as well as interest on the capital. The structure of the CLN is illustrated in Figure 6-3.

The protection seller in a CLN may be some arm of an existing financial institution, or it might be a specially created entity known as a *special-purpose vehicle (SPV)*. These are more or less independent legal entities created expressly for a purpose such as this, with credit reputations impeccable by design—that is, they generally have the highest credit rankings possible. They also tend to be iso-

FIGURE 6-3

Credit-Linked Note

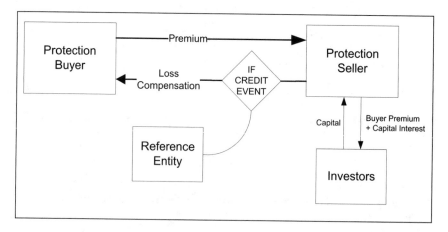

lated from the credit woes of any other entity. Among other things, the use of an SPV here helps mitigate any credit risk from the CLN issuer itself.

Plenty of variations on the basic theme of a CLN are possible. For example, the once-mighty Enron issued a series of *credit-sensitive notes* in 1998 that offered a coupon rate inversely tied to Enron's credit rating. As the company's Moody's or Standard & Poor's ratings decreased, the promised coupon rate increased. That coupon rate presumably skyrocketed as Enron self-destructed some years later. It would be interesting to know, however, if the investors actually received the coupon payments, given Enron's disappearing act.

OTHER CREDIT CONTRACTS

A handful of variations on and close relations to the instruments described above fill out the credit derivative market. Here are a few and what they're all about in a nutshell:

- **Portfolio CDS:** This credit default swap has more than one reference entity. Also known as a *multiname CDS*, it has a higher premium than a single-name CDS, due to the increased level of protection.
- **Basket default swap:** This form of portfolio CDS, also known as a *first-to-default CDS*, pays the protection buyer upon a credit default by any one of multiple reference entities, after which the agreement ceases to exist.
- **Binary CDS:** With this type of credit default swap, the protection buyer receives a fixed payment amount, rather than the difference between notional and market value, should a credit event occur. It is also known as a *digital CDS*.
- **Forward CDS:** This is a forward contract to buy or sell a CDS on a particular reference entity at a specified date in the future. As you would expect, the CDS spread for a forward CDS is the one that makes the value of the forward equal to zero.
- **CDS option:** This is an option, typically European style, that grants a right but not the obligation to buy or sell a CDS on some particular reference entity on some future date. A CDS option generally ceases to exist if a credit event occurs before the option expires.

PRICING CREDIT DERIVATIVES

As you'll see when we get to the pricing chapters (Chapters 8 through 10), there is a solid body of knowledge on how to determine the fair market value of forwards, futures, swaps, and options, and little disagreement among market participants on how one should price these price guarantees. This is not yet the case for performance guarantees or credit derivatives. Even though the market for credit contracts is impressive and growing every day, compared with the market for forwards, futures, swaps, and options, it is still rather small. This means, among other things, there is still a comparatively healthy debate on just how one should go about pricing these things, as there are limited markets for so-called price discovery.

One approach to pricing credit derivatives is the same one we'll use for pricing other derivatives in Chapters 8 to 10. In essence, this approach gets the value of a credit derivative by discounting the expected risk-neutral payoff of the derivative, using the risk-free rate of interest. We'll explain risk neutrality and the risk-free rate in those later chapters. And we've not yet explained discounting, but this just involves determining the value today of some future cash flow. The future cash flow in the case of a credit default swap, for example, is the payment from the protection seller to the protection buyer in the event of default by the reference entity—that is, the contract payoff.

Say you are a seller of a CDS where the reference entity is the corporate issuer of a bond with a face value of $10 million. To simplify, let's say that under the terms of the CDS, you will write a check to the protection buyer in one year's time for $10 million if the reference entity defaults over the course of the year. There is some probability of the default occurring, so there is some probability of your writing that check. To price this contract—that is, to determine how much premium you should charge the buyer—you want to know the *expected value* of that payment. Expected values are calculated all the time in finance by multiplying some future cash flow by the probability of it occurring. Say there is a 1 percent chance of the reference entity defaulting and you're writing a check for $10 million. The expected value of that payment is simply 1 percent of $10 million, or $100,000. You might set the premium, then, to at least $100,000.

There are at least a couple of complicating factors when doing this for real. In our example, we presumed the payout would total

$10 million, or 100 percent of the face value of the guaranteed bond. In reality, when companies default, some amount of their debt is "recovered," leading to the idea of a *recovery rate*. In this example, perhaps the terms of the CDS are such that the protection seller would have to pay only 60 percent of the $10 million, because that's the extent of the loss. The recovery rate, as you can sense, has a huge impact on the expected payoff of the derivative. And it's hugely difficult to predict.

Another not-so-easy feat is calculating a probability of default. In the example, we took a wild guess at 1 percent. In practice, there are a couple of ways one can obtain a probability of default. One is to use the credit spread between the yield of the reference entity's bond and an otherwise equivalent government bond—say, U.S. Treasuries. If the yield on a Treasury is 4 percent and the yield on the corporate bond is 4.25 percent, you can say the extra 0.25 percent compensates the bondholder for the risk of default. And from that credit spread, using a bit of algebra, you can back out a probability.

CHAPTER 7

Using Derivatives to Manage Risk

Risk, it is said, simply refers to the fact that more things can happen than will happen. Financial risk arises when things can happen to cause you a financial loss. *Financial risk management* is what you do to reduce the probability or degree of financial loss in the face of uncertainty. Derivatives are an excellent tool for a particular type of risk management known as *hedging*. Indeed, it's why they were invented in the first place.

Generally speaking, hedging involves recognizing and measuring the financial risk of an existing position and then taking on some new position with opposite exposure characteristics such that the gains and losses of the positions cancel each other out. In essence, you no longer care if the original position loses money, because the hedge position will make money to compensate. And if the hedge position loses money, no worries, the original position makes money to compensate—provided it's a good hedge, of course.

Imagine how you might manage an exposure to a nonfinancial risk: weather. Say you take an afternoon off work for a nice walk in the park. In investment terms, you are taking a position in a walk. There's only a slight chance of rain, but you bring along your umbrella, taking a position in that instrument, just in case you need one. Now, if it does not rain, you will have lugged an unused umbrella all day, thus "losing" on your umbrella position. But the position in the walk will have paid off nicely. If it does rain, you lose on the walk position but gain handsomely on the umbrella position. It's not a perfect analogy nor a perfect hedge, as the umbrella won't keep every drop of water off you. But at least you can count on a dry head on your walk home, whether it rains or not.

Derivatives are a natural financial risk management tool for two key reasons that we've already seen. First, because a derivative's value is determined chiefly by the value of its underlier, offsetting positions in a derivative and its underlier (long the derivative and short the underlier, or vice versa) tend to neutralize changes in the underlier's value. It's the playground seesaw thing: one side goes up; the other side goes down. Which is just what you want. Second, derivatives employ the power of leverage. On the playground, move the center point or fulcrum on the seesaw, and the kid farther from the fulcrum has a much easier time than the other kid. In finance, leverage allows you to replicate a payoff pattern of something you want to hedge at a lower cost than simply trading more of the thing itself. As we saw in Chapter 1, for example, you can buy stock options to replicate a stock portfolio's payoff for much less money than buying some desired amount of the stock itself. Hedging with futures also employs leverage, as in most cases you need only put up a margin, or portion of your position's value. For the speculator, leverage raises the stakes and can spell disaster if your bet is bad, or riches if your bet pays off. For the hedger, leverage lets you manage risk at a price far less than you might otherwise need to pay.

In this chapter, we'll look at risk management from the perspective of the classic derivatives user: someone who uses derivatives to hedge an exposure created by a position in some nonderivative instrument. Those who take positions in derivatives for reasons other than hedging—think market makers or arbitrageurs—also face financial risk. And the same leverage that makes derivatives such powerful hedging instruments makes them potentially devastating if not properly hedged. Many a career in derivatives has met a swift end when poor souls have forgotten to hedge a trade. Chapter 11, "Hedging a Derivatives Position," is all about this sort of hedging, which involves carefully quantifying the exposure of a derivatives position and using both derivative and nonderivative instruments to hedge it.

You've already seen several examples of hedging with derivatives in the preceding chapters. In the sections that follow, we'll revisit some of these for a second look and consider some alternative hedging strategies.

ALL ABOUT POSITIONS

We talk a lot about positions in this chapter, so it's worth reviewing some position-related concepts. A *position* is just an interest or stake in the financial value of something—some present or future asset or liability, to be exact.

Take a look at Table 7-1. With respect to forwards, futures, swaps, and call options, a long position connotes an interest or obligation with respect to buying the underlier. A short position implies an interest or obligation with respect to selling. The long party to a forward, for example, is obligated to buy the underlier, while the short party is obligated to sell. The long party to a call option is entitled to buy the underlier if he or she chooses to do so, in which case the short party is obligated to sell. The positional ramifications of a put option are just the reverse that of the call: the long party may have an interest in selling the underlier, in which case the short party is obligated to buy. Such obligations are sometimes known as *contingent liabilities*.

When hedging, the general idea is to choose a hedge position with an exposure opposite that of the thing you wish to hedge—in these cases, the underlier. So the decision whether to go long or short on your hedge position depends on whether you are long or short the underlier in the first place. And how can you tell? One way is by thinking of a long position in the underlier as connoting ownership and of a short position as a need, as shown in Table 7-2.

Say you own crude oil or will own it in the future. Consider yourself long oil. As the owner of oil, you are exposed to a decline

TABLE 7-1

Derivative Position Obligations and Rights

	Long Position	Short Position
Forward **Futures** **Swap**	Obligation to **buy** the underlier	Obligation to **sell** the underlier
Call option	Right to **buy** the underlier	Obligation to **sell** the underlier
Put option	Right to **sell** the underlier	Obligation to **buy** the underlier

TABLE 7-2

Underliers for Long and Short Positions

Long Position	Short Position
Present or future **ownership**	Present or future **need**

in the spot price of crude, because you won't be able to sell it for as much as you can today. To hedge the market risk of this long position, you might secure a short position in a forward or futures, or a long position in a put option, affording you the ability to sell your oil at a price you like. Conversely, if you will need oil in the future, consider yourself short oil. You are likewise exposed to spot price changes in the other direction. Should the price of oil increase, you will have to buy it for a higher price. You can hedge this short position with a long position in a forward or futures, or with a long position in a call option, affording you the ability to buy at a price you like.

Incidentally, there's a peculiar twist to the idea of a short position when the underlier is equity (stock). To be "short in stock" means you have borrowed shares, sold them, and taken the cash. This is known as *short selling*. The classic hope if you're a short seller is that the stock price will decrease, so when it comes time to return those borrowed shares, you buy them at a lower price than you received for selling them, pocketing the difference. Again, the idea of being short is analogous to a need. You will need shares in the future to return them to whomever you borrowed them from. To be long stock is just what you would imagine. You own the shares, plain and simple. We'll come across short selling again in Chapter 11, "Hedging a Derivatives Position."

HEDGING WITH FORWARD CONTRACTS

In Chapter 1, "Derivatives in a Nutshell," the tortilla maker bought forward contracts to lock in the price of corn for purchase in six months. And in Chapter 2, "The Forward Contract," the Gizmo Company bought foreign-exchange (FX) forwards denominated in U.S. dollars to lock in the price of a future purchase to be denominated in South Korean won.

In both cases, the hedger reduced the uncertainty of future prices. The hedged tortilla maker need not worry about the price of corn rising and cutting into the company's profits, and Gizmo need not worry about changes in the won-dollar exchange rate. (Recall that an exchange rate simply conveys the price of one currency in units of another.) Also, in both cases, the hedgers assumed long positions in the forward, as they intended to buy the underlier to satisfy their future need. And most important, both hedgers assumed an obligation to buy at the forward price, whether the underlier price rose or fell in the meantime.

Both of these examples had the hedger assume a long position in the forward contract, but consider the case where a short forward contract is what you need. Say you live in Chicago and purchased some property in Paris some time ago in euros, at a time when the U.S. dollar was much stronger against the euro than it is today. Back then, you could buy more euros per dollar than you can today. In other words, the price of euros (in dollars) has risen. Therefore, in dollar terms, your property investment has appreciated.

Say you plan to sell that property in six months, receiving euros, which you will then want to convert back to dollars. Can you lock in today the dollar value of the euros you expect to own in the future? You sure can. Just take a short position in a dollar-denominated FX forward contract to sell euros (however many you expect to receive from the buyer) in six months at today's exchange rate. Future ownership (of euros), future sell. But remember, if the dollar should *continue* to decline, so the dollar value of your investment climbs even more over the next six months, you won't realize that additional appreciation. You're locking in the dollar value today of those future euros, no matter what happens. Is there any way to avoid that? Sure. Buy FX put options instead, to sell euros in six months at today's rate. Future ownership, future sell. You'll need to shell out a premium, of course, but should the dollar weaken further you can just let those options expire worthless. If the dollar strengthens, lowering the price of euros in dollar terms, you can exercise the option and realize your gain. Table 7-3 summarizes when you should hedge to buy and when you should hedge to sell.

A forward hedge is really simple. The preexisting position in Gizmo's case is a future need for South Korean won. The value (if you will) of that position will decrease as the price of won increases. The value of the forward position also changes with the price of won, but in the opposite direction. Compared with other hedges,

TABLE 7-3

Underlier Positions and Hedge Guidelines

Long underlier → Present or future **ownership** → Hedge to **sell**
Short underlier → Present or future **need** → Hedge to **buy**

settling a forward hedge is uncomplicated: you simply take delivery of the goods and pay or receive the agreed-upon price.

HEDGING WITH FUTURES CONTRACTS

In Chapter 3, "The Futures Contract," Royal Mill used wheat futures to lock in the price of wheat for a purchase in six months. This might seem a lot like what the tortilla maker did with forward contracts, but there's one big difference: Royal Mill had no intention of actually buying wheat at the futures price, even though a futures contract commits the company to buy. When the delivery date came, Royal Mill bought wheat from its usual supplier—at a price greater than it had wanted to pay—and effectively canceled its long futures position by taking on a matching short position. The company paid more for the wheat than it had wanted to but made some money off the futures to compensate.

Just like the vast majority of all hedgers who use futures contracts, Royal Mill did not have to deal with delivery of the physical underlier. But the company did walk away with a financial gain, or trading profit, which it used to offset the fact that wheat prices had risen while it held the futures contract. Had the spot price of wheat fallen, Royal Mill would have experienced a loss on the contracts. But the price it paid on the spot market would have likewise fallen (i.e., the company would have paid a lower price to the grain supplier than it had been willing to pay), again neutralizing the change in the market price of wheat.

As you'll recall, a futures contract is just a highly standardized form of a forward contract, traded on an exchange where it is marked to market at the end of every trading day. In many ways, then, hedging a future need with futures is like hedging it with a forward: you figure out how much of the underlier you want to buy on some future date and go long the appropriate number of contracts. The big difference, though, is that the vast majority of futures contracts do not result in the delivery of the underlier. They are closed out on (or before) the delivery date. What the hedger cares about is the pure value change, not the literal delivery of the underlier.

Now, because futures contracts are so highly standardized, it's often difficult to effect a truly perfect hedge. With respect to price uncertainty, the FX forward hedge described for Gizmo Company is virtually perfect: Gizmo will get exactly what it needs, when it needs it, for the price it wants to pay. Not so for Royal Mill. For example, the delivery point of the contract wheat may be 1,000 miles or more from where the company needs it, so shipping costs alter the net hedge. Or the wheat specified in the contract may not be exactly the type of wheat Royal needs. So the spot price of the wheat it needs may change in a different way from the price of the contract wheat. Maybe the price of Royal's wheat goes up a lot and the price of the contract wheat goes up only a little, or maybe the prices change in opposite directions. In any of these cases, the company won't realize the offsetting gains and losses it had hoped for.

This is an example of *basis risk*, which comes into play when you hedge with something whose price doesn't change in exactly the same way as the price of the thing you are hedging. In the ideal case, the value of your hedge position is "perfectly negatively cor-related," as a mathematician would say, meaning it changes in the exact opposite way of your preexisting position. But this is simply not possible all the time. A little basis risk is generally okay, how-ever, and knowing how much is acceptable is what separates effec-tive hedgers from the not-so-effective.

So why do people hedge with a futures instead of a forward contract? Liquidity and credit risk. You simply may not find a coun-terparty willing to do the forward you need, and if you do, how sure can you be that they'll stick around when it comes time to deliver if the market moves against them? Now, for sure, there are many situations in which you can find a creditworthy counterparty willing to write you a forward contract. It happens all the time in the OTC markets, where buyers and sellers know how to find each other, and where they typically employ some form of *collateralization* (i.e., one party or the other pledges some cash or marketable securi-ties in the event they can't fulfill their obligation) to mitigate default risk. But when you can't find someone, it sure is nice to have those liquid futures markets.

Not every futures hedge position is a long position. Wheat growers, for example, are exposed to the spot price of wheat but in the opposite way from that of the miller. If the price of wheat decreases, they make *less* profit when it comes time to sell. So they can put on a hedge consisting of short positions, whose value will also change with the spot price of wheat but in the opposite way from that of a long position.

HEDGING WITH SWAPS

In Chapter 4, "The Swap Contract," the Gondor Corporation executed a plain-vanilla interest rate swap with Marlow Securities to effectively convert a preexisting floating-rate loan to a fixed rate. Entrepreneurs Boris and Chloe executed a swap with each other, allowing Boris to convert his preexisting floating-rate loan to fixed, and Chloe to convert her fixed-rate loan to floating. The Gondor example, where one party was a swaps dealer, is far more common than the Boris-Chloe example. Swaps certainly can be executed between hedgers, for virtually no cost, as it's in the interest of both parties to set the terms of the swap such that it has no value at the outset.[1] In practice, however, most swaps are actually executed with a swaps dealer, who "marks up" the fixed rate (or applies a *spread*, or *margin*, to the floating rate) such that the swap has some nonzero present value to the dealer.

Regardless of your counterparty, a swap mitigates uncertainty about the future price of money as conveyed by interest rates. And as with forwards and futures, parties to a swap are obligated to buy or sell at the predetermined rates, no matter what happens in the spot markets. Also, because swaps are generally traded in the over-the-counter market, they are more akin to forwards than futures. As forwards-in-disguise, then, swaps are inherently less liquid than futures and carry more credit risk. But in practice, the OTC swaps market is so darn vast that it's pretty easy to find a dealer to do a swap, and most swap transactions require one or the other party

---

[1] The theory here, and it makes some sense, is that each party is making the best of its comparative advantage over the other. The same idea is often applied in international economics in support of free trade (wherein countries are allowed to exploit their comparative advantage, making everyone theoretically better off) versus protectionism (where they are not).

to post collateral to mitigate the possibility of defaulting on their obligations.

You might have this question in your mind about Gondor or anyone who uses a swap to convert a floating-rate loan to a fixed rate: Why don't they just borrow at a fixed rate and forget about all this swapping? Excellent question. It turns out that often a fixed-rate loan is more expensive (that is, the present value of the interest charge is greater) than a floater. In these cases, it can be less costly in the long run to take out a floating-rate loan and convert it to fixed with a swap. And as you know, credit is a factor when lenders decide whether or not and how they will lend money. A business desiring a loan may simply not have good enough credit for a fixed-rate loan but can secure a floater. Bottom line, floating-rate debt is easier to come by, so there's a lot of it out there.

Alternatives to a Swap

In Chapter 9, "Pricing Swaps," we'll demonstrate how a swap is exactly the same as a bundle of forward contracts known as *forward rate agreements* (*FRAs*). This means a hedger could in theory use a portfolio of FRAs instead of a swap to convert a fixed-rate obligation into a floater or vice versa. But in practice, it's difficult to set up such a portfolio that exactly offsets your preexisting loan, which may include amortization or compounding or other features not commonly found in FRAs. No matter how unusual your situation, you can probably find any number of swaps dealers ready to concoct a hedge that fits like a glove.

And while we're on this vein of alternatives, you could also hedge your loan using exactly the same hedging instruments that swaps dealers are likely to use to hedge their exposure: interest rate futures contracts, government bonds, or some combination of the two. (You'll see how this is done in Chapter 11, "Hedging a Derivatives Position.") You would even save yourself the dealer's fee. But you'll have a *lot* of work to do constructing a hedge of futures and bonds with an acceptable level of basis risk. For example, eurodollar futures (a highly liquid contract traded on the Chicago Mercantile Exchange, whose underlier is a LIBOR loan) expire on set, quarterly dates. Those dates might not line up with the dates you need. Also, these contracts have notionals of $1 million, so if you don't have a loan principal rounded to the millions, you won't get a perfect hedge.

It comes down to packaging. Swaps dealers don't have as much of a problem here, as they hedge hundreds or thousands of swaps all at once as a portfolio of swap obligations, and this *diversification* is itself risk-reducing. (The swaps in the portfolio have a variety of exposure characteristics, and some of them are bound to cancel each other out for a natural hedge.) And because of the sheer size of a dealer's operation, the dealer simply has more "wiggle room" when it comes to basis risk than an individual hedger. What's more, maintaining a futures and bond hedge takes nearly constant work. With a swap, you let the dealer take care of that and get on with your own business.

When it comes to hedging an exposure to changing interest rates, swaps are the most popular of interest rate derivatives. But there are others. If you don't want to give up both downside (the prospect of loss) and upside (the prospect of gain) by locking in a fixed rate—remember, these are forwards—but just want to shed the downside in the event your floating rate goes up, you could use an interest rate cap instead of a swap. You'll pay a premium up front, as a cap is an option, but if rates decline, you'll get to enjoy it.

For example, say you take out a floating-rate loan of $1 million. At the outset of this loan, you have no idea what rate will be used to calculate your loan payments: 6 percent? 7 percent? Say you're comfortable with the prospect of making payments at a rate up to 6.5 percent but no higher, for a maximum payment of $65,000. Of course, you have to make the payment no matter how high rates go, but what if you could count on someone making up the difference between 6.5 percent and wherever rates happen to go? Say rates go to 7.5 percent, which is 1 percentage point higher than your limit. You could use a cap, with a notional of $1 million and strike price of 6.5 percent, such that you would receive $10,000 (1 percent of a million), or the payoff of the cap, which you then use to supplement your loan payment. If rates go to 8 percent, you receive $15,000. And so on.

HEDGING WITH OPTIONS

In Chapter 5, "The Option Contract," small investor Greta buys call options on a stock, but not to hedge! She is a speculator with a view that the stock of ZED Corporation is undervalued and its price will rise. In the example, it turns out she is right and makes a nice profit. However, in reality, the price of ZED could have fallen, causing her to lose 100 percent of her bet. Options can also, of course, be used for hedging. One common example is the *protective put*, to provide "portfolio insurance" against a decline in the value of a stock portfolio. Here's an example:

Boxwood Capital, a small hedge fund,[2] has a diversified portfolio of U.S. stocks whose current value is roughly $120 million. Boxwood wants to protect the portfolio against a large decline in value, and in particular does not want it to fall below $110 million. And the firm is willing to pay a premium for such insurance. So Boxwood buys put options on a market index, struck such that the firm will be compensated for a market decline taking the portfolio below the $110 million floor.

The instrument Boxwood uses is the SPX index option contract. It's a cash-settled, European-style option traded at the Chicago Board Options Exchange whose underlier is the S&P 500 index. The value of the index changes all the time, pretty much in step with the overall market, and conveys an average price (adjusted for stock splits and whatnot) of 500 different stocks. Calls and puts are available at a variety of stock prices above and below the current index value, at a variety of expiration dates.

Say the index is currently at 1,200, the current value of Boxwood's stock portfolio is $120 million, and the firm doesn't want it to fall below $110 million. So Boxwood buys 100,000 puts expiring in three months with a strike price of $1,100, for a premium of $6 per contract.[3] Why did Boxwood go long puts and not calls? Because it is hedging an ownership.

Now fast-forward three months. The S&P 500 index has fallen steeply to 1,050. And because the composition of Boxwood's portfolio is nearly identical to the S&P 500 index portfolio, its value has likewise fallen to $105 million. Damn. But its put options, struck at $1,100, expire in the money with a payoff of $50 each. So the 100,000 options together pay off to the tune of $5 million. Add that to the $105 million value of Boxwood's portfolio, and the net value comes to $110 million, just where the firm wanted to be. Now, this insur-

---

[2] Generally speaking, a *hedge fund* is just a firm that manages investors' money, not entirely unlike a mutual fund. However, hedge funds tend to invest money more aggressively than a typical mutual fund, using a combination of speculation, arbitrage, and whatever else the fund managers can dream up.

[3] In reality, Boxwood buys 1/100 of this number of contracts at a premium 100 times this amount, but that's just an operational detail we'll leave out for clarity. The math works out the same.

ance didn't come for free, of course, as the firm paid six bucks per contract—more than half a million dollars. Had the index been equal to or greater than the strike price of $1,100 on expiration, the firm would have lost the entire premium. And the "policy" was only for three months. If Boxwood wants to continue this hedge, the firm will need to keep buying puts.

The protective put is a common application of options, especially when stocks are trading at record highs. It's not a perfect hedge unless your stock portfolio matches exactly the portfolio of the index, but if set up properly, it can at least offer some income in the event of a major dip, to help offset the loss on your stocks. Also, when considering a protective put, it's crucial to consider the option premium. An option is not free, so money you spend on a premium lowers the net return of your portfolio. This insurance isn't always cheap. Between the portfolio mismatch and premium cost, deciding whether or not a protective put makes sense for a particular situation is not a trivial exercise—but hey, what is?

HEDGING WITH CREDIT DERIVATIVES

In Chapter 6, "Credit Derivatives," an investor holding $10 million of corporate bonds purchased a credit default swap from an insurance company to protect it in the event the bond issuer declared bankruptcy. As mentioned previously, credit derivatives in this sense provide a performance guarantee (i.e., guaranteeing that the bond issuer will perform up to its financial obligations and remain solvent), in contrast to the price guarantee inherently provided by forwards, futures, swaps, and options.

The CDS also differs from the other derivatives we've seen with respect to payoff. The payoff of a typical option, for instance, is proportional to the extent to which it expires in the money. If a 50-strike call option expires when the underlier is trading for $52, the payoff is $2. If the underlier is trading for $56, then the payoff is $6. And so on. It's the same for most forwards, futures, and swaps. A CDS like the one in our example, by contrast, pays the holder $10 million whether the underlier (the bond) is worth $8 million or $2 million. This sort of "binary" or all-or-nothing characteristic can also be employed in exotic versions of just about any derivative, especially options, but it's not an inherent quality of those derivatives, as it is with many CDSs.

And that's a sampling of what hedging with derivatives is all about. Next we turn to the valuation, or pricing, of derivatives. Assessing the value of a derivative is crucial no matter what you use them for. And by the way, the next three chapters on pricing include plenty of additional examples of risk management, so be sure to check those out if I've not quite slaked your thirst with the examples thus far.

CHAPTER 8

Pricing Forwards and Futures

The essence of pricing a forward or futures contract, and for that matter the swap, revolves around taking an observed spot price and adjusting it for time. With each of these contracts, you are dealing with a future transaction you are certain will occur. (With options, you don't have that certainty, so the pricing task is more difficult.) Knowing with certainty that a transaction will occur allows us to price a contract by adjusting the spot price for things like interest, storage costs, and other costs that stem from the deferral of the transaction. We can safely disregard any probability of the under-lier increasing or decreasing in value, because it just doesn't matter. Provided the contract is not canceled, the long party will buy, and the short party will sell.

Recall the delivery or contract price for a forward or futures contract. It's the fixed price at which the long party commits to buy and the short party commits to sell at some point in the future. The essence of this entire chapter is all about determining a delivery price. And here's the key to that: for a new forward or futures contract, the delivery price is the one—and only one—such that the value of the contract is zero. In a contract where the sole objective of each party is to lock in a price for a future transaction, neither party wants to incur a cost. And since a forward is zero-sum game, with one party's gain offset by the other's pain, the only fair price of a forward upon execution must be zero. Any other price gives one party a benefit and the other a cost. Now, again, we're only talking about the forward upon execution. Once the parties shake hands and time starts ticking, and the underlier's price starts changing, the value of a contract is a different story. But at the moment of execution, neither party has an advantage over the other.[1]

The delivery price of a new, zero-value forward contract is known as a *forward price*. Its analog for futures is the *futures price*. Because forward prices and futures prices are calculated intuitively the same way, and to simplify the text, whenever you read "forward price," you can safely assume it applies to a futures price, too. (There is, technically, a subtle difference between a forward and futures price due to daily settlement, a difference we won't go into.) We'll spend a fair amount of ink in this chapter on the various formulas for calculating a forward price. These formulas produce a forward price by adjusting a spot price for the costs and benefits of waiting for a delivery date, known collectively as *cost of carry* and encompassing such things as storage cost, interest charges, and the benefit or convenience of having a good in your possession.

It's not always easy when learning this stuff to get straight the differences between "delivery price" and "value" and "forward price." Just remember that the *delivery price* is the guaranteed price at which the long party will buy and short party will sell, set in stone when the forward is first executed, never to change over the life of the forward. The *value* is a measure, which changes over time, of how much better or worse off the parties are for having entered into the forward agreement. And a *forward price* is the delivery price of a theoretical new contract whose value is zero. (This makes a forward "price" quite a different thing altogether from a stock "price.") If it still seems the delivery price and forward price are the same thing, just think of it this way: A delivery price is associated with an actual forward contract (Farmer Joe agrees to sell 200 bushels of grapes to winemaker Leo for $5 per bushel next October). A delivery price may also include a fee paid from one party to the other.

---

[1] Notice I conditioned the zero-value example by saying it applies when the sole objective of *both* parties is to lock in the price for a future transaction. Oftentimes, only one of the parties has a real concern about a future transaction, and the other party enters into the forward only as a service to the other. Here in this chapter, however, we are talking about the broker/dealer who specializes in selling (or buying) forwards. The broker/dealer for OTC forwards typically requires a fee for the service and therefore adds some booty to the zero value, often by adjusting the delivery price. But theoretically, and certainly for the sake of learning these things, think of a forward value at execution as just a goose egg.

A forward price is the delivery price of a zero-value, theoretical forward contract that may or may not actually happen. It does not include any fees.

And what is the value of an existing forward or futures contract? As we'll see, for a forward, it's generally the present value of the difference between its delivery price and the current forward price. The value of a futures contract is the difference between the current futures price for that contract and the previous day's closing futures price. Forward contract value and futures contract value differ due to daily settlement, and you'll see further on in this chapter exactly why.

DISCOUNTING, PRESENT VALUES, AND FUTURE VALUES

If you're comfortable with the concepts and mechanics of discounting and continuous compounding, you can jump right over this section. If not, you will be delighted to know that the vast majority of math required for pricing forwards and futures involves just one mathematical procedure: adjusting monetary values for time. The fundamental concept here is that money invested (or lent) grows with time. Going forward in time, in which we calculate a *future value*, takes a known value today and calculates a value for a future date, given some interest rate or other rate that behaves like interest. Adjusting backward is known as *discounting*, and here we calculate a *present value*, given some future value and an interest rate.

Think of time as a line going off endlessly in either direction from a zero point at its center. The zero point represents a time at which you know the value of something. All points to the right represent a later time, and all points to the left an earlier time. Future valuation takes a monetary value known at time 0 (typically "now") and asks, "What does it grow to as we go forward in time?" Present valuation takes a monetary value known at a time 0 and asks, "What does it shrink to as we go back to some earlier time?" That earlier time is typically the present time. Take a look at Figure 8-1.

One of the reasons money can grow with time is, of course, interest. Interest is the price of borrowing money (or payment received for lending it) and is just a growth rate. For example, a present value of $100 (think of this as the investment or principal

FIGURE 8-1

Future Valuation and Present Valuation

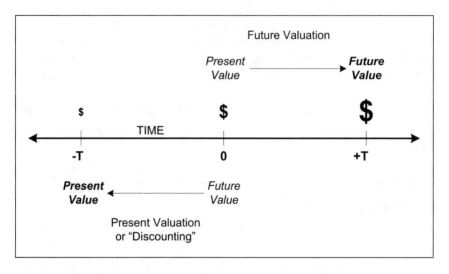

amount) in an account that pays 6 percent annually grows to $106 (a future value) in one year. Here's the math:[2]

$$FV = PV \times (1 + rt)$$
$$= 100 \times (1 + [0.06 \times 1]) = 100 \times 1.06$$
$$= 106$$

where:

$$FV = \text{future value}$$
$$PV = \text{present value}$$
$$r = \text{annual rate of interest}$$
$$t = \text{time in years}$$

The key to how much money actually grows is not just the interest rate but also the *compounding frequency*. In other words, we need to know the frequency at which earned interest is added to the

_____

[2] Notice we indicate multiplication either by the multiplication sign (×) or by squishing two symbols together (*rt*). We'll use both kinds of notation throughout, choosing whichever seems clearer.

principal in order for the earned interest itself to earn interest. In the one-year example, we assumed annual compounding, so it wasn't an issue. But say interest is compounded every six months. After the first six months, we have earned $3 of interest ($I$), like so:

$$I_{\text{1st 6 mo.}} = 100 \times (0.06)(0.5) = 100 \times 0.03 = 3$$

Notice we used a t factor of 0.5 for one-half year. This $3 of interest is added to the principal, giving us $103 on which to calculate interest for the second six months. Here then is the total value of this investment after one year:

$$I_{\text{1st 6 mo.}} = 100 \times (0.06)(0.5) = 100 \times 0.03 = 3$$
$$I_{\text{2nd 6 mo.}} = 103 \times 0.03 = 3.09$$
$$FV = PV + I_{\text{1st 6 mo.}} + I_{\text{2nd 6 mo.}}$$
$$= 100 + 3 + 3.09 = 106.09$$

So we earn a tad more interest—$6.09 instead of $6.00—by compounding every six months instead of annually. And what if we compound every three months, or quarterly?

$$I_{\text{Q1}} = 100 \times 0.015 = 1.5$$
$$I_{\text{Q2}} = 101.5 \times 0.015 = 1.5225$$
$$I_{\text{Q3}} = 103.0225 \times 0.015 = 1.5453$$
$$I_{\text{Q4}} = 104.5678 \times 0.015 = 1.5685$$
$$FV = PV + I_{\text{Q1}} + I_{\text{Q2}} + I_{\text{Q3}} + I_{\text{Q4}} = 106.14$$

We earn even more interest—$6.14—by compounding quarterly.

Clearly, the more frequently we compound, the more interest we earn. So how far does this go? What if we compound daily? Or every minute? Or how about continuously? Is there some limit to how much we can earn? Yes. The *limit* is in fact fundamental to calculus, which gives us a remarkably simple formula for calculating the end value of an investment where interest is compounded continuously. Here it is for our previous example:

$$FV = PV \times e^{rt}$$
$$= 100 \times e^{0.06(1)} = 106.18$$

So the most interest we can earn is $6.18, for a maximum future value of $106.18.

But what is this e that we raised to the power of our annual interest rate? It's Euler's number, the base of the natural exponential function e^x. The number represented by e is an irrational one that starts out 2.7182 . . . . Now you can ignore that fact and let your calculator worry about it. Any decent calculator has a button for raising e to some power, or exponent (if you don't have such a calculator, go get one). And don't let this Euler stuff scare you away. It really is the simplest way to deal with interest calculations.

For periods longer than one year, we simply increase the t factor. So for a future value over, say, two years, we have:

$$FV = PV \times e^{0.06(2)}$$
$$= 100 \times 1.1275 = 112.75$$

So far, we have calculated future values. How do we go backward in time, to calculate the present value of some known future value at a given interest rate? For this formula, just swap the FV and PV, and put a negative sign on the interest rate:[3]

$$PV = FV \times e^{-rt}$$

Let's give this a test drive by starting with our one-year future value of $106.18 and our interest rate of 6 percent. What is the present value, or principal required today to grow to this future value in one year's time? Using the PV formula and rounding the result to the nearest penny, we get:

$$PV = 106.18 \times e^{-0.06(1)}$$
$$= 106.18 \times 0.9418 = 100$$

Just as we expected. And what is the present value when the one-year future value is 100, again using 6 percent?

$$PV = 100 \times e^{-0.06(1)} = 94.18$$

---

[3] Recall from algebra that raising something to a negative power is equivalent to dividing 1 by the same thing raised to a positive. Therefore, if you prefer, you can think of the present-value formula as $PV = FV/e^{rt}$.

FIGURE 8-2

Examples of Present Value and Future Value

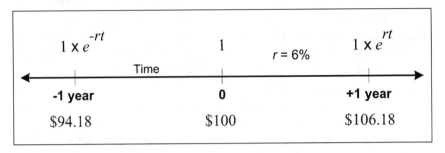

And that is how we calculate values as time glides in either direction, due to interest or any other factor that causes money to grow over time. Figure 8-2 shows how it all looks on a time line.

Formulas 8.1 and 8.2 are the future-value and present-value formulas for calculating changes in value as time glides in either direction, due to interest or any other factor that causes money to grow continuously with time. Notice the difference in the sign of the interest rate factor:

$$FV = PV \times e^{rt} \qquad \text{(Formula 8.1)}$$

$$PV = FV \times e^{-rt} \qquad \text{(Formula 8.2)}$$

where:

> FV = future value
>
> PV = present value
>
> e = Euler's number = 2.71828183 . . .
>
> r = annual rate of interest
>
> t = time in years

COST OF CARRY

Consider the value of a forward upon delivery. That's just the payoff, as illustrated by the payoff diagram, which we know is given by the difference between the spot price and delivery price. Recall from Chapter 1 the tortilla maker's long forward to buy 1,000 bushels of corn at $25. The spot price on the delivery date was $28, for a valuation of ($28 − $25) × 1,000, or $3,000.

What then is the value of a forward on some date before delivery? There are two basic components. The first is the spot-delivery difference we just talked about, which naturally changes with time. (The spot price changes over the life of a forward, but the delivery price does not; the difference between them must change as well. Easy.) The second component is cost of carry. This is the cost of maintaining or "carrying" a forward position over time. Consider storage. Commodity underliers such as corn and oil must be stored, and storage costs money. And who pays this cost? Until delivery day, the goods are held by the short party, so that party incurs this cost, which will affect the value of a forward. (Think what a merchant might say if you ask to buy something from her inventory but not for six months: "You want me to keep this stuff for six months and then you buy it from me? Okay, but you have to pay me for storage.")

Another cost of carry common to all forwards is interest. Now, interest is simply the cost of borrowing money or, put another way, the payment for loaning or investing it. And how is this a cost of carry? Consider that a long party to a forward contract is obligated to buy the underlier—but not, of course, until the delivery date. Were the long party to buy spot, he or she would be out some cash. But with a forward, the long party gets to hang onto that cash and can invest it, earning interest. The short party, of course, doesn't get that cash until delivery. So the short party misses the opportunity to invest the proceeds of the sale, thus incurring an *opportunity cost*. (To the short party, interest truly is a "cost" of carry; to the long party, it's actually a benefit, but we still call it cost of carry.)

Other costs of carry can include income paid to the holder of an underlier, such as dividends for stock underliers (these are periodic payments to the stockholder—i.e., the short party) and something less tangible known as *convenience yield* (the benefit of possessing the underlier, such as the ability to survive a shortage). We'll get back to all of these a bit later in this chapter.

THE IDEA BEHIND A FORWARD PRICE

By piecing together what we've seen so far, you can see that the value of a forward at any time is basically the sum of two things:

the difference between the ever-changing spot price and never-changing delivery price, plus the cost of carry (which can be a positive or negative value, as we will see in a bit). Here's how it looks as a basic formula for forward value:

$$\text{Forward Value}_{\text{Long}} = (\text{Spot Price} - \text{Delivery Price}) + \text{Carry}$$
$$\text{Forward Value}_{\text{Short}} = (\text{Delivery Price} - \text{Spot Price}) + \text{Carry}$$

Now think about what you know when setting up a new forward contract. You know the spot price, you know the carry, and you know the value has to be zero. You don't know the delivery price. The delivery price of a new contract—the forward price—is the only unknown factor at the outset of a deal. So to calculate a forward price, we just back it out of the basic valuation formula.

Consider again the formula for a long contract:

$$\text{Forward Value}_{\text{Long}} = (\text{Spot Price} - \text{Delivery Price}) + \text{Carry}$$

When crafting a forward, the parties have no control over spot price (call it s), nor over cost of carry (C), nor over the value of the forward (v), which must be zero. They can only tweak the delivery price (F, for forward price). Rearranging the basic formula, we get an algebraic expression that looks like this:

$$v = (s + C) - F$$

This equation just says the value of a forward is the result of adding spot price and cost of carry (which, remember, can be negative) and subtracting the forward price. Recall that this is basically how we calculated the value of the tortilla maker's forward, only we valued as of delivery date, so there was no carry. Knowing that v at inception is zero, we can plug that in and rearrange:

$$0 = (s + C) - F$$
$$F_{\text{Long}} = s + C$$

So a forward price is just spot plus cost of carry. And by "cost," we mean an actual cost to the short party. If it's a "benefit" to the short party, we subtract it.

Let's make our formula clearer by separating C into c (lower-case) for cost to the short party and b for benefit to the short party:

$$C = c - b$$

Ergo:

$$F_{Long} = s + c - b$$

Consider a one-year forward on a barrel of oil whose spot price upon execution is $100. By executing such a forward, the long party is obligated to buy that barrel of oil, but not for one year. If the long party bought today, he would be out $100. But he gets to keep that $100 for a year and put it to work earning interest. Let's say the interest rate is 6 percent with annual compounding and the rate is absolutely guaranteed, or risk-free. (More on this in the next section.) Upon execution of the forward and the simultaneous investing of $100, the long party can count on receiving $6 of interest on the same date he will buy the oil. The long party will also get his $100 back, giving him $106 to buy that barrel of oil. Therefore, the correct delivery price for this contract, assuming no other cost of carry, is $106.

And what does the short party think of this price? It suits her fine. On execution of the forward, she is obligated to sell the oil, but not for one year, so she loses the opportunity to invest the $100 and earn that $6. The extra $6 compensates her for the opportunity cost of selling forward versus selling spot. Clearly, with respect to interest, the fair delivery price for this deal is spot price adjusted for interest, or $106.

Now, oil is a physical good that must be stored, and storage costs money. The long party need not pay for storage between now and delivery price (he doesn't have it yet to store). The short party does. Say the annual storage cost of a barrel of oil is $7. This is another cost (an actual out-of-pocket cost this time, not an opportunity cost) to add to the interest we calculated. So now the fair price of this forward is $113, or $100 + $6 + $7.

THE RISK-FREE INTEREST RATE

Before we get to the formulas, we need to think about what interest rate we'll use. For virtually all derivative valuations, we use a *risk-free interest rate* for discounting. (For interest rate derivatives, we generally use a different rate for calculating payments.) The risk-free or "reference" rate is essentially a guaranteed rate of return on an investment with no risk of loss. Why use a risk-free rate? Strange as this may seem, it turns out we can safely price derivatives assuming all investors are perfectly risk neutral and don't really give a dang whether prices go up or down. This characteristic is known as *risk neutrality*, and we'll explain it later in Appendix C, "More Binomial Option Pricing." For now, suffice it to say we can disregard risk preferences when pricing derivatives and can therefore eliminate the "risk premium" component of an interest rate and use what's left over.

One risk-free rate commonly used for derivative valuation is known as *LIBOR*, an abbreviation of London Inter-Bank Offered Rate. We'll learn more about LIBOR in Appendix A, "All About Interest."

The risk-free rate is almost always lower than a rate of return that carries risk. Why? It's that risk premium again. Think of interest as a reward for taking risk. The more risk you take, the more you can expect to earn. The stock market, for example, generally provides a return greater than U.S. Treasuries, when returns are measured over a sufficiently long period of time. But as any stock investor knows, that market can also return quite a bit less than Treasuries, especially over a short period of time. Stocks are riskier than Treasuries over the long haul, so as such they return more to their investors. And consider the return of "investing" in roulette, blackjack, or a slot machine. You can make quite a handsome return, but only by taking the considerable risk of losing your investment (er, bet) entirely. A U.S. savings bond won't make you wealthy, but you can count on Uncle Sam to return your investment and at least a little bit more. Uncle Sammy the blackjack dealer offers no such assurance.

FORWARD PRICE FORMULAS

Enough of the background stuff! We're ready now for the formulas for calculating a forward price.

Basic Forward

The simplest of underliers requires no storage cost and generates no income (e.g., dividends). The only cost of carry is interest. The forward price (*F*) for such an underlier is just the future value of the underlier, given a spot price *S*, interest rate *r*, and time period *t*. It's given by Formula 8.3:

$$F = Se^{rt}$$ (Formula 8.3)

Example: You agree to buy from your brother 100 shares of stock in MGrove Inc. in six months. MGrove pays no dividends and is now trading for $15.50. The risk-free interest rate is 2 percent. What is the fair market forward price? We are given all we need for the right side:

$$S = 15.50 \times 100 = 1{,}550$$
$$r = 0.02$$
$$t = 0.5$$

The value of *e*, of course, never changes, and we let a calculator worry about converting it to a number anyway. So putting it all together, we can solve for *F*:

$$F = Se^{rt}$$
$$= 1{,}550 \times e^{0.02(0.5)}$$
$$= 1{,}550 \times 1.01005$$
$$= 1{,}565.58$$

The fair-market delivery price for this contract is $1,565.58, or $15.66 per share.

Forward with Storage

When an underlier incurs a fixed storage cost, the forward price is the future value of the sum of two things: spot (*S*) plus the present value of storage, *U*. (By "fixed" we just mean the storage cost does not change with the price of the underlier.) The forward price with storage is given by Formula 8.4:

$$F = (S + U)e^{rt}$$ (Formula 8.4)

Example: Indostan Energy agrees to buy from the Diablo Drillery 5,000 barrels of crude oil one year forward. The oil is selling on the spot market for $32 per barrel. The cost of storing this kind of oil is $1.50 per barrel per quarter, payable at the beginning of each quarter. The risk-free interest rate is 3 percent. What is the correct forward price for this deal?

First let's handle storage. For the formula, we need the present value of storage costs, from which we will calculate a future value. (Sounds weird, I know, but just hang in there.) Over the life of this forward, there will be four payments for storage made at the start of each quarter in the amount of $7,500 (i.e., 5,000 barrels at $1.50 each). Think of these as four cash flows. One occurs now (upon execution of the forward), one in three months, one in six, and one in nine. To calculate the present value of all storage, we just calculate the PV of each of the four cash flows and then add up the results. Notice that the PV of the first cash flow does not including any discounting:

$$PV_{storage} = CF_{0mo.} + CF_{3mo.} + CF_{6mo.} + CF + CF_{9mo}$$
$$PV = 7{,}500 + 7{,}500e^{-0.03(0.25)} + 7{,}500e^{-0.03(0.5)} + 7{,}500e^{-0.03(0.75)}$$
$$= 7{,}500 + 7{,}443.96 + 7{,}388.34 + 7{,}333.13$$
$$= 29{,}665.43$$

Now we have everything in present-value terms, so we just plug the following amounts into the formula to get the future value of the whole enchilada:

$$S = 32 \times 5{,}000 = 160{,}000$$
$$U = 29{,}665.43$$
$$r = 0.03$$
$$t = 1$$

Putting it all together we have:

$$F = (S + U)e^{rt}$$
$$= (160{,}000 + 29{,}665.43) \times e^{0.03(1)}$$
$$= 195{,}441.60$$

The fair-market delivery price for this contract is $195,441.60, or just about $39 per barrel.

When storage costs change with the spot price of the underlier, we call those *proportional storage* costs. Such costs are not unlike the cost of interest, which also depends on the price of the underlier. The forward price of an underlier with proportional storage cost, then, is the future value of the underlier, given a spot price S, annual interest rate r, and time period t, with the interest rate "adjusted" by the proportional storage cost u. It's given by Formula 8.5:

$$F = Se^{(r + u)t} \qquad\qquad \text{(Formula 8.5)}$$

What's an example of a proportional storage cost? Spoilage. If some portion of a good is expected to spoil, we can think of that as a "storage" cost to the short party.

Example: Juice-maker SqueezeMax agrees to buy 1,000 bushels of apples from apple grower Joe in three months. Joe knows from experience that stored apples lose 2 percent of their value to bugs, mice, and rot. Apples are currently selling wholesale for $6 per bushel. The risk-free interest rate is 4 percent. There is no precalculation this time, as we already have what we need:

$$S = 1,000 \times 6 = 6,000$$
$$u = 0.02$$
$$r = 0.04$$
$$t = 0.25$$

Putting it all together, we can solve for F:

$$\begin{aligned}
F &= Se^{(r + u)t} \\
&= 6,000 \times e^{(0.04 + 0.02)(0.25)} \\
&= 6,000 \times e^{0.015} \\
&= 6,090.68
\end{aligned}$$

The fair-market delivery price for this contract is $6,090.68.

Forward with Income

Income, such as dividends on a stock underlier, is like storage costs in reverse. It represents benefits to the short party. Now, the forward price is just the future value of spot, S, less the present value of income, I. So the delivery price is determined by Formula 8.6:

$$F = (S - I)e^{rt} \qquad\qquad \text{(Formula 8.6)}$$

Example: You agree to buy from your sister 400 shares of stock in Acme Industries in one year. Acme is currently trading for \$36 per share. Acme pays a quarterly dividend to its shareholders; the expected dividend is \$0.25 per share. The risk-free interest rate is 2 percent. What is fair market forward price?

As with storage, we need the PV of income. Over the life of this forward, there will be four dividend payments (cash flows) made at the end of each quarter for \$100 (i.e., 400 shares at 0.25 each). One of these payments occurs in 3 months, the next in 6, then 9, then 12. To calculate the present value of all dividends, we just calculate the PV of each of the four cash flows and then add up the results.

$$PV_{income} = Dividends_{3\ mo.} + Dividends_{6\ mo.} + Dividends_{9\ mo.} + Dividends_{12\ mo.}$$

$$= 100e^{-0.02(0.25)} + 100e^{-0.02(0.5)} + 100e^{-0.02(0.75)} + 100e^{-0.02(1)}$$

$$= 99.50 + 99.01 + 98.51 + 98.02$$

$$= 395.04$$

We are given all we need for the right side of the formula:

$$S = 36 \times 400 = 14{,}400$$
$$I = 395.04$$
$$r = 0.02$$
$$t = 1$$

So putting it all together, we can solve for F:

$$F = (S - I)e^{rt}$$
$$= (14{,}400 - 395.04) \times e^{0.02(1)}$$
$$= 14{,}287.88$$

The fair-market delivery price for this contract is \$14,287.88.

Sometimes underlier income is proportional to its spot price. For example, when the underlier is a stock index with dozens or hundreds of individual stocks, we treat the dividend income from such a "basket" as some percentage of the index spot price. (That's much easier than figuring the actual dividend stream of hundreds of stocks!) So as with proportional storage, we adjust the interest rate (r) by the proportional income factor (i) when calculating the future value of the underlier, as shown in Formula 8.7:

$$F = Se^{(r - i)t}$$

(Formula 8.7)

Example: You agree to buy from your broker 200 shares of the Midland stock index (MLX) in one year. MLX is an index composed of stock from the 50 largest agricultural companies in the midwestern United States and is currently trading for $54 per share.[4] MLX is expected to pay an annual dividend equal to 0.5 percent of its share price (i.e., 0.005 times the share price). The risk-free interest rate is 3 percent.

This is easier than it might seem. Again, there's no precalculation of PVs this time, as we already have what we need:

$$S = 200 \times 54 = 10,800$$
$$r = 0.03$$
$$I = 0.005$$
$$t = 1$$

Putting it all together, we solve for F:

$$F = Se^{(r - i)t}$$
$$= 10,800 \times e^{(0.03 - 0.005)(1)}$$
$$= 10,800 \times e^{0.025(1)}$$
$$= 11,073.40$$

The fair-market delivery price for this contract is $11,073.40.

Holding an underlier can have a less tangible benefit than income, known as a *convenience yield*. For example, if there's a shortage on a good, it can be quite nice (convenient) to have it on hand. Dealing with this convenience yield is computationally identical to dealing with proportional income. Just substitute the convenience yield (y) for the income rate (i), as in Formula 8.8:

$$F = Se^{(r - y)t}$$

(Formula 8.8)

---

[4] Don't call your broker. MLX exists only in my head.

Incidentally, convenience yields are often implied from, or backed out of, observed market prices and not explicitly entered into a formula as the other factors are. They are something of a fudge factor to make the equality between forward prices and their other input factors hold true.

Forward Price of Currency

When the underlier is a foreign currency, we consider not only the domestic interest rate but also the risk-free foreign rate (r_f). There's no need to go into details, but suffice it to say that exchange rates are influenced in part by prevailing interest rates in the respective countries. Bottom line, the foreign interest rate represents income to the short party and is just proportional income, as in Formula 8.9:

$$F = Se^{(r - r_f)t} \qquad \text{(Formula 8.9)}$$

Example: You agree to buy 5,000 Tuluvian krinkets from a currency dealer in nine months. Krinkets are currently trading for $0.35. (When dealing with foreign currency, just think of each unit of the other currency as something like a share of stock, which you buy with some amount of local currency.) The risk-free interest rate in Tuluvia is 2 percent. The risk-free interest rate in the United States is 6 percent. This is exactly like a forward on an underlier with proportional income, replacing i with r_f. Here's what we've got:

$$S = 5{,}000 \times 0.35 = 1{,}750$$
$$r = 0.06$$
$$r_f = 0.02$$
$$t = 0.75$$

Putting it all together, we solve for F:

$$F = Se^{(r - r_f)t}$$
$$= 1{,}750 \times e^{(0.06 - 0.02)(0.75)}$$
$$= 1{,}750 \times e^{0.03}$$
$$= 1{,}803.30$$

The fair-market delivery price for this contract is $1,803.30.

Forward Price Summary

Here are the forward price formulas in a nutshell:

Basic forward price	$F = Se^{rt}$	(Formula 8.3)
With fixed storage	$F = (S + U)e^{rt}$	(Formula 8.4)
With proportional storage	$F = Se^{(r + u)t}$	(Formula 8.5)
With fixed income	$F = (S - I)e^{rt}$	(Formula 8.6)
With proportional income	$F = Se^{(r - i)t}$	(Formula 8.7)
With convenience yield	$F = Se^{(r - y)t}$	(Formula 8.8)
Foreign-currency forward	$F = Se^{(r - r_f)t}$	(Formula 8.9)

Just remember that U and I are the present values of storage and income, respectively. If they are given as future values, you need to discount them before plugging them into these formulas.

Putting these all together, we get Formula 8.10:

$$\text{Forward Price} = (S + U - I)e^{(r + u - I - y - r_f)t} \qquad \text{(Formula 8.10)}$$

where:

$$S = \text{spot price}$$
$$U = \text{fixed storage costs}$$
$$I = \text{fixed income}$$
$$r = \text{risk-free interest rate}$$
$$u = \text{proportional storage cost}$$
$$i = \text{proportional income}$$
$$y = \text{convenience yield}$$
$$r_f = \text{foreign interest rate}$$

VALUING AN EXISTING FORWARD OR FUTURES POSITION

So far, we've explored calculating a forward price or futures price for the purpose of initiating a new contract. At inception, the value of a forward and otherwise identical futures are both the same: zero. After inception, their values must be calculated differently, due to the daily settlement inherent to futures contracts, which does not take place with forwards.

Forward Contract Value

The value of a forward contract after inception is the present value of the difference between its delivery price and the delivery price of a theoretical new contract, i.e., the current forward price. This applies to any forward contract. Think of this "theoretical new contract" as just one for which we calculate a delivery price —in order to get a forward price—and it has the same underlying quantity, delivery date, and any other feature of the forward contract we wish to value. Its delivery price, like that of all forwards at inception, is equal to the forward price F. So we have two forwards, one in our hands and one in our heads, whose only difference is the amount the long party will pay on delivery: F versus K. The value of the contract in our hands is thus the present value of the difference between F and K, as shown in Formulas 8.11 and 8.12:

$$\text{Forward Value}_{\text{Long}} = PV(F - K) = (F - K)e^{-rt} \quad \text{(Formula 8.11)}$$
$$\text{Forward Value}_{\text{Short}} = PV(K - F) = (K - F)e^{-rt} \quad \text{(Formula 8.12)}$$

Why do we discount? Because the difference between F and K is a future value, and we're interested in a present value. So we need to discount it to today.

Consider our previous example, wherein you executed a six-month forward contract with your brother to buy 100 shares of MGrove stock at a delivery price of $15.66 per share. Three months have gone by, and MGrove is currently trading for $15.80. What is the value of your position? Intuitively, we can expect the value to be positive, as we have a contract to purchase for $15.66 that is currently trading for $15.80. Let's see if that bears out.

First we calculate a forward price using a spot price of $15.80 and time to delivery T of three months, or 0.25 year. (The risk-free interest rate r has not changed.) Here then are the inputs:

$$S = 15.80 \times 100 = 1,580$$
$$r = 0.03$$
$$t = 0.25$$

Here's the current forward price:

$$F = Se^{(r-i)t}$$
$$= 1,580 \times e^{(0.03)(0.25)}$$
$$= 1,591.89$$

The forward price (i.e., the fair-market delivery price for a hypothetical new forward contract) is $1,591.89. Now we have what we need for the long forward value formula:

$$F = 1,591.89$$
$$K = 1,565.58$$
$$r = 0.03$$
$$t = 0.25$$

Putting the formula to work, we can find the value:

$$\text{Value} = (F - K)e^{-rt}$$
$$= (1,591.89 - 1,565.58)e^{-0.03(0.25)}$$
$$= 26.11$$

The value of our contract is $26.11.

There's an easier way to calculate the value of a forward contract when there are no costs or benefits to holding the underlier (that is, no cost of carry except for interest). It's just the difference between the spot price of the underlier and the present value of the delivery price, as shown in Formulas 8.13 and 8.14:

$$\text{Forward Value}_{\text{Long (No CC)}} = S - PV(K) = S - Ke^{-rt} \quad \text{(Formula 8.13)}$$
$$\text{Forward Value}_{\text{Short (No CC)}} = PV(K) - S = Ke^{-rt} - S \quad \text{(Formula 8.14)}$$

In the previous example, there was no cost of carry except interest. Here then are the inputs to valuing that contract, using this different approach:

$$S = 1,580.00$$
$$K = 1,565.58$$
$$r = 0.03$$
$$t = 0.25$$

Putting it all together, we can solve for forward value:

$$\begin{aligned}
\text{Forward Value} &= S - Ke^{-rt} \\
&= 1{,}580.00 - 1{,}565.58e^{-0.03(0.25)} \\
&= 26.11
\end{aligned}$$

As you can see, this is the same result as before.

Futures Contract Value

The value of a futures contract is rather different from the value of an otherwise identical forward contract because the payoff from a futures contract is realized at the end of every trading day. The value of a forward, recall, is generally realized at the end of the contract's term. So at any time, a futures contract's value is driven solely by how much its futures price has changed since yesterday. The value of a futures, then, is the difference between the current futures price and the futures price at the end of the previous trading day when everyone settled up.

Recall the Royal Mill from Chapter 3 and its 10 futures contracts to buy wheat. Say one day the futures price on those contracts closed at $3.10. By the middle of the next day, the futures price was at $3.20. What is the value of Royal Mill's position then?

$$\begin{aligned}
\text{Futures Value}_{\text{Long}} &= \text{Number of Contracts} \times \text{Bushels per} \\
&\quad \text{Contract} \times (F_{\text{Now}} - F_{\text{Yesterday}}) \\
&= 10 \times 5{,}000 \times (3.20 - 3.10) \\
&= 5{,}000
\end{aligned}$$

At the moment, Royal Mill's futures position has a market value of $5,000. This does not reflect, however, profits realized and collected previously. Recall that the futures price was $3 when Royal Mill put on these contracts, so prior to now, Royal had already collected $5,000, using the same math.

To calculate the value of an existing futures contract, we simply need the current futures price and the futures price from the previous day. The value is just the difference between the two. For position value, we need to know the number of contracts involved and whether one is long or short. Here's the formula for the value of a long position:

$$F_{\text{Long}} = (FP_{\text{Now}} - FP_{\text{Previous Close}}) \times \text{Number of Contracts},$$

where FP_{Now} is the futures price as it is calculated right now, $FP_{\text{Previous Close}}$ is the futures price at the end of the previous trading day, and F_{Long} is the fair market value of one long futures contract right now. Whether the value is positive or negative depends on whether the futures price has increased or decreased.

Another example: Say you are long 1,000 corn futures. The current futures price is $2.82 per bushel. The futures price at yesterday's close was $2.85. You can tell already your position has negative value, because the futures price is dropping; you are committed to buy at a price greater than you would have to with a brand-new contract. And sure enough . . .

$$\begin{aligned}
F_{\text{Long}} &= (FP_{\text{Now}} - FP_{\text{Previous Close}}) \times \text{Number of Contracts} \\
&= (2.82 - 2.85) \times 1{,}000 \\
&= -30.00
\end{aligned}$$

The formula for a short futures position is only slightly different. Here are both formulas, 8.15 and 8.16, together:

$$F_{\text{Long}} = (FP_{\text{Now}} - FP_{\text{Previous Close}}) \times \text{Number of Contracts}$$
$$\text{(Formula 8.15)}$$
$$F_{\text{Short}} = (FP_{\text{Previous Close}} - FP_{\text{Now}}) \times \text{Number of Contracts}$$
$$\text{(Formula 8.16)}$$

This all leads us to something rather peculiar about futures: they are never literally "canceled." Once you execute a contract, you are stuck with it till delivery. Alarming? No worries. To get out of a futures position (i.e., to rid yourself of its obligations and payoff potential), you simply execute a new, offsetting contract.

Say again you are long 1,000 corn futures. The current futures price is $2.82, and the futures price at yesterday's close was $2.85, just as before. Because you are losing money on the position (recall you're down $30.00), you decide to short 1,000 (at $2.82) to get out and not lose any more. By the end of the day, the futures price has dropped even further, to $2.80. Now consider the value of your two positions at settlement (for the short position, we use the futures price at the time of execution instead of the previous closing price):

$$F_{\text{Long}} = (\text{FP}_{\text{Now}} - \text{FP}_{\text{Previous Close}}) \times \text{Number of Contracts}$$
$$= (2.80 - 2.85) \times 1{,}000 = -50.00$$
$$F_{\text{Short}} = (\text{FP}_{\text{Execution}} - \text{FP}_{\text{Now}}) \times \text{Number of Contracts}$$
$$= (2.82 - 2.80) \times 1{,}000 = 20.00$$
$$F_{\text{Long}} + F_{\text{Short}} = -50.00 + 20.00 = -30.00$$

There you have it. The same result as before. At the end of the day, you are just where you were when you decided to bail, even though prices continued to decline. Now, in subsequent days, the two positions' settlements will cancel each other exactly, so you are effectively out of your long position.

No-Arbitrage Pricing

Hopefully by now, this manner of calculating the value of a forward seems reasonable enough, as the relationship between forward prices and costs of carry seem to make sense for the reasons given. But there is a stronger proof these relationships are true, based on a principle known simply as *no arbitrage*. All derivatives are priced using this principle, which basically says this: The fair price of any derivative is the one that prevents arbitrage.

Recall from the previous chapter that an arbitrageur seeks to profit from pricing errors—that is, cases in which two prices are available for essentially the same thing. The arbitrageur simply buys at the lower price and sells at the higher, making a profit with virtually no risk. Pretty cool, huh? Although this can and indeed does happen in practice, arbitrage opportunities are fleeting. Why? Because once an arbitrage opportunity is discovered, more and more trades will occur by market participants going for that riskless profit. (Free money is highly desirable, after all.) And this trading activity itself adjusts prices such that the arbitrage opportunity goes away. If this isn't clear, recall that a fundamental determinant of prices in a large and open market is supply and demand. As demand goes up or down, so do prices. Increased trading is just increased demand, so arbitrage is self-eliminating.

How might we arbitrage a mispriced forward? First consider an imaginary type of derivative we'll call a Now. A Now is just like a forward except that the delivery price is spot and the delivery date is right now. Suppose we come across a Now contract on MGrove stock offered for $15.00 when the spot price of MGrove is $15.50. What do we do? Buy the Now at $15.00, take delivery of the stock, sell it on the spot market for $15.50, and make 50 cents. Do it for a million shares, and make $500,000. Now, all that selling will drive the price down, which is why arbitrage opportunities are essentially self-destructing, but you get the basic idea.

That's a silly example, but it makes the point, and you arbitrage mispriced forwards the same way. You just have to consider the time value of money. Recall our example of a simple forward on MGrove stock? With spot at $15.50 and interest at 2 percent, the fair market six-month forward price (also known as the theoretical price) is around $15.65. Suppose there is a liquid market (ample buyers and sellers) for the contracts at $15.65. But suppose you come across someone offering the same six-month forward for $15.55. Clearly, that forward is priced below market. It's too cheap by 10 cents, and we can get that 10 cents as follows:

Now
- Buy (go long) a bunch of forward contracts at $15.55 each.
- Sell (go short) the same number of forward contracts at $15.65.

Six Months from Now
- Take delivery of MGrove stock, and pay $15.55 per share.
- Deliver those shares, and receive $15.65 per share.
- Pocket 10 cents profit per share.

There are other ways to arbitrage a mispriced forward (for instance, using stock and cash), but in any case, you always buy low and sell high. That's what we did here, buying at $15.55 and selling at $15.65. We won't go further into arbitrage, but just know it's out there in a big way. It is an awesome and pervasive force affecting nearly every one of the gazillion prices out there in the global financial marketplace.

Contango and Normal Backwardation

Now here are some colorful terms you may run across. In the previous chapter, you learned what goes into a forward price, and in this chapter, we noted how a futures price is calculated the same way. Now, when you calculate a futures price, it is going to be either greater than or less than the expected spot price on delivery, which is just today's spot price adjusted forward for interest—not for storage or any other cost of carry.

When a futures price is greater than expected spot, the market is said to be in *contango*. This will tend to be the case for underliers with high storage costs, such as gold and other precious metals. Look back at the forward price formulas to see the math that makes this so.

When a futures price is less than expected spot, the market is said to be in *normal backwardation*. Contango is more or less the "normal" situation, so "normal backwardation" just refers to the not-so-normal case.

CHAPTER 9

Pricing Swaps

How do we value a swap? There are two common ways.

THE SWAP AS A BUNCH OF CASH FLOWS

The easiest way to value a swap, and therefore the way it's often done in practice, is remarkably simple in concept: view each leg as a string of future cash flows (as if each leg were a bond), and add up their present values. That's it. Nothing difficult at all, but it can be rather tedious. You need to know the precise number of days between now and every cash flow, the precise interest rate fraction to apply to each for each accrual, and so on. But isn't this what computers are for? Precisely. To any old computer, the valuation of a swap is a snap, provided, of course, that some human gave it the right instructions. But let's not let computers have all the fun; let's compute the value of a plain vanilla ourselves with just paper and ink and our heads.

In the examples that follow, we'll refer to spot rates and forward rates and yield curves. A *spot rate* is a rate of interest for money borrowed right now, and a *forward rate* is for money to be borrowed in the future. A *yield curve* conveys interest rates (spot or forward) for various borrowing periods. Each of these is explained in detail in Appendix A, "All About Interest."

Speaking of interest, it can be helpful to keep in mind that it has two important but entirely distinct roles when it comes to interest rate derivatives. First, it is the underlier of these derivatives. More precisely, it is how we measure the price of the underlier, which is really just money borrowed or lent. Second, interest is used for discounting future values to present values (and occasionally vice versa). Because of this dual role of interest, we actually have two rates to keep in mind: a rate for pricing and a rate for discounting. Tangling matters even more, an interest rate, whether for pricing or discounting, is only for some given length of time. Interest rates vary by maturity, so when we speak of a rate, we're really speaking of an entire yield curve. Anyway, those are just some things to keep in mind.

An Existing Swap

Consider two businesses, the Finch Corporation and Radley Incorporated, which execute a two-year swap on March 1, 2006. Finch is using this swap to effectively convert a 3.9 percent fixed-rate loan obligation into a floating rate, perhaps believing rates will on average "float below 3.9 percent" over the life of the loan. Finch pays floating and receives fixed. Radley, then, pays fixed and receives floating. Now imagine today's date is May 23, 2007, or a bit less than a year before maturity. Let's calculate the value of the swap, to Finch, as of that date. (The value to Radley will be the same with the sign flipped.) This is a rather plain vanilla with quarterly payments and identical terms on each leg. Here are the details:[1]

Notional:	$1,000,000
Effective date:	March 1, 2006
Maturity date:	February 29, 2008
Discount curve:	LIBOR
Compounding:	None
Averaging:	None
Amortizing:	None
Fixed tenor:	3 months
Floating tenor:	3 months
Coupon date:	22nd
Stubs:	Short
Day basis:	Actual/365

---

[1] For simplicity, we'll ignore some picayunish details often found in actual swaps—things like reset offsets and reset adjustments.

Calendar:	New York
Adjustment:	Modified following
Fixed rate:	3.90 percent
Rate index:	LIBOR

We also need "the market," that is, LIBOR interest rates for three-month loans commencing at various points in the future—forward rates. These are captured nicely in a yield curve. We need two curves, actually, both a three-month forward curve for calculating payments and a spot curve for discounting them to today. Let's borrow the curves constructed in Appendix A, as shown in Figure 9-1. Table 9-1 shows the spot and forward rates from the curves, going out two years, which we'll use in our calculations.

We now have the swap terms, the market, and the date on which we want to value the swap. The previous payment, on both legs, was May 22, 2007, or yesterday. So today is the first day of the new coupon period. Now we can identify the remaining payments as our first step in calculating the value. The coupon date is the 22nd of the month, the fixed and floating tenors are both three months, and the swap maturity date is February 29, 2008. So the remaining payments must be as shown in Table 9-2. Figure 9-2 shows these dates on the calendar.

FIGURE 9-1

LIBOR Yield Curves

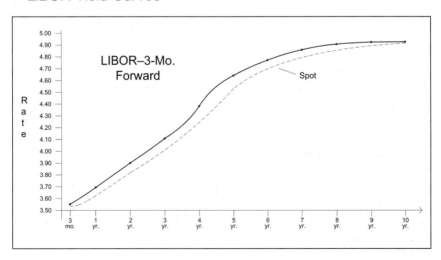

TABLE 9-1

Forward Rates

	Rate (percent)	
Term	**Spot**	**3-Month Forward**
3 mo.	3.53	3.55
6 mo.	3.54	3.64
9 mo.	3.59	3.67
12 mo.	3.63	3.71
15 mo.	3.67	3.73
18 mo.	3.70	3.80
21 mo.	3.75	3.81
24 mo.	3.78	3.84

TABLE 9-2

Payment Dates

Fixed Payment	**Floating Payment**
August 22, 2007	August 22, 2007
November 23, 2007	November 23, 2007
February 22, 2008	February 22, 2008
February 29, 2008	February 29, 2008

Why is the November payment on the 23rd and not the 22nd? Because the 22nd is a New York holiday (Thanksgiving), and the modified following business day convention tells us to take the next business day (unless it falls into the next month, in which case we take the previous business day, but that is not the case here). Note also that the final coupon period is quite brief—just six days (February 23 through February 29)—because the terms of this swap call for short stubs. Were it to call for long stubs, the February 22 payment would not occur. Instead, the final payment would fall on February 29, and the final coupon period would be longer than the three-month tenor by six days.

FIGURE 9-2

Swap Calendar

		May 2007							June 2007				

```
                          May 2007                           June 2007
            Su  Mo  Tu  We  Th  Fr  Sa       Su  Mo  Tu  We  Th  Fr  Sa
                     1   2   3   4   5                            1   2
             6   7   8   9  10  11  12        3   4   5   6   7   8   9
            13  14  15  16  17  18  19       10  11  12  13  14  15  16
            20  21 [22][23] 24  25  26       17  18  19  20  21  22  23
            27  28  29  30  31               24  25  26  27  28  29  30

                  July 2007                       August 2007                    September 2007
Su  Mo  Tu  We  Th  Fr  Sa       Su  Mo  Tu  We  Th  Fr  Sa       Su  Mo  Tu  We  Th  Fr  Sa
 1   2   3   4   5   6   7                    1   2   3   4                                    1
 8   9  10  11  12  13  14        5   6   7   8   9  10  11        2   3   4   5   6   7   8
15  16  17  18  19  20  21       12  13  14  15  16  17  18        9  10  11  12  13  14  15
22  23  24  25  26  27  28       19  20  21 [22] 23  24  25       16  17  18  19  20  21  22
29  30  31                       26  27  28  29  30  31           23  24  25  26  27  28  29
                                                                  30

              October 2007                       November 2007                    December 2007
Su  Mo  Tu  We  Th  Fr  Sa       Su  Mo  Tu  We  Th  Fr  Sa       Su  Mo  Tu  We  Th  Fr  Sa
     1   2   3   4   5   6                         1   2   3                                    1
 7   8   9  10  11  12  13        4   5   6   7   8   9  10        2   3   4   5   6   7   8
14  15  16  17  18  19  20       11  12  13  14  15  16  17        9  10  11  12  13  14  15
21  22  23  24  25  26  27       18  19  20  21  22 [23] 24       16  17  18  19  20  21  22
28  29  30  31                   25  26  27  28  29  30           23  24  25  26  27  28  29
                                                                  30  31

              January 2008                       February 2008
Su  Mo  Tu  We  Th  Fr  Sa       Su  Mo  Tu  We  Th  Fr  Sa
     1   2   3   4   5                             1   2
 6   7   8   9  10  11  12        3   4   5   6   7   8   9
13  14  15  16  17  18  19       10  11  12  13  14  15  16
20  21  22  23  24  25  26       17  18  19  20  21 [22] 23
27  28  29  30  31               24  25  26  27  28 [29] 30
```

Our job now is to calculate an amount for each payment, discount those amounts to their present values, and sum up all the present values. Let's start with the next fixed payment. We'll use the period start and end dates, plus the fixed rate and day fraction, to calculate the interest accrual over that period. Then we'll discount it to today, using the three-month spot rate. Here's the work:

Fixed Payment 5

Notional:	$1,000,000
Accrual start:	May 23, 2007
Accrual end:	August 22, 2007
Accrual days:	91
Payment rate:	3.90 percent
Day fraction:	91/365
Accrual rate:	$0.039 \times 91/365$
Payment future value:	$9,723.29
Spot rate:	3.53 percent
Days till payment:	91
Discount fraction:	91/365
Discount rate:	$0.0353 \times 91/365$
Payment present value:	$9,723.29/(1 + 0.0353 \times 91/365) =$ $9,638.46

Now let's do the first floating payment. The main difference here is the rate. Instead of the fixed rate, we need a LIBOR rate, and for this first floating payment, we choose the spot rate. Why not a forward rate? Because with plain-vanilla swaps, the floating rate for a coupon is fixed at the start of the period, which in this case is today. Forward rates converge to spot rates, so the forward rate for money borrowed now, "on the spot," is just a spot rate. For second and subsequent floating payments, we will use forward rates. Notice, too, that we will use a notional of –$1,000,000 to end up with a negative cash flow. Recall that Finch pays floating (negative cash flow) and receives fixed (positive cash flow). Here's the work for the next floating payment:

Floating Payment 5

Notional:	–$1,000,000
Accrual start:	May 23, 2007
Accrual end:	August 22, 2007
Accrual days:	91
Payment rate:	3.53 percent
Accrual fraction:	91/365
Accrual rate:	$0.0353 \times 91/365$
Payment future value:	–$8,800.82
Spot rate:	3.53 percent

Days till payment: 91
Discount fraction: 91/365
Discount rate: 0.0353 × 91/365
Payment present value: −$8,800.82/(1 + 0.0353 × 91/365)
                            = −$8,724.04

Now let's work out the next floating payment, number 6. The accrual period is three months in length, starting in three months, so we use the three-month forward rate three months out. And remember, even though it's a three-month *forward* rate, it's expressed as an *annual* rate, so we still need that day fraction. For discounting, we use the six-month spot rate (because the payment will occur in six months) and a day fraction with six months' worth of days in the numerator. Here's the work:

Floating Payment 6
Notional: −$1,000,000
Accrual start: August 23, 2007
Accrual end: November 23, 2007
Accrual days: 92
Payment rate: 3.55 percent
Accrual fraction: 92/365
Accrual rate: 0.0355 × 92/365
Payment future value: −$8,947.95
Spot rate: 3.54 percent
Days till payment: 184
Discount fraction: 184/365
Discount rate: 0.0354 × 184/365
Payment present value: −$8,947.95/(1 + 0.0354 × 184/365)
                           = −$8,791.07

Repeating this for all payments on both legs gives us a matrix like the one shown in Table 9-3.

As you can see, the fixed-leg coupons net to $29,283.23, and the floating-leg payments net to −$26,836.29. Combining these gives us the value of this swap to Finch: $2,446.94. Finch's view, that floating rates would be below its fixed rate of 3.9 percent, is turning out to be correct. The company is better off effectively paying a floating rate than having stayed with the fixed rate.

TABLE 9-3

Finch-Radley Swap from Perspective of Floating

Value as of May 23, 2007, with 4 Periods Remaining

	Payment	Notional	Accrual Start	Accrual End	Accrual Days	Payment Rate	Year Days	Payment Future Value	Spot Rate	Days till Payment	Payment Present Value
Fixed	5	$1,000,000	5/23/07	8/22/07	91	3.90%	365	$9,723.29	3.53%	91	$9,638.46
Fixed	6	1,000,000	8/23/07	11/23/07	92	3.90	365	9,830.14	3.54	184	9,657.79
Fixed	7	1,000,000	11/24/07	2/22/08	90	3.90	365	9,616.44	3.59	275	9,363.18
Fixed	8	1,000,000	2/23/08	2/29/08	6	3.90	365	641.10	3.59	282	623.79
										Net Fixed-Leg Present Value =	*$29,283.23*
Floating	5	($1,000,000)	5/23/07	8/22/07	91	3.53%	365	($8,800.82)	3.53%	91	($8,724.04)
Floating	6	(1,000,000)	8/23/07	11/23/07	92	3.55	365	(8,947.95)	3.54	184	(8,791.06)
Floating	7	(1,000,000)	11/24/07	2/22/08	90	3.64	365	(8,975.34)	3.59	275	(8,738.97)
Floating	8	(1,000,000)	2/23/08	2/29/08	6	3.64	365	(598.36)	3.59	282	582.21
										Net Floating-Leg Present Value =	*($26,836.29)*
										Swap Value =	*$2,446.94*

A New Swap

Now let's work out another swap valuation problem but for a different purpose. Instead of calculating the value of an existing swap, we will calculate the fixed rate, or swap rate, of a new plain vanilla. Recall that new swaps have a theoretical value of zero. The swap is just a stack of forward contracts, after all. So the job here is to calculate the fixed rate of a plain vanilla such that the swap value is zero. Sounds daunting, but once you see how it's done, it will daunt no more.

The counterparties here are Lakewood Securities (a financial firm that deals in swaps) and the Cornelia Corporation. The Lakewood-Cornelia swap differs from the Finch-Radley swap in three ways: it has a fixed tenor of six months and floating tenor of three months, it calls for long stubs instead of short, and it will commence today, May 23, 2007, and run for two years. Here are all the terms:

Notional:	$1,000,000
Effective date:	May 23, 2007
Maturity date:	May 29, 2009
Fixed rate:	???
Floating rate:	LIBOR
Discount curve:	LIBOR
Compounding:	None
Averaging:	None
Amortizing:	None
Fixed tenor:	6 months
Floating tenor:	3 months
Coupon date:	22nd
Stubs:	Long
Day basis:	Actual/365
Calendar:	New York
Adjustment:	Modified following

For the market, we'll use the same spot and forward curves from the previous swap. Now in Table 9-4 we'll identify the payment dates, and, of course, this time we have twice as many floating coupons as fixed coupons.

Now we set up a matrix exactly as before, using a spreadsheet (see Table 9-5, on page 121). But what fixed rate do we use? We'll start with a guess and see what happens. How about 3.9 percent, as before?

TABLE 9-4

Fixed and Floating Payment Dates

Fixed Payment	Floating Payment
Aug. 22, 2007	
Nov. 23, 2007	Nov. 23, 2007
Feb. 22, 2008	
May 22, 2008	May 22, 2008
Aug. 22, 2008	
Nov. 24, 2008	Nov. 24, 2008
Feb. 23, 2009	
May 29, 2009	May 29, 2009

It's no good—the swap has a nonzero value of $4,433.82 to the floating payer, so the fixed rate must be too high. Let's try 3.6 percent, as detailed in Table 9-6, on page 122.

The 3.6 percent gets us closer, but still no cigar.[2] But by continuing to try new fixed rates, we eventually find that 3.6697 percent gives us a value of zero. So the correct swap rate for the Lakewood-Cornelia swap is 3.6697 percent (see Table 9-7, on page 123).

Now recall Lakewood is not entering into this swap to convert a preexisting fixed-rate loan to a floating rate. Lakewood is a swaps dealer, contracted by Cornelia to make this swap. Let's say Lakewood is willing to do this swap for a fee of $10,000. Cornelia could write a check for that amount and do the swap at 3.6697 percent, or the parties could adjust the fixed rate to 4.1892 percent instead. This gives the swap a present value to Lakewood of $10,000, which to the company is nearly as good as a check. Table 9-8, on page 124, shows the matrix.

THE SWAP AS A PORTFOLIO OF FORWARD RATE AGREEMENTS

Now back to our original Lakewood-Cornelia swap with a zero value. To make it zero, we chose a fixed rate of 3.6745 percent.

---

[2] Computers are, of course, very good for this kind of trial-and-error calculation and are only too happy to do it for us. In this case, we used Excel's Goal Seek function to get our result in the blink of an eye.

TABLE 9-5

Lakewood-Cornelia Swap from Perspective of Floating-Payer Lakewood with Fixed Rate 3.9%

Proposed New Swap with Fixed Rate = 3.9%

	Payment	Notional	Accrual Start	Accrual End	Accrual Days	Payment Rate	Year Days	Payment Future Value	Spot Rate	Days till Payment	Payment Present Value
Fixed	1	$1,000,000	5/23/07	11/23/07	184	3.90%	365	$19,660.27	3.53%	184	$19,316.53
Fixed	2	1,000,000	11/24/07	5/22/08	180	3.90	365	19,232.88	3.54	365	18,575.31
Fixed	3	1,000,000	5/23/08	11/24/08	185	3.90	365	19,767.12	3.59	551	18,750.93
Fixed	4	1,000,000	11/25/08	5/29/09	185	3.90	365	19,767.12	3.59	737	18,431.08
									Net Fixed-Leg Present Value = $75,073.85		
Floating	1	($1,000,000)	5/23/07	8/22/07	91	3.53%	365	($8,800.82)	3.53%	91	($8,724.04)
Floating	2	(1,000,000)	8/23/07	11/23/07	92	3.55	365	(8,947.95)	3.54	184	(8,791.06)
Floating	3	(1,000,000)	11/24/07	2/22/08	90	3.64	365	(8,975.34)	3.59	275	(8,738.97)
Floating	4	(1,000,000)	2/23/08	5/22/08	89	3.67	365	(8,948.77)	3.63	365	(8,635.31)
Floating	5	(1,000,000)	5/23/08	8/22/08	91	3.71	365	(9,249.59)	3.67	457	(8,843.24)
Floating	6	(1,000,000)	8/23/08	11/24/08	93	3.73	365	(9,503.84)	3.70	551	(9,001.08)
Floating	7	(1,000,000)	11/25/08	2/23/09	90	3.80	365	(9,369.86)	3.75	642	(8,790.08)
Floating	8	(1,000,000)	2/24/09	5/29/09	94	3.81	365	(9,812.05)	3.78	737	(9,116.26)
									Net Floating-Leg Present Value = ($70,640.04)		

Swap Value = $4,433.82

TABLE 9-6

Lakewood-Cornelia Swap from Perspective of Floating Payer Lakewood with Fixed Rate 3.6%

Proposed New Swap with Fixed Rate = 3.6%

	Payment	Notional	Accrual Start	Accrual End	Accrual Days	Payment Rate	Year Days	Payment Future Value	Spot Rate	Days till Payment	Payment Present Value
Fixed	1	$1,000,000	5/23/07	11/23/07	184	3.60%	365	$18,147.95	3.53%	184	$17,830.65
Fixed	2	1,000,000	11/24/07	5/22/08	180	3.60	365	17,753.42	3.54	365	17,146.44
Fixed	3	1,000,000	5/23/08	11/24/08	185	3.60	365	18,246.58	3.59	551	17,308.55
Fixed	4	1,000,000	11/25/08	5/29/09	185	3.60	365	18,246.58	3.59	737	17,013.31
											Net Fixed-Leg Present Value = $69,298.95
Floating	1	($1,000,000)	5/23/07	8/22/07	91	3.53%	365	($8,800.82)	3.53%	91	($8,724.04)
Floating	2	(1,000,000)	8/23/07	11/23/07	92	3.55	365	(8,947.95)	3.54	184	(8,791.06)
Floating	3	(1,000,000)	11/24/07	2/22/08	90	3.64	365	(8,975.34)	3.59	275	(8,738.97)
Floating	4	(1,000,000)	2/23/08	5/22/08	89	3.67	365	(8,948.77)	3.63	365	(8,635.31)
Floating	5	(1,000,000)	5/23/08	8/22/08	91	3.71	365	(9,249.59)	3.67	457	(8,843.24)
Floating	6	(1,000,000)	8/23/08	11/24/08	93	3.73	365	(9,503.84)	3.70	551	(9,001.08)
Floating	7	(1,000,000)	11/25/08	2/23/09	90	3.80	365	(9,369.86)	3.75	642	(8,790.08)
Floating	8	(1,000,000)	2/24/09	5/29/09	94	3.81	365	(9,812.05)	3.78	737	(9,116.26)
											Net Floating-Leg Present Value = ($70,640.04)
											Swap Value = ($1,341.10)

TABLE 9-7

Lakewood-Cornelia Swap from Perspective of Floating Payer Lakewood with Fixed Rate 3.6697%

Proposed New Swap with Fixed Rate = 3.6697%

	Payment	Notional	Accrual Start	Accrual End	Accrual Days	Payment Rate	Year Days	Payment Future Value	Spot Rate	Days till Payment	Payment Present Value
Fixed	1	$1,000,000	5/23/07	11/23/07	184	3.67%	365	$19,660.27	3.53%	184	$18,175.71
Fixed	2	1,000,000	11/24/07	5/22/08	180	3.67	365	19,232.88	3.54	365	17,478.26
Fixed	3	1,000,000	5/23/08	11/24/08	185	3.67	365	19,767.12	3.59	551	17,478.26
Fixed	4	1,000,000	11/25/08	5/29/09	185	3.67	365	19,767.12	3.59	737	17,342.55
										Net Fixed-Leg Present Value =	$70,640.04
Floating	1	($1,000,000)	5/23/07	8/22/07	91	3.53%	365	($8,800.82)	3.53%	91	($8,724.04)
Floating	2	(1,000,000)	8/23/07	11/23/07	92	3.55	365	(8,947.95)	3.54	184	(8,791.06)
Floating	3	(1,000,000)	11/24/07	2/22/08	90	3.64	365	(8,975.34)	3.59	275	(8,738.97)
Floating	4	(1,000,000)	2/23/08	5/22/08	89	3.67	365	(8,948.77)	3.63	365	(8,635.31)
Floating	5	(1,000,000)	5/23/08	8/22/08	91	3.71	365	(9,249.59)	3.67	457	(8,843.24)
Floating	6	(1,000,000)	8/23/08	11/24/08	93	3.73	365	(9,503.84)	3.70	551	(9,001.08)
Floating	7	(1,000,000)	11/25/08	2/23/09	90	3.80	365	(9,369.86)	3.75	642	(8,790.08)
Floating	8	(1,000,000)	2/24/09	5/29/09	94	3.81	365	(9,812.05)	3.78	737	(9,116.26)
										Net Floating-Leg Present Value =	($70,640.04)
										Swap Value =	($1,341.10)

TABLE 9-8

Lakewood-Cornelia Swap from Perspective of Floating Payer Lakewood with Fixed Rate 4.1892%

Proposed New Swap with Fixed Rate = 4.1892%

	Payment	Notional	Accrual Start	Accrual End	Accrual Days	Payment Rate	Year Days	Payment Future Value	Spot Rate	Days till Payment	Payment Present Value
Fixed	1	$1,000,000	5/23/07	11/23/07	184	4.19%	365	$19,660.27	3.53%	184	$20,748.72
Fixed	2	1,000,000	11/24/07	5/22/08	180	4.19	365	19,232.88	3.54	365	19,952.54
Fixed	3	1,000,000	5/23/08	11/24/08	185	4.19	365	19,767.12	3.59	551	20,141.18
Fixed	4	1,000,000	11/25/08	5/29/09	185	4.19	365	19,767.12	3.59	737	19,797.61
								Net Fixed-Leg Present Value = $80,640.04			
Floating	1	($1,000,000)	5/23/07	8/22/07	91	3.53%	365	($8,800.82)	3.53%	91	($8,724.04)
Floating	2	(1,000,000)	8/23/07	11/23/07	92	3.55	365	(8,947.95)	3.54	184	(8,791.06)
Floating	3	(1,000,000)	11/24/07	2/22/08	90	3.64	365	(8,975.34)	3.59	275	(8,738.97)
Floating	4	(1,000,000)	2/23/08	5/22/08	89	3.67	365	(8,948.77)	3.63	365	(8,635.31)
Floating	5	(1,000,000)	5/23/08	8/22/08	91	3.71	365	(9,249.59)	3.67	457	(8,843.24)
Floating	6	(1,000,000)	8/23/08	11/24/08	93	3.73	365	(9,503.84)	3.70	551	(9,001.08)
Floating	7	(1,000,000)	11/25/08	2/23/09	90	3.80	365	(9,369.86)	3.75	642	(8,790.08)
Floating	8	(1,000,000)	2/24/09	5/29/09	94	3.81	365	(9,812.05)	3.78	737	(9,116.26)
								Net Floating-Leg Present Value = ($70,640.04)			
											Swap Value = $10,000

Sound familiar? Sound like a forward rate? It should. A swap can be viewed as a portfolio of a particular type of forward contract known as a forward rate agreement. And doing so can really help us understand how swaps are related to—and are in fact just a special collection of—another fundamental derivative.

The *forward rate agreement* (FRA) is an agreement between a buyer (the "borrower") and seller (the "lender") to execute a loan at a certain rate for a certain future time period. FRAs are typically cash settled, meaning the loan doesn't really take place, but this doesn't matter. Their true purpose is to provide a price guarantee. In fact, an FRA is just the same forward contract we learned about in Chapter 2, "The Forward Contract," where the underlier this time is borrowed money.

How might we use an FRA? One way is to reduce uncertainty about a single future interest rate payment based on a floating rate of interest. Say we have some preexisting obligation in three months' time to pay six months of interest on $100,000 using the six-month LIBOR then in effect. Let's also say we want to pay 3.25 percent, no matter what LIBOR turns out to be. We can achieve this by buying a forward contract known as a 3 × 9, or "three by nine," FRA (a term meaning the contract begins in three months and terminates in nine) with a delivery price of 3.25 percent. With such an FRA in place, we are obligated to pay 3.25 percent, and the short party is obligated to accept 3.25 percent for a six-month loan commencing in three months.

Now imagine three months have gone by and the six-month LIBOR is 3.5 percent (an annual rate, recall, for a six-month loan). Our original obligation requires us to pay, we'll say, $1,750 (i.e., 0.035 × 0.5 × $100,000). Remember, we only want to pay $1,625 (i.e., 0.0325 × 0.5 × $100,000). No worries! From our cash-settled FRA, we will receive 25 basis points from the short party, or $125 (i.e., [0.035 − 0.0325] × 0.5 × $100,000). So we shell out the $1,625 and combine it with this $125 to make our $1,750 payment.

Now imagine three months have gone by and the six-month LIBOR is instead 3 percent. Our original obligation requires us to pay $1,500 (i.e., 0.03 × 0.5 × $100,000). Hey, this is $125 less than we are willing to pay! A little bonus? No. Our 3 × 9 FRA requires us to pay 25 basis points, or $125 (i.e., [0.0325 − 0.03] × 0.5 × $100,000). So we still shell out the $1,625 but this time pay $125 on the FRA and the balance on the loan.

There we have two scenarios, one in which rates were higher than we would have liked and the other in which they were less, and in both cases, we paid exactly what we wanted to pay. That's what forwards are for.

And what if we had this same obligation, to pay six-month LIBOR on $100,000, every three months for the next two years? Perhaps it is our quarterly payment on a floating-rate loan. Could we not today execute a whole stack of FRAs—a 3 × 9 and 6 × 12 and 9 × 15 and so on? Sure could. Then, every three months, no matter where LIBOR fixes, we know our net payment would be based on a 3.25 percent annual rate, effectively converting our floating-rate obligation into a fixed-rate obligation.

This, of course, is just what a swap does. A position in one swap, then, will pay off exactly the same way as a position consisting of a stack, or portfolio, of FRAs. And when two positions have the same payoffs, their present value must be identical due to arbitrage. So lo and behold, this is how we know that a swap is equivalent to a portfolio of FRAs.

Let's look again at the Finch-Radley swap as a series of cash flows (see Table 9-9). In Table 9-10, on page 128, let's recast it as a portfolio of FRAs. We have four FRAs, each with a contract rate (a.k.a. "delivery price") of 3.9 percent. Finch is the short party, "selling money" at that interest. The payment rate each period is the difference between this delivery price and the current forward rate for the corresponding accrual period. The first payment rate, for example, is 3.90 percent minus 3.53 percent, or 0.37 percent. Otherwise the math is the same as before, giving us a net portfolio value of $2,446.94—the same as for the swap. (Recall this portfolio of FRAs has been in effect for 12 months. When it was initiated, the net value was, of course, zero, as with a swap.)

TABLE 9-9

Finch-Radley Swap from Perspective of Floating Payer Finch

Value as of May 23, 2007, with 4 Periods Remaining

	Payment	Notional	Accrual Start	Accrual End	Accrual Days	Payment Rate	Year Days	Payment Future Value	Spot Rate	Days till Payment	Payment Present Value
Fixed	5	$1,000,000	5/23/07	8/22/07	91	3.90%	365	$9,723.29	3.53%	91	$9,638.46
Fixed	6	1,000,000	8/23/07	11/23/07	92	3.90	365	9,830.14	3.54	184	9,657.79
Fixed	7	1,000,000	11/24/07	2/22/08	90	3.90	365	9,616.44	3.59	275	9,363.18
Fixed	8	1,000,000	2/23/08	2/29/08	6	3.90	365	641.10	3.59	282	623.79
										Net Fixed-Leg Present Value =	**$29,283.23**
Floating	5	($1,000,000)	5/23/07	8/22/07	91	3.53%	365	($8,800.82)	3.53%	91	($8,724.04)
Floating	6	(1,000,000)	8/23/07	11/23/07	92	3.55	365	(8,947.95)	3.54	184	(8,791.06)
Floating	7	(1,000,000)	11/24/07	2/22/08	90	3.64	365	(8,975.34)	3.59	275	(8,738.97)
Floating	8	(1,000,000)	2/23/08	2/29/08	6	3.64	365	(598.36)	3.59	282	582.21
										Net Floating-Leg Present Value =	**($26,836.29)**
										Swap Value =	**$2,446.94**

TABLE 9-10

Finch-Radley FRAs from Perspective of Fixed-Rate Seller Finch

Value as of 5/23/2007 with 4 Contracts Remaining

Payment	Notional	Accrual Start	Accrual End	Accrual Days	Contract Rate	Forward Rate	Payment Rate	Year Days	Payment Future Value
5	$1,000,000	5/23/07	8/22/07	91	3.90%	3.53%	0.37%	365	$922.47
6	1,000,000	8/23/07	11/23/07	92	3.90	3.55	0.35	365	882.19
7	1,000,000	11/24/07	2/22/08	90	3.90	3.64	0.26	365	641.10
8	1,000,000	2/23/08	2/29/08	6	3.90	3.64	0.26	365	42.74

Portfolio Value = $2,446.94

CHAPTER 10

Pricing Options

Option valuation is trickier than valuing a forward, futures, or swap, because each of those contracts involves a transaction we know with certainty will occur. How in the world do we value an option, involving a future transaction that may or may not occur? What is the fair market price of an instrument whose payoff is so wildly uncertain, depending as it does on the completely unpredictable price path of the underlier?

The basic idea involves the construction of an imaginary portfolio of non-option instruments—whose prices you can easily obtain—such that the portfolio payoff replicates that of the option. The price of such a portfolio gives you the price of the option, because two things with the same payoff must have the same value to prevent arbitrage. To create such a portfolio, you need a model of how the underlier's price changes. The binomial tree method, one of two option valuation methods we'll explain in detail, provides instructions for creating the replicating portfolio using a price path for the underlier that follows the pattern of a tree with very simple branches. The Black-Scholes method, which grows directly out of the binomial tree method, uses a tree with an infinite number of branches.

EYEBALL OPTION PRICING

Before we get into formal methods, let's see how to get some rough idea of an option's value using just our eyeballs, very simple math, and common sense to arrive at so-called *boundary conditions* for option values.

Option Value Versus Stock Value

The first thing to recognize when assessing the value of an option is that an option can be worth no more than a corresponding position in the underlier. Consider the call option. The lower the strike price, and the longer the time to expiration, the greater its value. The lowest a strike price can go is zero, and the longest time to expiration is infinity, and what's the value of a call option with a strike price of zero and no expiration? Such an option lets you have the stock at any time for free, as if you own it already. So its value is just the stock price. A call, then, can be worth no more than a long position in the stock. And like so many things with options, the same logic in pseudo-reverse says a put can be worth no more than a short position in a stock.

Intrinsic Value and Time Value

You can further get a rough idea of an option's value by assessing its *intrinsic value* versus *time value*. Intrinsic value is the difference between the strike price and the current stock price, or zero, whichever is greater. A 50-strike call option when the stock is trading at $53 has an intrinsic value of $3. A 50-strike put option when the stock is trading at $53 has no intrinsic value. We can express this mathematically, like so:

$$\text{Intrinsic Value of a Call} = \max(S - K, 0)$$
$$\text{Intrinsic Value of a Put} = \max(K - S, 0)$$

Time value comes from the optionality you get by holding an option. Some refer to it as the insurance value. This is why a 50-strike put when the stock is trading at $53, which has no intrinsic value, has *some* value, because who knows where the stock price will go before the option expires? Maybe the option will go in the money. And if it does, you're entitled to some payoff. If it doesn't, you're out no more than the premium. That opportunity for upside and shield from downside is worth something, and that something is known as time value. And the greater the time

before expiration, the more valuable this optionality becomes—
ergo, "time" value.

All unexpired options have some time value. If the option is in
the money, it also has some intrinsic value:

Out-of-the-Money (OTM) Option Value = Time Value

At-the-Money (ATM) Option Value = Time Value

In-the-Money (ITM) Option Value = Time Value +
Intrinsic Value

Notice that only ITM options can have intrinsic value.

You can use the idea of intrinsic value to get some idea of the
value of an option with a quick glance. If it's a call, just subtract
exercise price from stock price. If the result is positive, that's the
intrinsic value. If it's a put, just subtract stock price from exercise
price. If the result is positive, that's the intrinsic value. An option is
always worth *at least* its intrinsic value. We'll discuss more on this
in the following pages.

So now we have a boundary condition for option values. An
option value must lie between its intrinsic value and the value of the
underlying stock. Graphically, using the same x-y grid as a payoff
diagram, the value of an option must lie in the shaded region in
Figure 10-1.

FIGURE 10-1

Value Boundaries for a Call Option

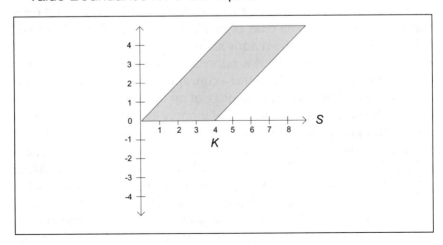

There are further boundary conditions for option values (e.g., the value is at least the difference between stock price and the *present value* of the exercise price), but now you know the basic idea. And with it you can easily figure in your head the range in which an option value sits. Consider our cZED62 from Chapter 5, "The Option Contract." When the stock ZED trades at $69, you know its value is at least $7 (intrinsic value, i.e., $69 − $62) but no more than $69. With ZED at $74, the option value is at least $12 but no more than $74. With ZED at $60, the option value is at least 0 (notice it's out of the money) but no more than $60. As you can see, when an option is in the money, most of its value comes from intrinsic value. A corollary of this fact—one you can add to your top-of-the-head tool kit—is that an OTM option is likely to be closer to 0 than stock price.

Granted, these are huge ranges, but they at least get you into the ballpark of where the actual value sits. Now let's move inside the park.

BASIC BINOMIAL OPTION PRICING

Way back in Chapter 1, "Derivatives in a Nutshell," we introduced the concept of arbitrage, one of our basic assumptions about the financial universe, stating that two things with the same payoff must have the same price. And in Chapter 5, "The Option Contract," you saw an example of position synthesis, or replication, where two positions with different assets can provide the same payoff and therefore have the same present value or price. And on the very first pages of Chapter 1, I introduced the idea of abstraction. This tried-and-true approach to learning starts by putting the mind on a simple case known to be true, often by making simplistic if unrealistic assumptions, and then adds small facts also known to be true until you have in your head a rather more complicated but useful truth. We shall now combine these concepts of arbitrage, replication, and abstraction to calculate the price of an option.

In the sections that follow, we'll apply two different methods for pricing an option. The first is the *binomial tree method*, and it's remarkably easy to understand when you start with the simplest case and move gradually from there. You can use and understand this powerful method with no more than algebra in your mathematical quiver. The second is the *Black-Scholes method*, and it grows directly and intuitively out of the binomial model. Once you get the binomial model, it's not a big deal to get what Black-Scholes is all about. Black-Scholes depends on calculus, but you certainly don't need to know calculus to use it. Black-Scholes also applies an additional powerful concept of risk neutrality, and I'll explain that just before we need it. Now, we don't cover two methods just for educational purposes. We really need them both in the real world. Black-Scholes only works for European options and certain American options. American put options, for example, require something like the binomial method.

A One-Step Binomial Tree

So consider again the stock ZED and a call option cZED62, which expires in six months with a strike price of $62. Imagine ZED is trading for $60 on the spot market. We are going to calculate the value of, or price, this cZED62. We'll first price cZED62 by making a seemingly ridiculous assumption that the price of ZED can change to one of only two possible values over a given period of time. It will either increase by 10 percent and trade at $66 or decrease by 10 percent and trade at $54. We call this model a *one-step binomial tree*, and it is, of course, unrealistic. But stick with me.

Now, if ZED rises to $66, the payoff of cZED62 will be $4. Should ZED fall to $54, then cZED62 will, of course, expire worthless—that is, have a payoff of 0. Figure 10-2 shows the situation graphically as a one-step (the price changes only once) binomial (two possible prices) tree (what mathematicians call the pattern in the figure).

Payoff of cZED62 if ZED = 66
$\max(0, S - K)$
$\max(0, 66 - 62)$
$\max(0, 4) = 4$

Payoff of cZED62 if ZED = 54
$\max(0, S - K)$
$\max(0, 54 - 62)$
$\max(0, -8) = 0$

The payoff of cZED62 is uncertain and depends entirely on whether ZED moves to $66 or $54. We want to know the price of this option with no more information than what we have already. And how do we do that? By creating a *replicating portfolio,* using compo-

FIGURE 10-2

One-Step Binomial Tree

nents we *can* price, whose payoff mimics the payoff of cZED62. And due to the law of no-arbitrage, two positions with the same payoff must cost the same. So, whatever the price of the replicating portfolio, it must also be the price of the option.

We build a replicating portfolio by purchasing some quantity of ZED stock and borrowing some quantity of money. We'll explain in a bit how we arrive at these quantities, but for now, just take them as given. You can think of our replicating portfolio as long a stock and short a bond, because "shorting a bond" is just another way of saying "borrowing some money." To be exact, we will borrow $17.47 at the risk-free rate of 6 percent for six months. We will use these borrowed funds, plus $2.53 of our own money, to buy 0.3333 share of ZED for $20 (i.e., 0.3333 × 60 = 20 = 17.47 + 2.53). Here's the composition of our replicating portfolio (RP) mathematically, with the quantity of ZED represented by the Greek letter delta (Δ) and the borrowed money represented by the letter B (it's a negative B, remember, because it's like shorting a bond):

$$RP = \Delta ZED - B$$

While we're here, let's calculate the cost of creating this portfolio, or its value at inception, using the delta and bond quantities mentioned previously:

$$
\begin{aligned}
RP &= \Delta ZED - B \\
&= 0.3333(60) - 17.47 \\
&= 2.53
\end{aligned}
$$

And this makes sense, as $2.53 is the amount of our own money we had to come up with to create the replicating portfolio; remember, we borrowed the $17.47. So the value of the replicating portfolio at time zero is $2.53.

Imagine that six months have gone by. Your debt has grown to $18 (i.e., $17.47e^{(0.06)(0.5)}$), and you need to pay it back. ZED is trading for either $66 or $54. Consider what you'll do with your replicating portfolio:

1. If ZED is trading for $66
   a. Sell your 0.3333 share, and collect $22 (i.e., 0.3333 × 66).
   b. Use $18 of it to repay your debt, and pocket the remaining $4.
2. If ZED is trading for $54
   a. Sell your 0.3333 share, and collect $18 to pay off your debt exactly (0.3333 × 54 = 18).
   b. Pocket nothing.

So, as you see in Figure 10-3, if ZED moved to $66, your payoff was $4, and if it moved to $54, your payoff was zero. These are the exact same payoffs had you bought a cZED62 instead of constructing the replicating portfolio.

Payoff of Replicating Portfolio if ZED = 66
$\Delta S - Be^{rt}$
$(0.3333)66 - 17.47e^{(0.06)(0.5)}$
$22 - 18 = 4$

FIGURE 10-3

Replicating Portfolio Payoff on a One-Step Binomial Tree

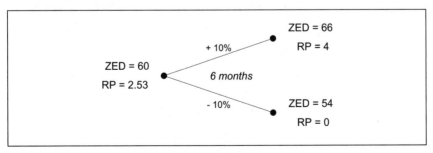

Payoff of Replicating Portfolio if ZED = 54
$\Delta S - Be^{rt}$
$(0.3333)54 - 17.47e^{(0.06)(0.5)}$
$18 - 18 = 0$

The replicating portfolio clearly, well, *replicates* a position in the option. So the value of the cZED62 at time 0 must have been $2.53, the cost of building the portfolio. In other words, a position in the option was equal to a position in the replicating portfolio:

$$cZED62 = \Delta ZED - B$$

Notice how the theoretical value of cZED62, $2.53, is consistent with the range we identified in the previous section of 0 to $60, the range between intrinsic value and stock price. Notice also that $2.53 is much closer to 0 than to $60, consistent with our intuition that out-of-the-money options are closer in value to 0 than stock price.

Now let's tackle this delta factor and how to calculate it. Delta tells us how much stock we need such that the sensitivity of the replicating portfolio to a change in the underlier is the same as the sensitivity of the option to a change in the underlier. Delta, then, is also a measure of the option price's sensitivity to changes in its underlier. (Delta also provides what is known as an option's *hedge ratio*, for reasons we'll cover later.) In our one-step tree, delta is given by the ratio of two differences: the difference between possible option values over the difference between possible stock prices. We can express this mathematically by using S_u for the stock price after an up move, S_d for the stock price after a down move, C_u for the option value after an up move in the stock, and C_d for the option value after a down move in the stock:

$$S_u = 66$$
$$C_u = 4$$
$$S_d = 54$$
$$C_d = 0$$
$$\Delta = (C_u - C_d)/(S_u - S_d)$$
$$= (4 - 0)/(66 - 54)$$
$$= 4/12 = 1/3$$
$$= 0.3333$$

We can generalize this delta formula, thus making it more useful later on, by denoting 1 plus stock return after an up move by the letter u and 1 plus the stock return after a down move by the letter d, and replacing the $(S_u - S_d)$ factor with the product of S and the difference between u and d (see Formula 10.1). A *return* is simply a proportional representation of how much an investment earns. In our one-step tree, the return is either 10 percent or –10 percent. So 1 plus return is how much of your original investment you have left, in proportional terms, after an investment period.

$$u = 1 + 0.10 = 1.10$$
$$d = 1 + (-0.10) = 1 - 0.1 = 0.9$$
$$\Delta(uS - dS) = C_u - C_d$$
$$\Delta = (C_u - C_d)/[S(u - d)] \qquad \text{(Formula 10.1)}$$
$$= (4 - 0)/[60(1.10 - 0.9)]$$
$$= 4/12 = 1/3$$
$$= 0.3333$$

Now the bond factor. We can calculate that with Formula 10.2. It uses the same inputs as the delta formula, plus the risk-free interest rate (r):

$$r = 0.06$$
$$B = (dC_u - uC_d)/[e^{rt}(u - d)] \qquad \text{(Formula 10.2)}$$
$$= (dC_u - u\,C_d)/[e^{(0.06)(0.5)}(u - d)]$$
$$= (0.9(4) - 1.10(0))/[e^{(0.03)}(1.10 - 0.9)]$$
$$= 3.6/0.2061$$
$$= 17.47$$

Putting this all together, we get the one-step binomial option-pricing formula for a call option (Formula 10.3):

$$C = \Delta S - B \qquad \text{(Formula 10.3)}$$

where:

$$S = \text{stock price}$$
$$\Delta = (C_u - C_d)/[S(u - d)]$$

C_u = call value after up move

C_d = call value after down move

u = 1 + stock return after up move

d = 1 + stock return after down move

$B = (dC_u - uC_d)/[e^{rt}(u - d)]$

An Alternative Approach

Now we consider an alternative approach when using a one-step binomial tree to price an option. It's a tad less intuitive but does the same thing: it gives us the price of our cZED62. And it will help demonstrate another fundamental concept of derivative pricing, the concept of risk-neutral pricing. So let's switch gears to this alternative approach.

In our first climb up the binomial tree, we created a replicating portfolio—or synthetic option, as it is sometimes known—by borrowing money and buying stock. This is known as a levered position, as it entails *leverage*, which simply means you borrow money to buy something. Buying something with borrowed money is, of course, more risky than buying something with your own money. If the value of the thing you buy should fall below what you owe, you can get into a heap of trouble right quick. And when you think about it, buying something with a call option is more risky than buying it outright. If the value of the underlier falls below the strike price and the option expires, you lose 100 percent of your investment. This, in a nutshell, is one of the reasons we model an option position with levered stock positions.

We did not know which payoff of the synthetic option would actually occur, but it did not matter; the payoff would exactly mimic the payoff of the real option. And we could easily price the components of the portfolio, which is all we needed to get a price for the option. Our alternative approach constructs a replicating portfolio in which the payoff *is* certain, but it includes a component we can't price directly. It expresses the valuation problem by asking, "What is the value of a position of one *long* cZED62?" It answers that question by constructing a replicating portfolio consisting of some quantity delta of the stock ZED as before, plus a *short* position in the option cZED62, such that the payoff of the portfolio is certain whether the spot price of ZED moves up 10 percent to $66 or down 10 percent to $54. So here we don't directly know the cost of the portfolio (it includes the option, after all—the thing we want to price in the first place), but this time we do know the payoff with certainty. In other words, we have just one variable: the price of the option, which it turns out we can calculate with some algebra.

Now we're already familiar with the (really important) concept of delta. In our formulas, it is just some proportional quantity of stock. For example, a delta of 0.50 is one-half of a share. A delta of 0.07 is seven one-hundredths of a share, a delta of 1.0 is exactly one share, and a delta of 0 is no shares. (Of course, you can't really buy fractions of shares; in practice, you multiply delta by a multiple of 10 or 100 to get a whole number of shares.) Using delta, along with a positive sign to represent a long position and a negative sign to represent a short position, the contents of the replicating portfolio can thus be represented like this:

$$+(\Delta \times ZED) - cZED62$$

or:

$$+\Delta ZED - cZED62$$

Say you own this portfolio. The positive sign in front of ΔZED signifies a long position in some quantity Δ of ZED stock. You've bought some ZED, so any future payoff of that stock is yours. In other words, its payoff is positive from your perspective. It's your asset, if you will. The minus in front of cZED62 signifies a short position in cZED62. You've sold, or written, this call option, and any positive payoff to that option belongs to the other party. Its payoff is negative from your perspective. It is your liability.

By modifying things just a bit, we can express the value of the portfolio (i.e., the cost of creating this portfolio) with a simple algebraic expression:

$$RP = \Delta ZED - cZED62$$

This says the value of the portfolio is equal to the cost of Δ shares of ZED less the cost of one cZED62 option. We have then three unknowns: RP (the replicating portfolio), ΔZED, and cZED62. If we can figure out two of them, we can deduce, or solve for, the third.

Let's start with delta. To find it using this new approach, imagine that six months have gone by. We need a delta such that the value of the portfolio is the same whether ZED is trading for $66 or $54. In algebraic terms, then, we want the following equation to be true:

$$\Delta 66 - 4 = \Delta 54 - 0,$$

where $\Delta 66 - 4$ is the payoff with ZED trading for $66 and $\Delta 54 - 0$ is the payoff with ZED trading for $54. With a pinch of algebra, we can solve this equation for delta:

$$\Delta 66 - 4 = \Delta 54 - 0$$
$$\Delta 66 - \Delta 54 = 4$$
$$\Delta(66 - 54) = 4$$
$$\Delta 12 = 4$$
$$\Delta = 4/12 = 0.3333$$

That's the same delta as before. But let's plug this delta back into the original equation to be extra sure it works:

$$\Delta 66 - 4 = \Delta 54 - 0$$
$$(0.3333)66 - 4 = (0.3333)54$$
$$18 = 18$$

Yep. This proves the value of delta is correct. And as a little bonus, it also tells us that the value of the portfolio at expiration under either scenario is $18. We'll use this factoid in a moment.

First let's see what our formula looks like at time zero, now that we know delta. And we know from before that the spot price of ZED is $60:

$$RP = \Delta ZED - cZED62$$
$$= (0.3333)60 - cZED62$$
$$= 20 - cZED62$$

Now we're down to two unknowns: portfolio value and the price of cZED62. Can we figure out the portfolio value? Sure can. Recall that the value of this portfolio in six months is $18 whether the stock moves to $66 or $54. So the portfolio value is just the present value of $18. Can we calculate the present value of $18? Sure can. We just need a period of time and an interest rate. The period is, as we know, six months. But what interest rate should we use? We know the payoff of this portfolio with complete certainty, that is, without risk. So the discount rate should be the risk-free interest rate. Let's say it's 6 percent and use continuous compounding as before:

$$PV(18) = 18e^{-(0.06)(0.5)}$$
$$= 17.47$$

So the present value of the payoff is $17.47, which must be the portfolio value. That is:

$$17.47 = 20 - cZED62$$

Now we have just one unknown, the value of cZED62. We can solve for it with just a smidge more algebra:

$$17.47 = 20 - cZED62$$
$$cZED62 = 20 - 17.47$$
$$= 2.53$$

The correct price of this option, also known as its *fair market value* or *theoretical value*, is $2.53—the same result as before.

And how can we verify this price? By imagining the construction of a portfolio using this option price and delta and seeing what happens under both of the two possible price paths for the stock. Recall the portfolio contents and costs of its components:

$$RP = \Delta ZED - cZED62$$
$$= (0.3333)60 - 2.53$$

Imagine it is time 0. We just follow the above equation like a recipe, and any cash required we borrow at the risk-free interest rate:

1. Sell cZED62, and collect the $2.53 premium.
2. Borrow $17.47 at 6 percent.
3. Use the premium and borrowed funds to buy 0.3333 share of ZED for $20 (i.e., 0.3333 × $60).

Next, imagine that six months have gone by. Your debt has grown to $18 (i.e., $17.47e^{(0.06)(0.5)}$). You need to pay this back. And ZED is trading for either $66 or $54.

1. If ZED is trading for $66, the option is in the money, so you must sell the holder ZED for $66 or cash-settle by paying the holder $4.
   a. Sell your 0.3333 share of ZED for $22 (i.e., 0.3333 × $66).
   b. Use $18 of the $22 to repay your debt.
   c. Use the remaining $4 to cash-settle the option.
2. If ZED is trading for $54, the option is worthless, so you owe nothing to the option holder, but you still must repay your debt.
   a. Sell your ZED on the spot market, and collect $18 (i.e., 0.3333 × $54).
   b. Use the proceeds to repay your debt.

In either case, you break even. There's nothing exciting about that, but it does prove the value of our option is correct.

Still not convinced? Recall that arbitrage is not allowed in our land of derivatives. If we can demonstrate how one *could* perform an arbitrage if the price is *not* $2.53, then we further demonstrate the correctness of our price.

So imagine you had the opportunity to buy cZED62 for less than $2.53—let's say $2.43. We can prove such a price is cheap by 10 cents by demonstrating how you can make money no matter what, just by doing this:

1. Borrow 0.3333 share of ZED, and sell it short for $20 (i.e., 0.3333 × $60).
2. Use $2.43 of your proceeds to buy one cZED62.
3. Invest the remaining $17.57 at 6 percent.

Imagine that six months have gone by. Your investment has grown to $18.10 (i.e., $17.57e^{(0.06)(0.5)}$). Cash it in. Now you need to return those ZED shares you borrowed no matter what.

1. If ZED is trading for $66, the option is in the money, so you will want to buy ZED for $66 or cash-settle by receiving $4.

    a. Cash-settle your cZED62, and collect $4. Now you have
      $22.10 on hand (i.e., $18.10 + $4).

    b. Use $22 to buy 0.3333 share of ZED (i.e., 0.3333 × $66).
      Return that to your ZED lender.

    c. Keep the remaining $0.10 as your profit.

  2. If ZED is trading for $54, the option is worthless, so you
    do nothing with it, but you do need to return those shares
    of ZED you borrowed.

    a. Use $18 of your $18.10 to buy 0.3333 share of ZED on
      the spot market (i.e., 0.3333 × $54). Return that to your
      ZED lender.

    b. Keep the remaining $0.10 as your profit.

You make a dime no matter what.

In other words, you've made a riskless profit, that is, an arbitrage. And derivative valuation is based on the assumption that arbitrage opportunities don't exist. Now, you can debate that assertion long into the night, pointing out one example after another of market inefficiencies and real arbitrage profits that people have really made, but when the sun comes up the next morning and computers all over the planet start calculating the values of derivatives, trust me, they will assume arbitrage opportunities cannot exist. At least not for long.

We could also examine the case where you find an opportunity to buy cZED62 for more than $2.53—let's say $2.63—and prove such a price is "rich" by 10 cents by demonstrating how to make another riskless profit through arbitrage. We just do things in reverse: write the option and buy the stock. At the end of the period, we again pocket a dime no matter what.

I know one thing you might be thinking about now: "So you made 10 cents—big whoop." Yes, it might seem a lot of bother for a dime until you consider that most U.S. equity option contracts entitle the holder to buy or sell 100 shares of the underlier. So the price of the contract would really be 100 × $2.63, or $26.30, and the payoff 100 × $0.10, or $10.00. And traders often buy or sell not just one contract (a *one-lot*) but hundreds of contracts as a single trade. So multiply that $10 again—say, by 500—and now you've made a profit of $5,000. Do 20 or 30 or 100 trades like this in a day, and you can make yourself quite a lot of money.

A Multistep Binomial Tree

I know what else you might be thinking: "Stock prices don't change
like your little tree." Right. "This binomial tree thing is bogus." No,
it's just that we're still working with an abstraction and need to get
more concrete. As I've demonstrated the method so far, underlier
prices can follow one of just two possible paths. That's not a good
model of reality, as clearly the number of possible price paths is
way more than two. But we can improve our model—that is, make
it more like reality—by simply shortening the branches and adding
more of them. A two-step tree, for instance, has three leaves (each is
a possible price for ZED) and four possible price paths.

For example, Figure 10-4 divides the single six-month step into
two three-month steps. As before, the price of ZED at the outset can
move to one of just two values, either up by 5 percent or down by
5 percent, to one of the two middle nodes. At each of those nodes,
ZED can again either go up by 5 percent or down by 5 percent, ultimately taking us to one of the three end nodes. So there are four
possible paths. Notice how the two middle paths take you to the
same node, because increasing and then decreasing by 5 percent is
the same as decreasing and then increasing by 5 percent. This idea
that more paths take you to the "middle" of the possible end prices
than to the "edges" is an important phenomenon that we'll get back
to when we cover probability distributions later in this chapter.

FIGURE 10-4

Two-Step Binomial Tree

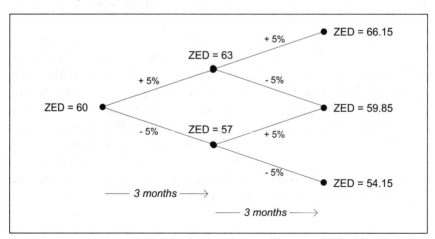

Notice that our two-step tree is really just three one-step trees. So we basically iterate through the tree, working right to left, till we are at the starting node. In other words, to calculate the price of an option with this tree, we create a replicating portfolio just as before, but whose payoff is certain no matter which of the *four* paths are taken, then we back out the price of the option from the present value of that payoff. We basically need an option value at each node, and we get those by repetitively applying the one-step process. If you're interested, we walk through all the steps in Appendix C, "More Binomial Option Pricing," where we also provide the generic formulas.

Taking It to the Limit

If you took a look at Appendix C, you saw how the math can get a little hairy. But hopefully, you are at least reasonably convinced that binomial trees really do allow us to price options, and the deeper the tree (to mangle a metaphor), the better the price. A tree that perfectly models reality, one that provides for *every* possible price path, would require an infinite number of steps. And wouldn't you know there's a way to do basically just that—by turning to the friendly field of calculus and its awesome concept of the limit. The Black-Scholes model for option valuation, which we'll turn to next, is based in part on this idea.

There's an important practical ramification of this idea of deeper and deeper trees that also demonstrates nicely the imperfection of pricing something in the real world with a theoretical model. Think back to how we priced an option by building a replicating portfolio on the one-step tree. That replicating portfolio is only good for that one step of the tree. Once we know which of the two paths the price is taking, we need to get rid of the old replicating portfolio and build a new one. Same thing at the next step, and the next step, all the way to the end.

Liquidating and recreating this portfolio is known as *dynamic replication*. And as the number of steps goes past a couple or three, it starts getting tough to do that, with the transaction costs and time involved and whatnot. And when the number of steps goes to infinity with Black-Scholes, it's truly impossible. This dynamic-replication requirement is one of the things that makes option pricing more difficult than forward pricing. With forwards, you can set up a replicating portfolio and forget about it. Not so with options.

Risk-Neutral Valuation

Here's another sidebar worth noting before we get to Black-Scholes, but it is just a sidebar, and not something you have to understand to apply Black-Scholes. In our option-pricing examples so far, we've relied heavily on no-arbitrage arguments to prove that our calculations are correct. In the financial universe, this law against arbitrage is like the law against exceeding the speed of light in the physical universe. It's just, well, the law.

There's another idea with nearly equal standing in this land, and it goes by the name of *risk-neutral valuation*. This idea says that the theoretical value of any derivative—any derivative, not just an option—is equal to the expected value of the derivative's payoff in a risk-neutral world, discounted at a risk-free rate of interest. An *expected value* is just some value in the future, considering some probability. A *risk-neutral world* is one in which investors don't care about risk. They are neither risk-averse nor risk-inclined. Hedgers in reality *do* wish to mitigate risk, and speculators, of course, seek out risk to potentially profit from it.

So this risk-neutral assumption seems wildly bogus at first glance. But as happens every so often in the world of thinkers, one can prove this assertion. And it's an assertion worth proving because doing so allows us to greatly simplify our pricing calculations by using a risk-free rate, as we've been doing all along. Appendix C, "More Binomial Option Pricing," illustrates the basic proof of risk neutrality.

BLACK-SCHOLES OPTION PRICING

Step back for a minute, and think about how we approached the problem of option valuation using the binomial tree method. We constructed a model of how the real world operates (changes in stock price follow a binomial tree) and then observed facts from the model (a carefully constructed portfolio gives the same payoff no matter which path is followed, etc.). It's a bit like testing a new design for an aircraft wing. Before building a pair for real and sticking them onto a plane for a real flight, the designers typically build a model of the proposed new wing, place it in a wind tunnel, crank up the air, and observe facts about how air flows around the wing. If it's a good model, they can reasonably assume air will flow over the real wing in a similar way. That is, the facts they observe from the model in the wind tunnel will apply to the real world—with some consideration, perhaps, for the differences between the wind tunnel and the real sky. The point is, the better the model, the more reliable the facts. And this is where Black-Scholes comes in. It uses a better wind tunnel.

The basic idea behind Black-Scholes is really the same basic idea behind the binomial tree method: the value of an option equals the price of a levered stock portfolio that replicates the payoff of the option. The binomial tree method constructs such a portfolio supposing that a price path follows a tree (from its trunk to one of its leaves) with a fixed number of branching levels, where at each branch, the stock price can change to one of two possible new prices. Given enough branches, the binomial tree is not a bad model for price changes in the real world. Black- Scholes uses an even better model by essentially supposing a tree with an infinite number of branches.

The method we call "Black-Scholes" is named for Fischer Black and Myron Scholes, who in the 1970s along with Robert Merton developed the Black-Scholes formula for pricing European options on non-dividend-paying stock. Their work was a real groundbreaker in the world of finance, so much so that in 1997 it earned Scholes and Merton the Nobel Prize in economics.[1] There are actually two main components to Black-Scholes: the *Black-Scholes formula* for pricing an option, which we'll explain entirely in the sections that follow, and the *Black-Scholes partial differential equation*, which we'll summarize briefly for the mathematically curious.

Partial differential equations (PDEs) are one of the workhorses of calculus. They express how things change with respect to various contributing factors. The Black-Scholes PDE expresses how an option price and its factors change with respect to one another between two points in time, where the length of time between those points is infinitesimally small. It's given by Formula 10.4:

$$\frac{\delta f}{\delta t} + rS\frac{\delta f}{\delta S} + \frac{1}{2}\sigma^2 S^2 \frac{\delta^2 f}{\delta S^2} = rf \qquad \text{(Formula 10.4)}$$

This eyeful basically says that over this ultra-teeny period of time, the change in price is a function the option price *f*, stock price

---

[1] Fischer Black had passed away by then, and Nobel Prizes are not given posthumously.

S, stock volatility σ (a measure of the "changiness" of the stock price), time t, and the risk-free interest rate r. You can read the symbol δ as "the change over an infinitesimally small period of time in the value of," so the term $\delta f/\delta t$, for example, expresses the ratio between very small changes in option price to very small changes in time. The equation makes a number of assumptions, which we'll detail in a later section in this chapter, mostly with respect to how stock prices change over time. Bottom line, we've got this equation that says how changes to these factors are related to one another. What we want, of course, is an option price or a value for f in the PDE. The Black-Scholes formula gives us such a value by solving the Black-Scholes PDE for f.

Now, we won't go any further into the Black-Scholes PDE. That's the stuff of books way more mathy than this one. But we will explain the formula, because this handy recipe is followed billions of times each day in the world of derivatives, so it's worth a few pages. If you understood the basics of the binomial tree method, then Black-Scholes will even make some sense.

Volatility

The Black-Scholes formula has five inputs, and one of them, volatility, we've not yet covered. *Volatility* is a measure of how a stock return changes. Recall that *return* is the growth rate (or shrink rate if negative) of a stock price over time. So we're talking here about a stock's return, not its price. Now, if a stock's return changes a lot (frequently and by significant amounts, in either direction), its volatility is said to be high. If it doesn't, then its volatility is said to be low. Volatility is given as a number between 0 and 1 and pertains to some period of time. So if you see a stock with an annual volatility, or "vol," of 0.30, you can read it as saying the stock return changes 30 percent (up or down) over the course of a year. The return of stock with a volatility of 0.05 changes 5 percent. And so on. Technically, volatility is the standard deviation from the probability distribution of stock returns (we'll discuss probability distributions later in this chapter), but just think of volatility as a measure of how changeable a stock price is.

Volatility is an absolutely crucial ingredient in the option price recipe—arguably *the* most critical. Yet, wouldn't you know, it's the one factor we cannot observe. It's true. Nobody can tell you the current volatility of any stock, anywhere, at any time. But we must have one, and there are, fortunately, a couple of ways to get one. First, we can calculate *historical volatility* by calculating it from past stock price changes. Unfortunately, one of our bedrock assumptions is that past price changes cannot foretell future price changes, so anything derived from past price changes is really, well, dubious at least. A second, more reliable source is *implied volatility*. Calculating this is a neat trick, and you might even think it bogus. But it actually works. Besides, if everyone is doing it, if everyone is punching the same number into his or her Black-Scholes calculator, it sort of doesn't matter, right? Sort of.

We get implied volatility by observing the market prices—the prices at which traders are actually buying and selling options—and deducing the volatility from those prices. Think of it this way: Black-Scholes requires five inputs and produces one output. If we have the output from some other source and four of the inputs, we can deduce mathematically or imply the missing input using algebra. Ignore for a minute the complicated Black-Scholes formula, and picture a trivial formula like this:

$$x = a + b$$

If we're given a and b, we just add them to find x. But if we're given, say, x and a, we can find b by just rearranging the formula:

$$b = x - a$$

So we subtract the given a from the given x to find b. Basic algebra. It's the same idea for implied volatility. We observe the output of Black-Scholes (the market price of an option) and four of its inputs (stock price, strike, time, interest rate) and plug those into a rearranged version of the Black-Scholes formula to get volatility.

Now I'm tempted to show you such a rearranged version of Black-Scholes, but trust me, it's just a big pile of *not*-so-basic math you can find elsewhere if you really need it. The point is, we get implied volatility by seeing a market price and asking, "What volatility factor would we have to plug into Black-Scholes to produce that price?" But you may be asking a different question right about now: What's the point? What's the point of a formula to calculate an option price if you just use the market option price anyway?

It does perplex. But remember, there's more than one option traded for a given stock, and it's the stock volatility we're after. You might have 10 call options on IBM, for instance, differing only by strike price (one option to buy at $50, another to buy at $55, and so on). Say we're interested in the 50-strike call. Could we not imply the volatility of IBM from the market price of the 55-strike, and plug that into Black-Scholes for the price of the 50-strike? Yes! It's the volatility of the underlier we're after, so "backing out the volatility input" from Black-Scholes doesn't seem quite so stupid after all.

But this leads us to another conundrum worth noting, the so-called constant-volatility assumption of Black-Scholes, which stems from the Black-Scholes assumption about how stock prices change. Intuitively, a stock should have just one volatility at a time, right? It's like the speed of a car. You can't be driving at both 60 and 65 mph at the same time, any more than you can weigh 195 and 205 at the same time. You would think the implied volatility from options differing only by strike price would be the same. But alas, they typically are not. And here we approach the misty lands at the edge of Black-Scholes territory. For if you were to imply the volatility from, say, the market prices of seven otherwise identical calls on ZED, you are as likely as not to get seven different volatilities for ZED. Graphically, it might look like Figure 10-5.

Weird, huh? This says ZED has a volatility of, well, take your pick! And did you notice that it looks a bit like a smile? It lends one of the names given to this phenomenon, the "volatility smile." Now, graphs of implied volatilities don't always turn out this way, and a snarl or sneer is as likely as a smile, but the point is that you don't get a straight line, as you would expect. The phenomenon is more formally known as *skew*.

And whence derives this peculiar thing? Well, the first thing you might wonder, as many do, is whether the problem is with Black-Scholes. Considering some of its assumptions we'll see in a later section of this chapter—constant interest rates, lognormal stock price distributions, etc.—it's no surprise its results lead to things like skew. (It's *not* a perfect formula for the real world, clearly, but it's nearly so, given its well-defined assumptions, and that's a lot.) Skew might also point to some rather intuitive, if difficult to quantify, possibilities such as investor preference for one strike over another. If demand for, say, a deep-ITM option is different from a deep OTM, you would expect the market to bear different prices, and this is something Black-Scholes doesn't consider.

FIGURE 10-5

Volatility Smile or Skew

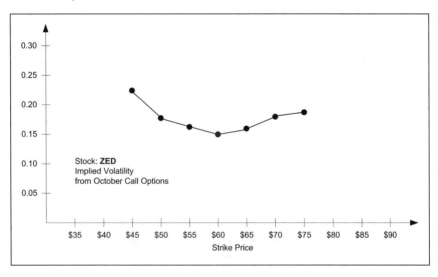

So the way people deal with this skew thing is to modify the model (i.e., build a different wind tunnel) for stock price changes. They price options with models different from Black-Scholes—models with names like *jump-diffusion* and *stochastic volatility*, to name a couple. And they consider things such as *kurtosis*, having to do with the "peakiness" and "tail thickness" of a distribution. Now, we shan't go down any of these those roads in this slender text, but at least you know some people do, people who might while away their minutes at the coffee pot talking about things like "leptokurtotic distributions" with their colleagues.

Oh, and one more important and related thing: not only do implied volatilities exhibit weirdness across options with different strikes, they also do not line up when you sample the same option (option with the same strike) across different expiration months, or terms. It's the same intuition as before. You would expect the implied volatility from two market options that differ only in expiration to be the same. But alas, you do not, getting instead something often termed *volatility term structure* and graphically looking something like Figure 10-6.

So now we have volatility anomalies across two dimensions, strike space and term space. These two anomalies are so closely related and have such similar practical effects that they are often

FIGURE 10-6

Volatility Term Structure

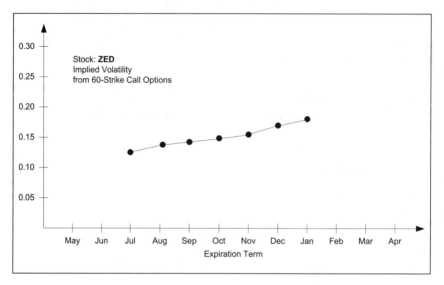

FIGURE 10-7

Volatility Surface

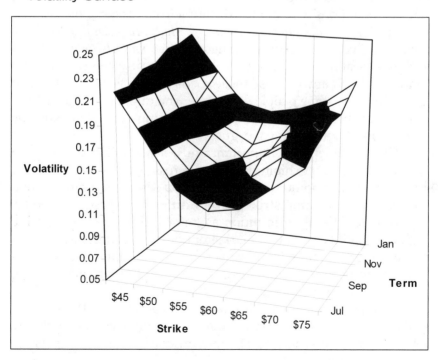

merged into one three-dimensional graphical representation. The resulting image, known as *volatility surface*, is simply a representation of implied volatility across strike space and term space at once. Volatility surfaces look something like Figure 10-7.

The Five Option Price Factors

Table 10-1 shows all five inputs to the Black-Scholes option-pricing formula—that is, the five factors affecting the price of an equity option. Whether you care about how Black-Scholes works or not, if you plan to work with options, it's a good idea to get really comfortable with these factors and how each affects the price of an option. Let's summarize those effects by examining what happens to the value of an option as each of these factors increases or decreases.

- **Stock Price (S):** Increasing stock price increases the value of a call and decreases the value of a put. Makes sense, right? A call is an option to buy at a set strike, so the more you would have to pay *without* the call, the better off you are as a holder of the option. A put is an option to sell at a set strike, so the relationship is, of course, reversed. You want your strike price to be more than you could get by selling spot, so as the stock price increases, the value of a put option decreases.
- **Strike Price (K):** The strike price is just the stock price in reverse. Increasing strike price decreases the value of a call and increases the value of a put. Remember, the difference between stock price and strike price chiefly determines the value of an option, so increasing the strike price is like decreasing the stock price, and decreasing strike price is like increasing stock price. And we already know how changes in stock price affect the option value.

TABLE 10-1

Black-Scholes Pricing Factors

S	Stock price
K	Strike price
t	Time to expiration
σ	Volatility
r	Interest rate

- **Time to Expiration (*t*):** Increasing time to expiration increases the value of calls *and* puts. The more time that remains, the more values the underlier can potentially take on, so the more likely it is for an option to expire in the money. Just consider the extremes: Whether you are holding a call or a put, you'd certainly like an option that never expires more than one that expires tomorrow, right?
- **Volatility (σ):** Like time to expiration, increasing volatility increases the value of both calls and puts. The intuition is the same as well. The more "changy" a stock price is, the more likely it is that an option on that stock will expire in the money, whether it is a call or a put. Volatility, you should know, is *the* most interesting price factor to option traders. So much so that "trading options" is often known as "trading volatility," because that's the most dynamic of price inputs. Now, stock prices also change continuously and unpredictably, but options are all about probability. And as we will see later in this chapter, volatility, as the standard deviation from a probability distribution, is literally an indicator of the probability of future stock price values.
- **Interest Rate (*r*):** Increasing interest rates increases the value of a call and decreases the value of a put. The intuition isn't as obvious as with other factors, because it involves opportunity costs. Here's the thing: Say you have a choice between buying a stock for $50 or buying a 50-strike call option, and you buy the option. This means you have 50 bucks (less the price of the premium) to put into an interest-bearing savings account. While waiting to exercise the option, that savings earns interest. The higher the interest rate, the more you earn—for holding an option instead of buying the underlier. Now suppose you have a choice today between selling a stock for $50 or instead buying a 50-strike put. If you choose the option, you *don't* have that $50 to invest as the call holder does. While waiting to exercise the option, you don't earn any interest. So the higher the interest rate, the greater the opportunity cost of earning interest. The higher the interest rate, the more you *don't* earn. So a call holder benefits by higher interest, while the put holder takes a hit.

TABLE 10-2

Effect of Factor Changes on Option Prices

Change in Factor	Effect on Call Value	Effect on Put Value
Increase S	Increase	Decrease
Increase K	Decrease	Increase
Increase t	Increase	Increase
Increase σ	Increase	Increase
Increase r	Increase	Decrease

Table 10-2 summarizes the effect of the five pricing factors on the price of an option. This is information worth getting to the top of your head if you plan to work with options.

The Black-Scholes Formula

Conceptually, you can think of Black-Scholes as just another function, taking inputs and generating output. For a call value, then, it's like this:

Call Value = Black-Scholes (S, K, t, σ, r)

And in mathematical terms, Formula 10.5 is the Black-Scholes formula for the value of a European call option on a non-dividend-paying stock, using the factors defined in this section and some mathematical expressions we'll explain in a minute:

$$c = SN(d_1) - Ke^{-rt}N(d_2) \qquad \text{(Formula 10.5)}$$

where c is the value of a European call option, S is current stock price, K is strike price, $N(\ )$ is the cumulative normal distribution function (more on this in the next section), and d_1 and d_2 are these guys:

$$d_1 = \frac{\ln\left(\frac{S}{K}\right) + (r + \sigma^2/2)t}{\sigma\sqrt{t}}$$

$$d_2 = d_1 - \sigma\sqrt{t}$$

What a mess, eh? Well, sure, it's mathy, but they don't give out Nobels for pound cake recipes. And it's not so bad if you take it one piece at a time.

First, though, just take a look at the Black-Scholes formula together with the binomial tree formula to see a resemblance:

Black-Scholes: $c = SN(d_1) - Ke^{-rt}N(d_2)$
Binomial tree: $c = S\Delta - B$

The two formulas say basically the same thing! The value of a call option is equal to that of a portfolio consisting of some long position in stock (Δ shares in the binomial tree model, $N(d_1)$ shares in Black-Scholes) and some short position in a bond (B in the binomial tree model, $Ke^{-rt}N(d_2)$ in Black-Scholes). And a short position in a bond, recall, is just the borrowing of some money. Black-Scholes gives more precise quantities of stocks and bonds for the replicating portfolio, for a more precise option value.

The Normal Distribution

We can appreciate how Black-Scholes gets its precision by examining and understanding the formula. As always, feel free to jump off here and skip ahead. We're about to get into some statistics and calculus, and no problem if those aren't your cups of tea. No need to know this stuff for most purposes. But if you're still curious and don't mind some math, let's go for it.

First, let's figure out this *cumulative normal distribution* function, or $N(\ )$ in the formula. It tells us how many shares of stock we need to buy (S) as well as how much money to borrow as some portion of the discounted strike price (Ke^{-rt}). Now, the arguments to $N(\ )$, that is, d_1 and d_2: just think of them as some numbers. What does the cumulative normal distribution function return for a given input x? What does $N(x)$ tell you? A statistician would tell you it gives the probability of a normally distributed random variable having a value less than x. A mathematician would tell you it gives the area beneath the normal probability distribution curve to the left of x. And here's a refresher in case those last two sentences mean nothing to you:

The basic thing to understand here is a *probability distribution*, which is a tool for telling us about the expected values of some *random variable* (RV). A random variable represents the numerical result from a *sampling*. There are a bazillion candidates for random variables out there. Consider the weight of a pumpkin--that's a perfectly autumnal RV. How much does a ripe pumpkin weigh on average? What's the likelihood of it weighing more than 10 pounds? Less than 2 pounds? A probability distribution exists to answer questions just like these.

Imagine spending one autumn visiting pumpkin stands and selecting pumpkins at random for weighing. You record each weight in pounds and then count the pumpkins at each weight. A nice way of presenting your data is to use a *histogram* where the height of each bar gives the number of pumpkins having a certain weight. So the *x*-axis is for weight, and the *y*-axis is for counts, as in Figure 10-8.

Now, just by looking at our histogram, we can glean some facts about the pumpkins. The highest bars are around 15 pounds, telling us this is the average or *mean* weight. (It's 16.11 pounds, to be precise.) Another, less intuitive fact is something called *standard deviation*, which measures how "bunched up" the data points are around the mean. To understand this important statistic, first remember that each bar of the histogram is like a stack of pumpkins. Think about any one of these pumpkins—say, one of the pumpkins in the 7-pound stack. Now consider the difference between the mean weight (say, 15) and the weight of this pumpkin (7), which is 8 pounds (i.e., 15 − 7). A pumpkin on the 19-pound stack has a difference of −4 (i.e., 15 − 19). Imagine calculating this difference for every

FIGURE 10-8

Sampling Histogram

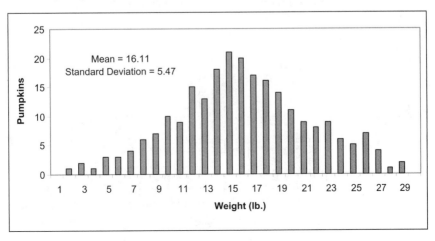

pumpkin, squaring all the results (to make them all positive values), and taking the average of your results. That average is known as the *variance*. For these pumpkins, it turns out to be 29.94. Now take the square root of variance, to undo the effect of squaring and return things to the original units. The result is the standard deviation, or for these pumpkins, 5.47.

The important thing to remember about standard deviation is best illustrated graphically. It measures the "bunchiness" or dispersion of a random variable. Figure 10-9 shows another hypothetical pumpkin sampling. In this new distribution, you can see how pumpkin weights are, on average, farther from the mean, which is again 16.11. Thus, although the mean is the same, the standard deviation is higher, at 6.39. The greater the standard deviation, the greater the dispersion.

Now, everything we've said so far about pumpkin weights pertains only to this particular sampling. But if the random variable samples meet certain conditions—that they are identically distributed (every sampling has the same probability characteristics) and independently distributed (the weight of one pumpkin does not affect the weight of any other pumpkin)—then we can safely say *any* pumpkin has a weight that is *normally distributed*. This essentially means if you were to sample every single pumpkin at every stand, a histogram of the precise (not rounded) weights would be shaped as in Figure 10-10.

FIGURE 10-9

Sampling Histogram with Greater Dispersion

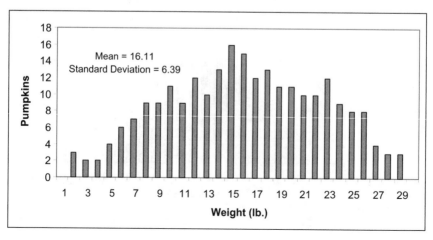

FIGURE 10-10

Normal Distribution

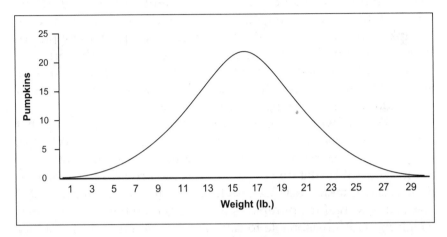

The normal distribution is perhaps the most widely used probability distribution of them all and is sometimes called a bell curve distribution for its shape. Again, think of the normal as a histogram for an entire *population* of random variable values, as opposed to just the *sample* pumpkins. A population mean is typically denoted by the Greek letter mu (μ). Population variance is typically depicted by the symbol sigma-squared (σ^2), and standard deviation by sigma (σ), as shown in Figure 10-11.

FIGURE 10-11

Population Mean and Standard Deviation

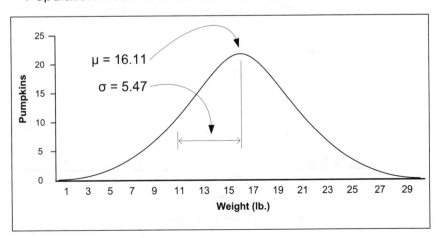

Now let's move on to the good stuff. First, recall that the numbers along the x-axis (horizontal) represent possible values for the random variable. In our case, these are pumpkin weights. The height of the curve over a given point is the proportional number of pumpkins having that weight. We can see that quite a few pumpkins weigh around 15 pounds, whereas only a few weigh more than 25 pounds. Now, the key thing to observe from a distribution is *the area beneath the curve,* which translates directly into a probability of the random variable taking on some value or another.

Let's start with an extreme case. What is the probability that a random variable will take on some value, any value? Why, it's 100 percent of course, or the entire area under the curve, or just 1, if you will. And what do you suppose is the probability of the random variable taking a value less than or equal to the mean of 15? Well, because half the pumpkins weigh less than the mean and half weigh more, it's reasonable to say there is a 50 percent probability of that being the case. And what is the area beneath the curve to the left of the mean? Fifty percent. So it turns out this is true for any value of x: the probability of the random variable taking on a value less than x is just the area beneath the curve to the left of that point. In our pumpkin distribution, for example, the area beneath the curve to the left of 9 pounds is 10 percent of the total area. Thus, there is a 10 percent probability that a pumpkin chosen at random will weigh no more than 9 pounds (see Figure 10-12).

FIGURE 10-12

Area Beneath the Normal Curve

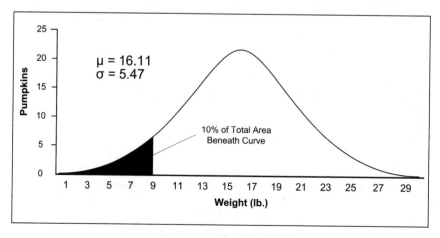

$\mu = 16.11$
$\sigma = 5.47$

10% of Total Area
Beneath Curve

The area to the left of the 21-pound mark happens to be 81 percent, which is the probability of a pumpkin weighing no more than 21 pounds. For $x = 26$, the area is 96 percent. And this brings us to the raison d'être for this little lesson. That area beneath a curve, which measures the probability of a random variable taking on some value less than the x-value at which the area stops, is known as the *cumulative normal distribution*.

Calculating an area beneath a curve is where the calculus comes in—*integral calculus*, in fact, as the area beneath a curve is known as the integral of the function the produces it.[2] You can imagine that there are many possible normal distributions. And calculating integrals is a lot of work, even for computers. To reduce this drudgery, someone a long time ago imagined a normal distribution with a mean of 0 and standard deviation of 1. Such a distribution is known as the *standard normal distribution*, and the cumulative normal distributions for the standard normal have been calculated for scads of x-values and documented in numerous textbook appendixes and programmed into a great many computer programs and calculators. How does this help us? It turns out that the cumulative normal of any normal distribution can be easily calculated from the cumulative normal from the standard normal distribution. Whoohoo! A labor-saving device if ever there was one.

Summarizing a bit, the cumulative normal distribution function $N(x)$ returns for a given value x the area beneath the normal distribution curve to the left of x. This area is equal to the probability of a normally distributed random variable having a value less than x. The cumulative normal distribution for any normal distribution is derivable from that of the standard normal distribution. In the Black-Scholes formula, $N(d_1)$ tells us that the number of shares of stock in a replicating portfolio is equal to the probability of a standard normally distributed random variable having a value equal to d_1. Voilà.

And that's all you need to know to understand what's going on in the formula. But while we're here, let's jump off the path and consider how we can connect the pumpkin thing with the option-pricing thing. Imagine you stumbled across an undocumented button on your kid's computer that did something slightly out of the ordinary. Let's say, hmm, let's say it turned back time for the

---

[2] The other type of calculus you might recall is *differential calculus*, which is concerned with the slope (rise over run) of the curve at a single point.

entire earth for exactly one day. Reasonable? Okay. Now imagine you sample the closing price of the stock ZED one day. Then you press the button, wait for a day, and again sample the closing price of ZED. It's different from before because that's just how random processes work. So you do this again and again several hundred times, and then use your data to calculate mu and sigma and use those to plot yourself a distribution curve just like we did with pumpkin weights. Now you have a probability distribution for stock prices.

For better or worse, we don't have world-replay buttons on our computers like that. But Black, Scholes, and Merton essentially imagined they *did* have such a button and made an important assumption about the resulting curve. Did they assume stock prices were normally distributed? Not exactly. We won't go into all the reasons why, but they assumed stock price *returns* are normally distributed, which happens when stock *prices* are lognormally distributed. And we'll explore that further when we cover all the Black-Scholes assumptions in the next section.

APPLYING BLACK-SCHOLES

Now back to the formula:

$$c = SN(d_1) - Ke^{-rt}N(d_2)$$

That $N(\ )$ function is really the trickiest part of Black-Scholes. The rest, calculating the d_1 and d_2 values, is just algebra:

$$d_1 = \frac{\ln\left(\frac{S}{K}\right) + (r + \sigma^2/2)t}{\sigma\sqrt{t}}$$

$$d_2 = d_1 - \sigma\sqrt{t}$$

There are some square roots and exponents and Euler's number e in there. The natural log function $\ln(\ )$ is something your calculator is only too happy to calculate for you. The function $\ln x$, which you might recall as the inverse of the natural exponential function, returns the number you need to raise e to in order to get x.

So let's fill up the tank and fire up this Nobel Prize–winning contraption. Say we want to again value our old friend cZED62, a European call option on the stock ZED that expires in six months with a strike price of $62, this time using Black-Scholes. We'll use the exact same factors as before plus a volatility factor. Let's choose 0.15. Here's the math:

$$S = 60$$
$$K = 62$$
$$t = 0.5$$
$$\sigma = 0.15$$
$$r = 0.06$$

$$\text{Call Value} = \text{Black-Scholes}(S, K, t, \sigma, r)$$
$$c = SN(d_1) - Ke^{-rt}N(d_2)$$

$$d_1 = \frac{\ln\left(\frac{S}{K}\right) + (r + \sigma^2/2)t}{\sigma\sqrt{t}}$$

$$= \frac{\ln\left(\frac{60}{62}\right) + (0.06 + 0.15^2/2)0.5}{0.15\sqrt{0.5}}$$

$$= \frac{\ln(0.9677) + 0.0356}{0.1061}$$

$$= 0.0267$$

$$d_2 = d_1 - \sigma\sqrt{t}$$
$$= 0.0267 - 0.15\sqrt{0.5}$$
$$= -0.0793$$

$$c = SN(d_1) - Ke^{-rt}N(d_2)$$
$$= 60N(0.0267) - 62e^{-(0.06)(0.5)}N(-0.0793)$$
$$= 60(0.5107) - 62(0.9704)(0.4684)$$
$$= 30.64 - 28.18$$
$$= 2.46$$

Black-Scholes tells us the fair market value of this option is $2.46. Compare this with the $2.53 from the one-step binomial tree. And it, of course, falls in the range of 0 to $60, which we identified using the rough method. And again we see the value falling much closer to the bottom of that range, as we expect with most OTM options.

Black-Scholes Assumptions

Black-Scholes is darn good, but it's not perfect. It's still based on a wind tunnel test that draws facts from a model—a very good model, but still a model. We can tell how the model differs from the real world by examining the assumptions made by Black-Scholes about stock price changes. There are three biggies.

First is the Black-Scholes assumption about how stock prices change over time. As noted earlier in this chapter, it assumes stock returns are normally distributed. Not prices, mind you, but returns. Normally distributed random variables can take values less than zero, and stock prices are always positive, so they can't be normally distributed. But stock *returns* can be negative, and thanks to something in mathland known as the *central limit theorem*, assuming they are independently and identically distributed, we can say they are normally distributed; that is, histograms of very large samplings will take on the familiar shape of a bell curve. One can also assert, as Black-Scholes does, that returns are normally distributed by assuming stock price paths follow a *stochastic* or essentially unpredictable process. Think of process in this sense as the path created as the value of something—in this case, returns—changes over time. Black-Scholes further assumes that returns follow a special form of stochastic process known as Brownian motion, a type of Weiner process, or a process in which the random variable changes continuously and whose changes are normally distributed.

Now, it so happens there's this distribution called the *lognormal*, which essentially plots the logs (the number you have to raise *e* to) of a normally distributed random variable that follows a process known as *geometric Brownian motion*. And mathematically, it can be shown that if a stock price is lognormally distributed, its return is normally distributed. Bottom line, Black-Scholes assumes that stock *returns* are normally distributed by assuming that stock *prices* are lognormally so. Figure 10-13 pairs up a normal and lognormal distribution to give the basic idea.

You might wonder about the asymmetric shape of the lognormal distribution and how that fits with reality. If you think about it, the U.S. stock market over many decades has been a bull market. Over long periods of time, the value of stocks overall has increased. (Of course, over relatively short periods, it can be a bear market, with stock prices decreasing.) The lognormal model, if you look at it and think about it, fits with that fact. The left slope is steeper than

FIGURE 10-13

Normal and Lognormal Distributions

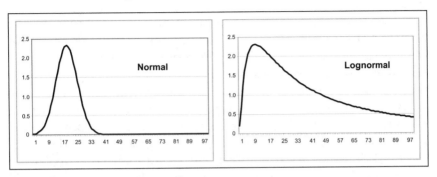

the right, which says there are fewer price decreases than increases. So in this respect, it's not a bad model of reality.

And before we leave the lognormal distribution, here's a fact you'll want to know: the binomial distribution (the distribution produced by the binomial tree we used in the previous section) approaches the lognormal as you add levels to the tree. So there's another reason we like the lognormal and a key link between the binomial tree method of option pricing and Black-Scholes.

The normal distribution, of course, is where we get the volatility values required by the formula. Now, stemming from the Black-Scholes assumption about normally distributed stock returns, Black-Scholes also assumes there is only *one* such distribution applicable to the price of an option, irrespective of its strike price or term. This is where the skew thing, and the warped volatility surface, gets Black-Scholes into trouble. This assumption is often known as the constant-volatility assumption of Black-Scholes, and like other assumptions, it just doesn't jibe with what we see empirically.

The second huge assumption of Black-Scholes is that markets are frictionless. This means one can trade continuously with no transactions costs, taxes, or other encumbrances of any kind. This assumption is required by the dynamic hedging involved in maintaining the replicating portfolio of stocks and bonds. Recall from the binomial tree method that the replicating portfolio changed slightly at every step, and with a tree of infinitely small steps, the portfolio changes continuously. Only a frictionless market would permit such a thing.

Third, Black-Scholes assumes constant interest rates. In other words, interest rates don't change over the course of a contract. But, of course, they can and do.

Are stock prices *really* lognormally distributed? Probably not. Are markets *really* frictionless? Definitely not. Trading does involve commissions and other costs, truly continuous trading is impossible, etc. Are interest rates constant? Not usually. Still, owing to widespread acceptance of Black-Scholes, we can say clearly the markets believe that these assumptions are reasonable. Further, nobody is limited to Black-Scholes as it comes out of the box. Indeed, a great many fine minds are forever at work modifying and extending Black-Scholes—for example, to deal with the implied-volatility anomalies we discussed earlier—all in pursuit of the elusive "real" value of an option.

Why all the interest in a better and better price? Why isn't Black-Scholes good enough? Because the better your pricing *analytics*, as they are known, the better you are at spotting pricing errors in the market—that is, people offering to buy or sell at the "wrong" price. And as we'll explore further in the next chapter, and as you may have already gathered, pricing algorithms also provide hedging instructions. So if your analytics tell you that something in the market is mispriced, you can lock in the difference between the market price and what you believe to be the actual price by hedging according to those same analytics, thus realizing an arbitrage. So arbitrage is indeed attainable even today, but you need damn good analytics to pull it off.

Put-Call Parity

So far, we've dealt only with call options. There is a variation of the Black-Scholes call option formula for valuing put options, shown in Formula 10.7, but it's good to know that put prices are mathematically linked to call prices due to an important concept known as *put-call parity*. To get some intuition behind the put-call parity, imagine that you form a portfolio by buying 100 shares of a $5 stock, buying one put option to sell (100 shares of) that same stock at $5, and writing one call option to buy it at $5. If you think through a sample of possible prices for the stock, you will quickly see that the value of this portfolio at expiration is $5, no matter what. So the value of the portfolio must be the present value of $5.

Algebraically, then, we arrive at the put-call parity for European options in Formula 10.6:

$$S + p - c = Ke^{-rt} \qquad \text{(Formula 10.6)}$$

where:

S = stock price
p = put option price
c = call option price
K = strike price for both call and put
e^{-rt} = discount factor
$Ke^{-rt} = PV(K)$ = present value of strike price

The put-call parity can be arranged into whatever form we like, depending on what we're after. To wit, here are four expressions of put-call parity for European options on non-dividend-paying stock:

$$S = c - p + Ke^{-rt}$$
$$c = S + p - Ke^{-rt}$$
$$p = c - S + Ke^{-rt}$$
$$Ke^{-rt} = S + p - c$$

So owing to the put-call parity and math we shall not delve into, Formula 10.7 is the Black-Scholes formula for valuing European put options on non-dividend-paying stocks:

Put Value = Black-Scholes (S, K, t, σ, r)
Put Value = $p - Ke^{-rt}N(-d_2) - SN(-d_1)$ $\qquad$ (Formula 10.7)

where, as before, $N(\ )$ is the cumulative normal distribution function and d_1 and d_2 are again these guys:

$$d_1 = \frac{\ln\left(\frac{S}{K}\right) + (r + \sigma^2/2)t}{\sigma\sqrt{t}}$$

$$d_2 = d_1 - \sigma\sqrt{t}$$

Effect of Discrete Dividends

So far, we've dealt only with options on stocks that don't pay dividends. Dividends are payments made by stock issuers to their stockholders, typically at some interval like every three months. Think of these as *discrete dividends* (versus continuous dividends, which we'll get to next). When a dividend is paid, it immediately lowers the value of the stock, because receiving a dividend is like partially cashing in your investment in the issuer. Another way to think of this is that some portion of a dividend-paying stock price is the present value of all future dividend payments. Now imagine that you are pricing a call option with a nine-month term. Of course, you need a stock price, but the current stock price includes the present value of, say, three dividend payments, *which the option holder will not receive*. A more appropriate stock price is one from which the present value of those three dividends has been removed, known as a *dividend-adjusted stock price*.

Now, companies are free to change their dividend payments from time to time, but it so happens they don't change all that much, so at any time, there is a decent consensus on the future expected dividends from a stock issuer. So to price an option on such a stock, we first calculate the present value of the expected stream of all dividends paid before option expiration. (This is easier than it sounds. Just look back to our earlier explanation of calculating present values. Do that once for each dividend, and sum the results. There's your present value of the dividend stream.) We subtract that present value from the stock price and then plug this dividend-adjusted stock price into our option valuation formula in lieu of the regular stock price. If and when issuers pay dividends that deviate from expectations or simply announce their intention to do so, this, of course, immediately affects the dividend-adjusted stock price; this is why dividend announcements and unexpected dividend payments affect option prices.

To modify the Black-Scholes formulas to work for options on dividend-paying stocks, we simply replace all occurrences of the factor S (stock price) with $S - PV(D)$, the dividend-adjusted stock price where D represents future dividend payments to be paid before expiration (see Formulas 10.8 and 10.9):

Call Value = Black-Scholes (S, D, K, t, σ, r)

$\qquad D$ = discrete dividends

$\qquad c = (S - PV[D])N(d_1) - Ke^{-rt}N(d_2)$ (Formula 10.8)

Put Value = Black-Scholes (S, D, K, t, σ, r)

$\qquad p = Ke^{-rt}N(d_2) - (S - PV[D])N(-d_1)$ (Formula 10.9)

$$d_1 = \frac{\ln\left(\frac{S - PV[D]}{K}\right) + (r + \sigma^2/2)t}{\sigma\sqrt{t}}$$

$$d_2 = d_1 - \sigma\sqrt{t}$$

Effect of Continuous Dividends

Think of discrete dividends as money that "drips" out of the underlier at some regular interval. Not only can an underlier drip like this, but some underliers "leak" money continuously. The value of foreign currency, for example, when priced in local currency, decreases continuously by the foreign risk-free interest rate. Or a stock index, with a great many component stocks all dripping discrete dividends on their own schedules, can be seen as leaking a continuous stream.

For option pricing, we think of these leaks as *continuous dividends*. Just like discrete dividends, they affect the price of an option by effectively lowering the value of the underlier. And they, too, decrease the value of the stock by the present value of the expected dividend stream over the life of the option. We use slightly different math to arrive at that present value, however, because continuous dividends are actually just like continuously compounded interest. So the dividend rate is treated like an interest rate and affects the value of the underlier (see Formulas 10.10 and 10.11):

Call Value = Black-Scholes (S, D, K, t, σ, r)

$\qquad d$ = continuous dividend rate

$\qquad c = Se^{-dt}N(d_1) - Ke^{-rt}N(d_2)$ (Formula 10.10)

Put Value = Black-Scholes (S, D, K, t, σ, r)

$$p = Ke^{-rt}N(d_2) - Se^{-dt}N(-d_1) \qquad \text{(Formula 10.11)}$$

$$d_1 = \frac{\ln\left(\frac{Se^{-dt}}{K}\right) + (r + \sigma^2/2)t}{\sigma\sqrt{t}}$$

$$d_2 = d_1 - \sigma\sqrt{t}$$

And here's a little bonus. You can use the continuous-dividend option-pricing formulas for options on two other kinds of underliers: stock indexes and foreign currency. For an index, S is just the index price (i.e., an average of a bunch of individual stocks), and d is the approximate total dividend flow from all the dividend-paying stocks in the index. For foreign currency, S is the spot price in local currency (i.e., the currency you want the option value in) of one unit of foreign currency. And d is the risk-free interest rate paid in the foreign country.

American Options and Early Exercise

So far, we've restricted our discussion of Black-Scholes to the valuation of European options, which can only be exercised on the expiration date. Americans, of course, can be exercised any time up to and including expiration. And here's the basic question: Is it ever wise to exercise an American option before the expiration date? Yes, but not as often as you might think. First, it is *never* wise to exercise early an American call option on a non-dividend-paying stock. It *may* be optimal to exercise early an American call or put on a dividend-paying stock, depending mostly on the size of the dividend. And it may be optimal to exercise early an American put on a non-dividend-paying stock if it's deeply in the money.

Consider the case of a non-dividend-paying stock. Imagine holding 100 American call options with a strike price of $30 on a stock currently trading for $50, and the options don't expire for another three months. If you exercise, you get to buy 10,000 shares of stock (remember, each option is to buy 100 shares) for $300,000 instead of the going price of $500,000, saving a whopping $200,000! Who could pass up an opportunity like that? You should. Why? Because there are two alternatives to exercise in which you are better off.

First, you can simply sell the option and lock in a profit of *more* than $200,000. That's just the intrinsic value, recall, so you know the option must be worth more than that. And this is cash you get to keep no matter what; if you exercise and hold, remember, the stock price can tank and take those gains with it. If you exercise and sell immediately, the most you get is intrinsic value. So selling the option is always better than exercising.

If you can't sell the option, you can still take that $300,000 and, rather than using it to purchase stock, invest it at the risk-free rate. After three months, the stock price will either be above the $30 strike price or below it. If it is above, cash in your investment, use $300,000 to buy the stock, and pocket the interest as a bonus. If it is below, cash in your investment and use some portion of the $300,000 to buy the stock, and again pocket the interest. In either case, you are better off (because of the interest) than if you had exercised and held the stock.

You still might be thinking, "What if I believe the stock price is sure to fall? Shouldn't I exercise and sell immediately if I can't sell the option, to at least lock in the intrinsic value?" If you really believe the stock price will fall, then you should sell the stock short. If the stock price falls as you expect, you make money from the short stock position—and you haven't given up the opportunity to exercise your option.

In the case of American options on dividend-paying stocks, it may be optimal to exercise early, just before or after the dividend payment, in order to get the dividend and future dividends. (Remember, it goes to the stockholder.) The basic idea for a call is to compare the present value of all remaining dividends with the sum of the option value and the interest you will lose on K by exercising. If the former exceeds the latter, go for it. You only do this immediately before the dividend pays, because doing so earlier gains you nothing and gives up optionality. Because option value and forgone interest change over time, you need to reevaluate for early exercise before every dividend. While it may not be wise to exercise before the next dividend, it could be wise to exercise just before the next or a later one.

In the case of an American put on a dividend-paying stock, the same intuition applies but in reverse. And you make the decision just *after* a dividend is paid. If the present value of interest on the strike price (which, remember, you don't get if you don't exercise) is greater than the present value of remaining dividends and option value, you should exercise. Here you don't mind giving up remaining dividends and optionality, because you'll make more by selling the stock and investing the proceeds.

Unlike an American call on a non-dividend-paying stock, it turns out it may be optimal to exercise an American put on a non-dividend-paying stock—if it is very deep in the money. Imagine, for instance, that a stock price is nearly zero and the strike price of your put is $5. You'll never get more than $5 because the stock price can't go below zero. And you might as well collect the payoff now, so you can put it to work earning interest.

WHICH METHOD TO USE?

Black-Scholes cannot be applied to all types of options; for some, you must use a tree method. Here's the lowdown.

For European calls and puts on non-dividend-paying stocks, use Black-Scholes in its simplest form. For European calls and puts on dividend-paying stocks, use Black-Scholes modified for discrete or continuous dividends, whichever the case may be, using the formulas laid out earlier.

For American calls on dividend-paying stocks, you can arrive at an approximate option value using Black-Scholes by applying it twice and taking the maximum of the two results. On the first application, you assume exercise (just before the dividend date), and for the second, you assume no exercise. It's just an approximation; the tree method is a better choice.

For American puts, Black-Scholes is simply not a choice. You must use a binomial tree method because an analytical method for pricing an American put option simply does not exist. An *analytical* solution is one in which you plug factors into a function and get a result. A nonanalytical method is more of a brute-force or trial-and-error approach, which the tree method really is, once you think about it. A faithful explanation of why no analytical solution exists would go well beyond the scope of our little book. It's an example of a "free boundary" problem, and these things are *hard*, like trying to predict precisely where water will flow when poured from a bucket onto a flat surface. If you can solve this one, the Nobel committee is waiting to hear from you.

Incidentally, there is an extension of the binomial method known as the *trinomial method*, often used in practice for pricing options. It's the same basic idea as the binomial, but instead of assuming a stock can change to one of two prices at each node, we assume it can also remain unchanged. As a result, there are three possible values—ergo the name. It makes for a more complicated tree, but as it turns out, the math can actually be simpler and therefore faster to perform in a time crunch. And when it comes to option pricing, there is always a time crunch.

And while we're on the subject of alternative methods, we should touch briefly on the *martingale* approach to pricing. Like Black-Scholes, it is based on a continuous-time model, meaning time intervals are infinitesimally small. (Time intervals in the discrete-time binomial and trinomial models are also small, but not infinitesimally so.) As it relates to the pricing of derivatives, a martingale is a stochastic (unpredictable) price process with no discernible trend. Using the martingale approach, you apply formulas and constructs assuming stock prices are martingales, that is, moving with no trends. Only they don't. Over time, stock prices tend to drift up. And discount bond prices are expected to increase as well. So there are transformations you can apply to make derivative underlier prices behave like martingales, and these are known as *equivalent martingale measures*. We won't go into these, but at least you know now that Black-Scholes with its partial differential equation is not the only game in town when it comes to cool pricing models.

PRICING OPTIONS ON FUTURES

The first thing to remember with regard to pricing options on futures is that a futures price (like a forward price) is just a spot price adjusted for carry. So options on futures are like options on stock, but the value on expiration is not the difference between exercise and stock prices; rather, it is the difference between exercise and a futures price.

If you hold a call option on a futures with a strike price of $35 and the futures price on expiration is $39, exercising the option gives you $4. It also gives you a long position in the futures, which you can either unwind immediately (for little or no cost) or hold if you so choose. The option writer is obligated to take a corresponding short position in the futures. If you hold that futures option and the futures price at expiration is $34, your option expires worthless. Oh well. Same thing in reverse for a put option. Your option is in the money when its strike price exceeds the futures price and is otherwise out of the money—or at the money if strike happens to equal the futures price.

Now, to calculate an option on a futures contract, we use Black-Scholes with just two changes. First, the underlier is a futures contract potentially initiated at time t (expiration) and going on to a delivery date we'll call t' (read "t prime"). So the futures contract we might do at expiration is $F(t, t')$. Now notice we have three dates: the date when the option is executed, which we'll denote t_0; t when the option expires and the futures commences; and t' when the futures contract delivers. The first change to the formula, then, is to replace the S factor with $F(t_0, t')$. Second, to account for daily interest received on a replicating portfolio including lent funds in the amount of $F(t_0, t')$, we treat the underlier as if it has a continuous dividend, using the risk-free interest rate for the "dividend" rate. Using Black-Scholes in this way, modified this way for future options, is known as *Black's model*. Here is Black's model in Formulas 10.12 and 10.13:

Call Value = Black $(F(t_0, t'), d, K, t, \sigma, r)$

$F(t_0, t')$ = underlier futures price

d = continuous dividend rate

$$c = F(t_0, t')e^{-dt}N(d_1) - Ke^{-rt}N(d_2) \qquad \text{(Formula 10.12)}$$

Put Value = Black $(F(t_0, t'), d, K, t, \sigma, r)$

$$p = Ke^{-rt}N(-d_2) - F(t_0, t')e^{-dt}N(-d_1) \qquad \text{(Formula 10.13)}$$

$$d_1 = \frac{\ln\left(\dfrac{F(t_0, t')e^{-dt}}{Ke^{-rt}}\right)}{\sigma\sqrt{t}} + \frac{\sigma\sqrt{t}}{2}$$

$$d_2 = d_1 - \sigma\sqrt{t} = \frac{\ln\left(\dfrac{F(t_0, t')e^{-dt}}{Ke^{-rt}}\right)}{\sigma\sqrt{t}} - \frac{\sigma\sqrt{t}}{2}$$

CHAPTER 11

Hedging a Derivatives Position

We've discussed already how derivatives can be used to hedge exposures stemming from positions in nonderivative instruments. In this chapter we'll delve into how to hedge a position in derivatives.

HEDGING SWAPS AND OPTIONS

Consider options dealers or market makers, who as a matter of course buy and sell derivatives all day long, taking on new exposures with every new trade. If they do nothing, on some of the exposures they will likely gain, and on some they will lose, depending on how the market moves thereafter. But in general, dealers are not interested in making upside profits; that's the dominion of the speculator. Dealers want to make money on every trade, no matter what, and are willing to forgo upside along with downside in order to make that happen. And they do so by hedging, managing the exposure created by taking on a new position in a derivative. Notice how this contrasts with our "classic" hedger from the earlier chapter, who used derivatives to hedge an exposure stemming from some nonderivative.

We'll examine derivatives risk management from the perspective of two market makers: the swaps dealer and options dealer. The swaps dealer can hedge nicely with offsetting positions in interest rate futures or bonds, and the options dealer can hedge most of his or her exposure with offsetting positions in the underlier. We choose the swaps dealer and options dealer because they illustrate two very different hedging requirements. The swaps dealer (and any dealer of forward-based derivatives) can manage risk with a *static* hedge. This essentially means the dealer can form the hedge position and more or less forget about it until it's time to close it. The options dealer, in contrast, can only manage risk with a *dynamic* hedge. This is a hedge position that must be monitored and adjusted nearly continuously for as long as the hedge is required.

Hedging a Swap

Imagine you're a swaps dealer who just executed a one-year, fixed-for-floating LIBOR swap with some business entity using the swap to effectively convert a preexisting floating-rate debt into a fixed rate. As the party to receive fixed, you are said to have sold the swap. (The party who pays fixed is said to buy.) The swap has a notional of $1 million and fixed rate of 3.5 percent. Its coupon frequency is three months, so every quarter for the next two years, you will make a payment based on a floating rate of interest on an imaginary $1 million loan and will receive a payment based on a rate of 3.5 percent, or $8,750 (i.e., $1,000,000 × 0.035/4). You are thus exposed to changing interest rates. Should they increase, so will the net of your payments and receipts, effectively causing you a loss. And should they decrease, so will your payments, effectively making you money. How the heck do you manage that exposure? And how, by the way, do you make some money whether interest rates rise or fall?

To get your mind around swap hedging, first thing you do is chop the big problem into a bunch of smaller problems. Remember, a swap is equivalent to a portfolio of forwards. In other words, executing this two-year quarterly swap is economically equivalent to taking short positions in a series of three-month floating-rate agreements (FRAs)—one for each of the swap coupons. On each FRA expiration date, you would make a payment if rates exceed the delivery price or receive a payment should rates be below. Just like your swap obligation.

Now all you need is some hedging instrument with the same payoff characteristics as your FRAs, something in which you can take offsetting positions such that every three months, you will receive money if rates increase and make a payment if they fall. The Eurodollar futures contract, an exchange-traded instrument whose underlier is a LIBOR loan and whose payoff characteristics are similar to that of an FRA, is just such a hedging instrument. Another instrument is a government bond that makes quarterly payments and whose price changes are correlated with LIBOR, such as U.S. Treasury bonds. Both Eurodollar futures and U.S. Treasuries are used a zillion times a day by swaps dealers around the world to hedge their exposures.[1]

So let's use futures to hedge the swap. We'll look first at just one coupon period in the middle of the swap, but the idea is the same for the entirety of any plain-vanilla swap. Let's express the swap coupon in terms of a payoff diagram for the swap dealer in Figure 11-1.

By virtue of the swap, the dealer has a short position—hence the idea that you are the seller of the swap—on forward LIBOR at a delivery price of 3.5 percent (or $8,750, as we calculated previously) and a delivery date 12 months out. Now, short forward positions always make money when the spot price is below delivery price. So, for example, if LIBOR settles at 3.4 percent, the dealer will make a

FIGURE 11-1

Short Swap Payoff

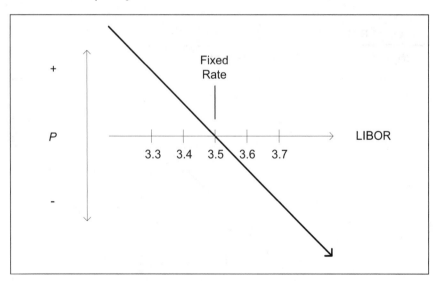

----

[1] Futures that expire within four or five years tend to be much more liquid than futures for periods further out, so dealers tend to use them for so-called front terms. For periods further out, bonds tend to be the favored hedging instrument.

gain of $250 (i.e., $1{,}000{,}000 \times [0.035/4 - 0.034/4]$). By the same rea-
soning and math, they will lose $250 if rates increase to 3.6 percent.

Now consider the payoff of a short position in a Eurodollar
futures (EDF) contract with a delivery date 12 months out and
delivery price of 3.5 percent. (If your intuition tells you that should
be a long EDF position, note that a short EDF position is effectively
a long position in the interest rate, which is what we really want.)
Eurodollar futures have a notional of $1 million. The actual under-
lier is 3 months of LIBOR interest, so in dollars, the delivery price
is $8,750—just like our coupon. Figure 11-2 shows the short EDF
payoff.

Now we're getting somewhere. A combined short position in
the swap coupon and short position in the EDF gives us the net
exposure shown in Figure 11-3. No more worries about rising interest rates.

But wait! The dealer isn't writing a swap just for the fun of it.
Dealers would like to make some money for their trouble. So instead
of an EDF with a delivery price of 3.5 percent, let's use 3.4 percent
instead. That shifts the futures payoff line to the left, which raises
the net payoff, as shown in Figure 11-4.

FIGURE 11-2

Short Eurodollar Futures Payoff

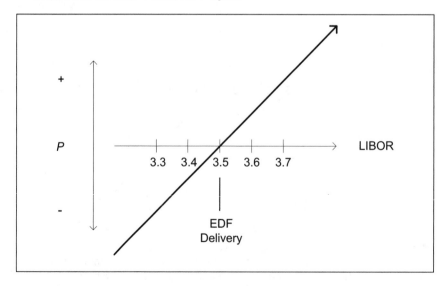

FIGURE 11-3

Net Swap and Eurodollar Futures Payoff

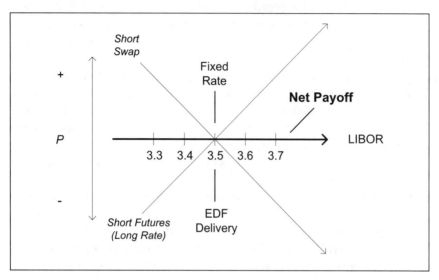

FIGURE 11-4

Net Swap and Eurodollar Futures Payoff with Dealer Profit

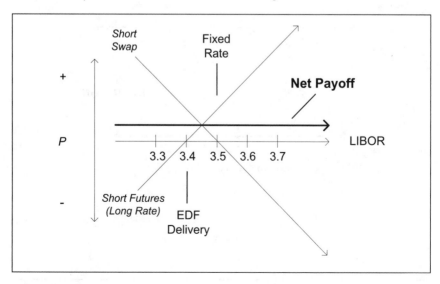

The dealer can now bank on a profit whether interest rates rise or fall. And what if the dealer takes the other side of the swap, so they receive floating and pay fixed? Same hedge, different side. Instead of short futures positions, they take long futures positions with delivery prices slightly higher, for positive net payoffs, as in Figure 11-5.

Now a couple of practical points are in order, because swaps in practice aren't hedged exactly as I've shown, but the idea is the same. First, you can't exactly choose the delivery price of a new futures contract. Recall that it's set such that the initial value of the contract is zero. You can, though, adjust the fixed rate of the swap you are willing to sell. And this is how it works in practice; the fixed rate is set some number of basis points away from the breakeven rate such that the dealer makes some money. Second, we've seen just one coupon of a multicoupon swap. And due to the term structure of interest rates, each coupon is bound to have a different breakeven rate, but we want a single fixed rate for the entire swap, right?

If this intrigues you, then take a look back at Chapter 9, "Pricing Swaps," and see how we chose the breakeven fixed rate, or swap rate, by setting up each leg of the swap as a series of cash flows, one

FIGURE 11-5

Net Long Swap and Long Eurodollar Futures Payoff with Dealer Profit

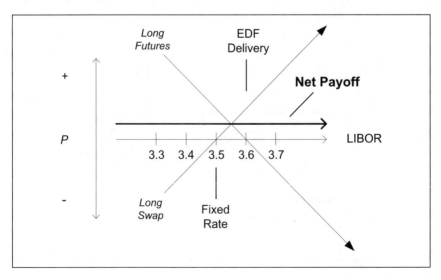

using forward interest rates (which generally differed from one coupon to the next) and another using a fixed rate, which we chose by trial and error till we found the breakeven rate. Constructing a swap in this fashion also makes it easy to deal with different tenors on each leg. Bottom line, the swaps dealer is likely to make money on some coupons and lose money on others, but the net payoff across all coupons will work out as if the dealer makes a few bucks on each one, just as in our simple example.

The dealer can also adjust the fixed rate to make some set target profit. Recall that in the Lakewood-Cornelia swap in Chapter 9, "Pricing Swaps," Lakewood was in the same position as our swaps dealer in this chapter, receiving fixed and paying floating. The company fiddled with the fixed rate till the present value of the swap came to $10,000, which was its fee in essence for doing the swap. Table 11-1, on the next page, shows the cash flows.

Hedging an Option

The writer of an option contract automatically takes on a risk that the option will go in the money and be exercised. Note that this applies to anyone who takes a short position in an option, not just dealers per se. When a long option is exercised in the money, the dealer is obligated to buy stock from the option holder for more than it is worth (for puts) or sell the option holder stock for less than it is worth (for calls).[2] Figure 11-6 shows the payoff diagrams for short option positions.

The payoff diagrams make the bad news perfectly clear: the exposure is huge—theoretically unlimited for written calls. The good news is the exposure can be significantly reduced by assuming offsetting positions in stock such that the net change in value of the option and stock positions remains near zero. For example, later in this chapter you'll learn about a crucial measure known as *delta*, which quantifies the sensitivity of an option price to changes in the underlier price. Delta tells the short party (e.g., the dealer) how many shares of stock he or she needs per contract written. A delta of 60 gives the correct *hedge ratio*, or how much offsetting stock the short party needs in the hedge position per option contract.

---

[2] As in previous chapters, our discussion of option hedging will focus on equity options, but the same concepts apply to many other kinds of options as well.

TABLE 11-1

Lakewood-Cornelia Swap from Perspective of Floating-Payer Lakewood

Fixed Rate = 4.1892%

	Payment	Notional	Accrual Start	Accrual End	Accrual Days	Payment Rate	Year Days	Payment Future Value	Spot Rate	Days till Payment	Payment Present Value
Fixed	1	$1,000,000	5/23/07	11/23/07	184	4.19%	365	$19,660.27	3.53%	184	$20,748.72
Fixed	2	1,000,000	11/24/07	5/22/08	180	4.19	365	19,232.88	3.54	365	19,952.54
Fixed	3	1,000,000	5/23/08	11/24/08	185	4.19	365	19,767.12	3.59	551	20,141.18
Fixed	4	1,000,000	11/25/08	5/29/09	185	4.19	365	19,767.12	3.59	737	19,797.61
									Net Fixed-Leg Present Value = $80,640.04		
Floating	1	($1,000,000)	5/23/07	8/22/07	91	3.53%	365	($8,800.82)	3.53%	91	($8,724.04)
Floating	2	(1,000,000)	8/23/07	11/23/07	92	3.55	365	(8,947.95)	3.54	184	(8,791.06)
Floating	3	(1,000,000)	11/24/07	2/22/08	90	3.64	365	(8,975.34)	3.59	275	(8,738.97)
Floating	4	(1,000,000)	2/23/08	5/22/08	89	3.67	365	(8,948.77)	3.63	365	(8,635.31)
Floating	5	(1,000,000)	5/23/08	8/22/08	91	3.71	365	(9,249.59)	3.67	457	(8,843.24)
Floating	6	(1,000,000)	8/23/08	11/24/08	93	3.73	365	(9,503.84)	3.70	551	(9,001.08)
Floating	7	(1,000,000)	11/25/08	2/23/09	90	3.80	365	(9,369.86)	3.75	642	(8,790.08)
Floating	8	(1,000,000)	2/24/09	5/29/09	94	3.81	365	(9,812.05)	3.78	737	(9,116.26)
									Net Floating-Leg Present Value = ($70,640.04)		
									Swap Value = $10,000.00		

FIGURE 11-6

Short Option Payoffs

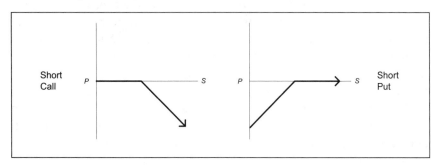

Now, an option's delta changes with price, which changes all the time, illustrating why options require dynamic hedging. Delta tells you how to construct the hedge, but it changes continuously, so the contents of a hedge must be adjusted all the time. Whoa! Is it even possible to hedge an option? A perfect hedge is indeed practically impossible, but it turns out the option dealer doesn't need a perfect hedge, just a reasonably good one.

Synthetic Options

A position that offsets the payoff of an option is often known as a *synthetic option*, as it replicates the payoff of the option, using instruments other than the option itself. How do we make one? Recall first how we priced an option by constructing an imaginary replicating portfolio, a portfolio whose payoff mimicked that of the option. The price of the replicating portfolio gives the price of the option, because two portfolios with the same payoff must cost the same due to arbitrage. If you think about it, then, to hedge an option position, one could simply create an actual replicating portfolio based on the theoretical portfolio presumed by the pricing formula and take the opposite side of it.

This is true in theory. But in practice it's virtually impossible, because the composition of the replicating portfolio presumed by the pricing formula changes all the time—at each branch of the tree if we use the binomial method, and continuously if we use Black-Scholes. Changing the composition of a portfolio means trading, and trading costs money (broker fees, etc.), so the transaction costs of a continuously changing portfolio quickly approach infinity. And that's a bit more money than most of us have to spend.

While we cannot construct a perfect replicating portfolio, we can construct an approximate replicating portfolio by quantifying the sensitivities of an option price to its input factors—sensitivities known as *the Greeks*—and then constructing a portfolio with those same sensitivities. It's not perfect and requires constant maintenance, but zillions of these portfolios are constructed every day, so it can't be all bad. A perfect options hedge is nearly impossible in practice, because multiple factors affect an option price, and each Greek addresses just one of them. So you can be perfectly hedged with respect to one Greek but exposed with respect to another. Option hedging can be quite a juggling act.

THE GREEKS

To understand what the Greeks are all about, first recall the five inputs to an option pricing formula: strike price, underlier price, volatility, time to expiration, and interest rates. Four of these (all except strike price) change all the time over the life of an option, so we say the option price is sensitive to changes in each of those factors. The Greeks tell us how the price of an option changes as these pricing input factors changes, giving us instructions for constructing the synthetic option. Table 11-2 provides their common names and what they measure.

Only four of these, by the way, are actually letters in the Greek alphabet. "Vega" is not a true Greek but somehow was adopted as one. For the purist, the Greek letter for sensitivity to volatility is

TABLE 11-2

The Five Greeks and Corresponding Sensitivities

Greek	Measures Option Price Sensitivity to Changes in . . .
Delta	Underlier price
Gamma	Underlier price
Vega	Underlier volatility
Theta	Time to expiration
Rho	Interest rates

kappa, which you might see in some academic texts. And don't be tripped up by the coincidence of there being five Greeks and five factors to an option price. There is no Greek for strike price (because it never changes), and there are two Greeks related to underlier price.

Calculating the Greeks is a rather complicated affair that we won't delve into, but for the mathematically curious, each is a partial derivative from the Black-Scholes partial differential equation. Using the Greeks, thankfully, is much less complicated than calculating them. But to use them, we first need to understand precisely what each of them tells us. Every Greek expresses a ratio of a change in one thing to a change in another thing, as depicted in Table 11-3.

A delta of 0.50 (often expressed as simply "50" without the decimal point) tells us that for a $1 increase in the underlier price, the price of the option increases by 50 cents. Vega, theta, and rho also tell us how the option price changes per unit change in underlier volatility (1 percent change), time to expiration (one day), and the risk-free interest rate (1 percent), respectively. Gamma is a bit different. It expresses how *delta* changes with underlier price. A gamma of 10, for example, tells us the delta of an option changes by 10 units per $1 change in the underlier. In a bit, you'll see why that's so important. While we're here, notice how delta and vega are

TABLE 11-3

The Greeks as Ratios

Greek	Ratio	Example
Delta (Δ)	Change in **option price** / Positive change in **underlier price**	$0.50/$1.00 = 0.50 (expressed as "50")
Gamma (Γ)	Change in **delta** / Positive change in **underlier price**	3/$1.00 (expressed as "3")
Vega (*V*)	Change in **option price** / Positive 1% change in underlier **volatility**	0.35/1% = 0.35 (expressed as "35")
Theta (Θ)	Change in **option price** / One-day change in **time-to-expiration**	$0.05/day = 0.05 (expressed as "−.05")
Rho (P)	Change in **option price** / Positive 1% change in **interest rates**	0.02/1% (expressed as ".02")

much greater numbers than the rest. This is true for most options, and tells us the two greatest sensitivities are to underlier price and volatility. As a result, most option hedgers spend most of their time worrying about these.

Table 11-4 contains an assortment of facts about, and properties of, the Greeks. These can come in handy if you ever need to apply them for real.

TABLE 11-4

Properties of the Greeks

Greek	Ratio	Facts
Delta (Δ)	Option price / Underlier price	• Typically expressed as a percent without the sign ("50"). Intuition: Delta 50 means option price changes at a rate 50% of that of the underlier.
		• Positive for long calls: 0 to 100. Negative for long puts: 0 to −100.
		• Approximately 50 (−50) for ATM calls (puts); near 100 (−100) for deep in the money (ITM); near 0 for deep out of the money (OTM).
		• Can view as "probability of option expiring ITM."
		• As underlier price increases, call delta approaches 100, and put delta approaches 0. With decrease, call delta approaches 0, and put delta approaches −100.
Gamma (Γ)	Delta / Underlier price	• Typically expressed as a percentage without the sign ("3").
		• Positive for long positions (calls or puts); negative for short positions.
		• Typical range: 0 to 10 for long, 0 to −10 for short.
		• Greatest when ATM. Near 0 for deep ITM or OTM.
Vega (V)	Option price / Volatility	• Typically expressed as % without the sign ("35").
		• Positive for long positions (calls or puts); negative for short positions (just like gamma).
		• Greatest for ATM; smallest for ITM and OTM.
		• Decreases as expiration approaches (opposite of theta).

Greek	Ratio	Facts
Theta (Θ)	$\dfrac{\text{Option price}}{\text{Time to expiration}}$	• Technically expresses rate of loss with passage of time, so is always positive.
		• By convention, expressed in dollars gained or lost per day ("−.05").
		• Positive for long positions (calls or puts); negative for short positions.
		• Relative size negatively correlated with gamma: large positive gamma goes with large negative theta, and vice versa.
		• Grows as expiration approaches (opposite of vega).
Rho (P)	$\dfrac{\text{Option price}}{\text{Interest rates}}$	• Typically expressed in dollars gained in option value per 1% increase in risk-free interest rates (".02").
		• Positive for long calls; negative for long puts.

Greeks and Option Pricing

One of the interesting things about the Greeks is where they come from. They are, in essence, by-products of the option-pricing formulas. In the Black-Scholes pricing formula, for example, delta is just $N(d_1)$ for calls and $N(d_1) - 1$ for puts. And this connection between hedging and pricing makes sense when you consider that pricing an option is based on the idea of a replicating portfolio. For now, just think of the Greeks as values you can use to construct a hedge portfolio—values someone else has been kind enough to calculate for you.

The Delta Hedge

Delta hedging is the basic routine for the option market maker, or dealer, and it goes like this: The dealer expresses a willingness to buy an option for some *bid* price less than model price, or to sell it for some *ask* or *offer* price greater than model price, where *model price* (MP) is simply the theoretical value produced by a pricing method such as Black-Scholes. The difference between a bid and model price, or offer and model price, is commonly known as "edge." Someone comes along—say, a hedger—and buys the option at the offer. The dealer now has a position in the option. He or she imme-diately establishes a *delta-neutral* hedge position in the underlier and then adjusts that hedge over time to remain delta-neutral. When the two positions are closed, if the hedge was successful, then the dealer realizes the edge (or something close to it, if the vega and other sensitivities weren't too outrageous) as his or her profit. We'll walk through an example with numbers in just a minute.

Delta hedging is also, by the way, the daily grind for the option arbitrageur. But instead of quoting bids and offers, arbitrageurs scan the market for "mispriced" options, or option bids above model price and offers below. When they spot one, they take a position in it. Like the dealer, they immediately establish a delta-neutral hedge posi-tion, which they adjust over time to remain delta-neutral. When the positions are closed, the arbitrageurs realize the edge as their profit.

Now you might be thinking, "What's the difference between a so-called mispriced option and an option bid or offered by the dealer?" Think of an option dealer's offer price as analogous to a car dealer's retail price, where model price is analogous to cost. Car dealers as a matter of course sell cars for some price greater than cost, and the option dealer is doing the same. So market makers publish bids below MP and offers above, for the benefit of "cus-tomers" willing to pay the edge. Arbitrageurs essentially look for market makers who place bids above MP and offers below MP by mistake, who are then forced to pay the difference whether they want to or not. It's like a car dealer who mistakenly sells a car for less than what the dealership paid for it. The dealer loses the differ-ence. And the car buyer gets a great deal.

So imagine a 30-strike call option whose model price one morning is $1.85. You are a dealer and offer it for $2.00, for a theoret-ical edge of $1.50 per contract (recall each contract is for 100 shares of the underlier). Someone comes along and buys 20 calls from you. Your goal now is to realize the theoretical edge of $300.00 (i.e., 20 × $1.50). The option delta is 79. This tells you that, for a delta-neutral hedge, you need 79 shares of the underlier for each contract. So you buy 1,580 shares of the underlier (i.e., 79 × 20). Throughout the day, you monitor delta and adjust your hedge accordingly by buying or selling stock. At the end of the day, say your option holder exercises and you close out your stock position. Your profit/loss (P/L) on the option trade is negative, meaning you lose money. But your P/L on the stock is positive by a greater amount. The net of option and stock P/L is your profit. Table 11-5 lays out the numbers.

TABLE 11-5

Option Dealer Hedge

	Options	Strike Price	Option Profit/Loss	Stock Price	Delta	Stock Buy (Sell)	Stock Position	Stock Profit/Loss
9 A.M. Dealer writes 20 calls @ $2.00 (MP = $1.85) and buys stock	20	$30	$4,000	$31.50	79	$1,580	$1,580	
10 A.M. Delta goes down; dealer sells stock				$31.00	78	(20)	1,560	($10)*
11 A.M. Delta goes down; dealer sells stock				30.50	60	(360)	1,200	(360)
12 noon Delta goes down; dealer sells stock				30.00	54	(120)	1,080	(180)
1 P.M. Delta goes up; dealer buys stock				31.00	78	480	1,560	
2 P.M. Delta goes up; dealer buys stock				32.25	98	400	1,960	
3 P.M. Delta goes up; dealer buys stock				33.50	99	20	1,980	
4 P.M. Holder exercises. Dealer settles	20	30	(8,000)	34.00	(1,980)	0	4,850**	
Total P/L			(4,000)					4,300

* For our purposes, we only realize profit/loss when we sell stock. To calculate it, we simply multiply the number of shares by the change in stock price while we held it. For example, 20 × (31.00 − 31.50) = −10.

** Notice the 1,080 shares were purchased at four different prices. Here's the P/L calculation: 1,080(34.00 − 31.50) + 480(34.00 − 31.00) + 400(34.00 − 32.25) + 20(34.00 − 33.50) = 4,850.

At the end of the day on the option trade, you lost $4,000 (the call option went well into the money). However, on the stock transactions, you gained $4,300, for a net gain of $300—exactly the theoretical edge.

Now, for the purposes of this example, we've simplified the deltas and stock prices by rounding and restricted our update intervals to hourly, but otherwise this is how to delta-hedge a written call with a long position in the underlier. You just might need to do it more often, using stock prices and deltas more precise than these. Hedging a written put, by the way, works the same way, but you maintain a short position in the stock instead of a long position as we did in the example. And for hedging long positions in calls and puts, it's just the reverse. (Remember, dealers buy options as well as write them, and they hedge long options in the same way to capture the edge.) Table 11-6 sums it up.

A long position in the underlier simply means you buy stock and hold it. A short position means you short sell the stock. To sell a stock short, you literally borrow shares belonging to someone else and immediately sell them on the open market. After some period of time, you purchase new shares and return them to the lender. If the price of the stock has fallen over that period, you make money; it if has risen, you lose money. Short selling is very different from simply selling stock that you own, as we did in the delta-hedging example. Short selling is traditionally used by the speculator who believes a stock price will fall.[3] It just so happens that it's also an indispensable tool for the options hedger. Figure 11-7 shows payoff diagrams for both long and short stock positions to illustrate.

This is an appropriate point to revisit what we mean exactly by "model price." In the most practical sense to options dealers or arbitrageurs, it is simply the price of an option they can synthesize with confidence. And the "better" a model price in this sense, the better they are in quoting, or spotting mispriced options. Consider the previous example. We supposed a model price of $1.85, but if a dealer believed the model price was really $1.75, he or she could make not $300 but $500 on the trade—provided he or she could synthesize the hedge. Alternatively, a dealer who believed the model price was $1.95 might not even bother doing the trade at all. (In reality, disagreements in model prices are generally not as wide as these simple examples.)

---

[3] The speculator can also, as you know, buy put options.

TABLE 11-6

Option Positions and Underlier Hedge Positions

Option Position	Hedge Position
Short call	Long underlier
Short put	Short underlier
Long call	Short underlier
Long put	Long underlier

FIGURE 11-7

Long Underlier and Short Underlier Payoffs

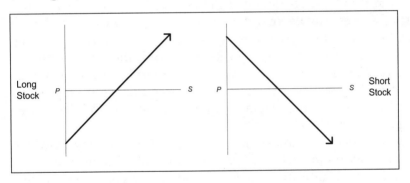

This is why the better your model, the better you will be as a dealer or arbitrageur. It also explains why firms spend great gobs of money in developing ever-better pricing models, or *analytics*. It also illustrates *model risk*, or the risk that your pricing analytics are simply wrong. Suppose a dealer mistakenly believes a model price to be $1.50 when it's really $1.30, and the dealer buys 500 contracts at $1.40, expecting to make $5,000 in edge, when really the dealer will *lose* $5,000. Ouch.

Now, there are complicating factors that make delta hedging a bit more complicated in practice than in our example. For one, we disregarded transaction costs. And if your hedge requires a short sale of stock, regulations in the United States may dictate that short selling is permitted only after an uptick (increase) in the stock price.

Using Gamma

Gamma is a measure of how delta changes with underlier price. The delta of a high-gamma option changes more rapidly than that of a low-gamma option. The practical effect to the option hedger is straightforward: the higher the gamma, the more quickly an option becomes unhedged as the underlier price changes. It's a speed thing. If gamma is high, you'd better monitor your hedge like a hawk. If it's low, you'll have a bit more time.

Using Vega

Vega indicates how the price of an option changes with underlier volatility. This means you can have a perfect delta hedge all day long and still lose money if the volatility of the underlier changes significantly. Oops. So what is the option hedger to do? Plenty, and most of it goes way beyond the scope of an introduction to derivatives. One obvious vega hedge is another option position with the same vega, but going the opposite way. And, there are securities based on a *volatility index*, and these can certainly be used to hedge baskets of options or options whose prices are highly correlated with the market, but for a simple option on a single underlier, these often are of little help.

Another tool is the *spread trade*, an option strategy in which you take simultaneous positions in different options (say, both November and December options with otherwise identical features), such that the value of the combined position is sensitive to changes in volatility. These "calendar spreads" can be effective because changes in volatility are closely related to the passage of time. The greater the time to expiration, the greater the probability of underlier price changes. Anyway, that's the basic idea.

Using Theta and Rho

Theta and rho measure, respectively, the sensitivity of an option price to changes in time and to changes in the risk-free interest rate. Thankfully, these sensitivities tend to be far smaller than sensitivities measured by delta and vega, so the option dealer need not worry about these quite as much.

Still, there are ways to hedge theta and rho. For example, a calendar spread can be used for theta, as can a position in a bond—

another instrument whose value is closely related to the passage of time. Bonds are also sensitive to changes in interest rates, so they can be used as well for rho hedging. Another liquid instrument for rho hedging is interest rate futures such as Eurodollar futures—the same ones we used for hedging swaps in the previous section.

MORE ON RISK MANAGEMENT

So what other fun stuff goes on in the heady world of financial risk management? One thing you might hear about is the idea of *value at risk* (*VAR*). Risk managers and regulators tend to like VAR, because it gives a concrete answer to a mushy question: What's the most money a position might lose? VAR is an example of a general topic of *scenario analysis*, which involves analyzing potential future scenarios to help you prepare for or avoid them. To be precise, VAR expresses the maximum loss you can expect to incur over a given time period T with probability P.

For example, a swaps dealer might run some VAR calculations at the end of the day and see that the most he or she can expect to lose over the next 30 days, with 95 percent probability, is $12.5 million. If the dealer is uncomfortable with a VAR greater than, say, $10 million, then he or she probably will want to unwind some of the portfolio to bring it down. A portfolio manager might use VAR to compare two nearly identical investment opportunities, to see which one has greater risk. And industry regulators can use VAR to set capital requirements (how much money a financial institution is required to keep on hand to weather adverse market conditions). An agency might recommend—or enforce—that a swaps dealer keep "five times VAR" in reserves.

How is VAR calculated? Mostly by *simulation*. Recall how the value of a financial instrument depends on some set of factors. A floating-rate loan is affected heavily by changing interest rates, an option is affected by underlier price and volatility and such, and so on. One popular type of simulation is known as *Monte Carlo*. This involves running a computer program that supposes different values for those factors (typically using randomly generated numbers in some form or another) and calculating the value of the position under those factors. Then the program does so again, using different factor values. Then again, and again and again. The key, of course, is to run as many simulations as possible. The more you try, the better you can make inferences about the future.

It's no wonder, of course, why risk management is so important in the world of derivatives. As the sheer number of derivatives positions increases, so does the global risk. There are shelves full of books now just on "derivatives disasters," and we'll look at some of them in the Epilogue. The good news is, each disaster provides both a wake-up call to the importance of risk management and valuable real-world—not hypothetical—examples of what can happen. And if you spend any time looking at the disasters, you'll notice that not all of them had to do with the type of risk we've covered so far in this chapter. There's more than one type of risk.

The exposures we've dealt with are all examples of *market risk*, sometimes called *price risk*, or the risk associated with changing market prices. But there are other types of financial risk that tools like our forwards, futures, swaps, and options are ill suited to handle. One of these is *operational risk*, or the risk that flaws in a firm's internal processes and policies could cost it substantial sums of money. Consider the trading firm that lets a rogue trader rack up huge speculative positions on behalf of the firm, due to insufficient oversight. If those speculations don't pay off, the firm can suffer dearly. When we discussed option hedging, you probably got a sense of *model risk*, or the risk that your pricing models aren't right. This can really mess up a hedge! Another type is *legal risk*, or the risk of a change in laws that affect your ability to manage an existing position. Another huge one is *credit risk*, or the risk that your counterparty won't honor its responsibilities and will leave you with a loss. We'll encounter that one, in fact, in the very next chapter.

CHAPTER 12

Derivatives and the 2008 Financial Meltdown

There was, of course, no single cause of the economic earthquake of 2008. The epicenter was certainly the U.S. housing market, but beyond that, it's hard to pinpoint any one thing. Was it the ascension of home prices to unheard-of levels—and the forgetting that price bubbles are called price bubbles because they really do tend to burst now and again? Was it the lowering of lending standards so more people could realize the American Dream of owning a home? Was it the giddy mortgage originators who might lend money to a border collie, knowing they could sell off the mortgage to someone else the next day? And what about the derivatives, those usual suspects when things go terribly wrong in the markets? Was it the CDS or CDO or synthetic blah blah blah things nobody living an actual life could possibly understand? Were they one of the reasons we got into that god-awful mess? Why, yes, it turns out, they were.

For the short story of how derivatives played a role in the crisis, we need look no further than the *credit default swap* (*CDS*). It's basically loan insurance. The buyer of one of these "policies" makes regular payments to the seller in return for the peace of mind that, should a third-party or "reference entity" default on a loan obligation, the buyer will receive a payment (perhaps a very substantial one) from the seller. It's just insurance on someone else's loan.

If you think of the CDS as loan insurance, then it's a bit easier to see how it played one of the starring roles in the lead-up to the Great Recession. The lowering of lending standards, in the years just after the turn of the millennium, meant more people could, and did, take out loans to buy houses. These new mortgagees, the so-called subprime borrowers, were *by definition* likelier to default than were borrowers who could meet more stringent credit requirements. A number of folks who noticed this fact used the CDS (loan insurance) as a vehicle for placing bets that more subprime borrowers would default than were expected to. The sellers of CDS contracts (loan insurance companies) thought these were very safe bets that were unlikely to pay off, so they were only too happy to collect the wagers (loan insurance payments) and use them to pay mouthwatering bonuses to some of their employees.

Did the CDS sellers make arrangements to have adequate money on hand in case the bets did pay off? In a word (a two-letter one at that), no. They just didn't think these bets would ever pay off, or weren't careful enough with their math to realize the magnitude of their potential obligations, or both. And unlike what insurance companies actually called insurance companies had to do, no regulator told them they had to be ready to make good on those obligations.

Now zip forward a few happy-go-lucky years to 2008. Housing prices had stopped climbing. It wasn't a crash in house prices but just enough of a gradual slowdown that subprime borrowers began defaulting in greater than expected numbers. These surprisingly high default rates caused a number of problems. One of them was that the CDS bets started paying off. And how. The CDS buyers—the gamblers—went to the casino window to collect their winnings, only to find the casino owners basically wetting their pants. The house didn't have the money. There were so many of these CDS writers on the hook, many of them affiliated with or part of major Wall Street banks and insurance companies, that the U.S. government had no choice but to bail out at least some of them and cover their, um, backsides. So Uncle Sam used his own borrowing power and good credit (and authority to raise taxes) to come up with many billions of dollars to make good on the bets of the CDS buyers.

The bailout, which took care of not only the CDS writers but lenders and others in the mortgage market as well, didn't keep the stock market from tanking—laying waste to countless retirement and college savings accounts and putting just about everyone in a really bad mood. Consumer spending slowed, people lost their jobs, and unemployment rates climbed into double digits for the first time in who can remember how long. The close of 2008 didn't offer much to feel good about in America, unless you were a Democrat, in which case you at least had the hopeful results of the presidential election to get your mind off your not-so-hopeful 401(k) balance.

No doubt about it, derivatives played a role in the crisis. It's worth noting we're talking about credit derivatives, which are a relatively new addition to the derivatives family and very different from traditional derivatives like stock options and commodity futures, which had been humming along for well over a century before the term *subprime* had even been coined. Those traditional derivative contracts are *price* guarantees and are primarily traded on regulated exchanges, unlike credit derivatives, which are *performance* guarantees and are generally traded in the comparatively unsupervised and uncoordinated over-the-counter (OTC) markets. Indeed, a plausible argument can be made that credit derivatives aren't derivatives at all, but insurance policies gussied up as "financial derivative securities" to keep insurance regulators at bay. Still, credit derivatives are considered derivatives and thus are subject to scrutiny, and for you to truly understand their role in the crisis, you'll need more than the flyover provided so far.

BONDS

To understand the 2008 credit debacle, we first need to remind ourselves of the security at the root of the whole darn thing: the bond. Now, a traditional bond is a security wherein some entity, historically a large corporation or government or municipality, finances its operations by borrowing money from investors. (Bonds are thus known as *debt securities*, in contrast to stocks, which are a type of *equity security*.) The entity borrowing money is said to *sell* a bond to the investors, who *buy* it by lending some principal in order to receive interest or "coupon" payments at some rate of interest for some period of time, after which the investors get their principal back. Figure 12-1 shows the cash flows associated with a typical bond.

Only rarely do bond investors buy directly from issuers. Rather, a bond dealer typically stands between them, matching up buyers and sellers and earning a profit as any dealer does, by selling to investors (their customers) at some price greater than what the dealer pays to issuers (the dealer's suppliers). Dealers also facilitate exchanges between investors who already hold bonds, long after the original issuer is out of the picture, in the so-called secondary market. As you might expect, the higher the price at which a dealer

FIGURE 12-1

Bond Cash Flows

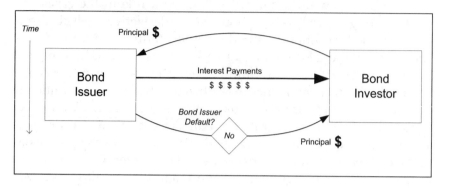

can sell his bonds, the more money he makes, a motivation that will play into this story later on.

The return to an investor on a bond investment is known generally as the bond's yield, and to make sense of the rest of this discussion, you need to know what determines yield. One key factor is the difference between the coupon rate and prevailing interest rate. For example, a bond paying its investors 5 percent when the prevailing interest rate is 4 percent clearly has positive value. Another huge factor is the market's perception of the creditworthiness of the bond issuer, or how likely the issuer is to pay coupons and to return the principal at the bond's maturity. An issuer that does not live up to these expectations is said to default. Naturally, investors would very much prefer that the issuers of their bonds do not default. But the risk, which varies by issuer, is always there. As a result, a portion of any bond's yield is given by what's known as a risk premium.[1]

Now, one of the fundamental laws of the financial universe is that the return on an investment is proportional to the risk incurred by the investor. The greater the risk, the greater the expected return. In bond markets, then, with all else equal, bonds from issuers more likely to default offer yields greater than those from more creditworthy issuers. A high-yield bond, then, is one that pays a comparatively nice return to its investors but has a greater chance of default than a bond with a lower yield. Bottom line, it's essential that investors have some reliable measure of a bond's likelihood of default.

---

[1] Technically, the risk premium is the difference between the yield on a (risky) bond and that of a security considered risk-free, such as a U.S. Treasury bond.

BOND RATINGS

In the United States, the job of determining the creditworthiness of bond issuers is handled mostly by two venerable ratings agencies: Moody's and Standard & Poor's. Their job is not an easy one. But they do their best, analyzing things like the historical track record of issuers, the riskiness of their business, the quality of the issuer's leadership, and who knows what else. At the end of they day, they stamp each bond with one of several standardized ratings, which the bond market then uses in setting prices. Just to keep our pencils sharp, it's worth noting here that a bond's price is inversely proportional to its yield. The lower the yield, the higher the price, and vice versa.[2] Each of the ratings agencies uses slightly different ratings, but for our purposes, let's say the highest rating is AAA, which is followed by AA, then A, then B, then BB, then BBB, where a "triple-A" is considered least likely to default (low risk → low yield → high price) and a "triple-B" is the most likely (high risk → high yield → low price).

You can certainly imagine how crucial is the role of the ratings agency. It's not unreasonable, in fact, to assert that the very integrity of the bond market depends on how well the ratings agencies do their jobs. In a perfect world, these agencies will employ the most robust and reliable methods of calculating the risk of a bond's default and will do their sacred work with complete objectivity, unbiased by any conflict of interest. Would that it were so. The good people at the ratings agencies are human like the rest of us and don't always get things right. And as they are compensated primarily by bond issuers and dealers, one can reasonably question just how objective they can really be. But there we are.

MORTGAGE-BACKED BONDS

A residential mortgage is essentially a type of bond. When a married couple borrow money to buy a house and promise to pay interest on the loan as well as pay back the principal, they have in

---

[2] To get some intuition for this price-yield thing, consider the formula for the simplest form of yield, known as current yield, which is $Y = AI/MP$, where Y = yield, AI = annual interest, and MP = market price. Say a bond is supposed to pay $500 annual interest. A market price of $10,000 implies a yield of 5 percent (i.e., $500/$10,000), and a market price of $9,000 implies a yield of 6 percent (lower price, higher yield).

essence "issued a bond" to their lender (or mortgage originator, as that party is known). Figure 12-2 shows how the cash flows associated with a mortgage are essentially the same as for a traditional bond. The essential difference is how principal is repaid. With a traditional bond, principal is repaid at the end of the term in one lump sum. With a mortgage, an increasingly larger portion of each payment includes some principal payment, such that the principal is entirely repaid by the end of the mortgage term.

Now, even though a mortgage is a bond, it is a rather small one, so it's not worth a bond dealer's time trying to sell such a security to investors. But imagine you are a bond dealer and buy up, say, 1,000 mortgages from originators. For each mortgage, you pay some amount of money for the right to the remaining interest and principal payments. Now you have this giant "super bond" made of smaller bonds (mortgages), which will generate income with every monthly mortgage payment. And now you've got something substantial enough to sell off to investors. Say you paid $100 million for your pool of mortgages. You might turn around and sell the super bond to investors for $110 million, transferring the rights to the mortgage payments to them and keeping the $10 million difference as your profit.

But what should be the yield on such a mortgage-backed bond (MBB)? The problem here is that you have not one bond issuer but a thousand. Some homeowners have impeccable credit histories and can be counted on to be not so much as late on a single payment. Other homeowners will have less pristine credit, or maybe some just come on hard times and go into default or at least become tardy on

FIGURE 12-2

Mortgage as Bond

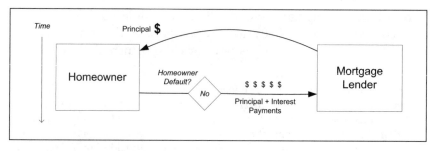

their payments. Unlike the case of a $100 million bond from a single corporate or government issuer, no single bond rating makes sense. The solution is, instead of offering the super bond as one security, to package it into some number of smaller bonds, as shown in Figure 12-3. In the figure, the riskiness of mortgages is indicated by stars, where a five-star mortgage goes with homeowners with very high credit ratings, four stars refer to those with slightly less pristine credit, and so on down to one-star mortgages, which are associated with subprime borrowers who are most likely to default. Each of the

FIGURE 12-3

Mortgage-Backed Bonds

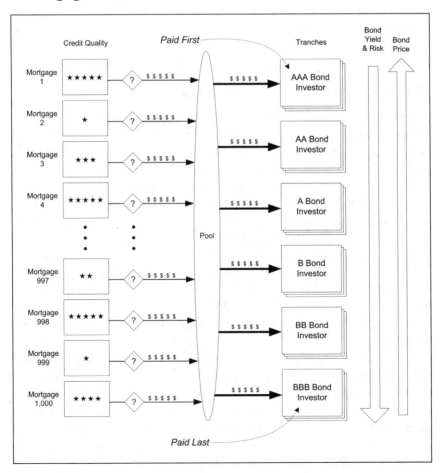

bonds created out of the pool has its own payment structure and corresponding rating (more on that in a moment) and is known, descriptively enough, as a *tranche*—the French word for slice.

So imagine you've sliced the virtual super bond into a number of actual bonds, one for each of our bond ratings, each structured to pay monthly interest as mortgage payments come in from homeowners whose creditworthiness ranges from very high to low. Here's how it works: The triple-A bondholders enjoy the lowest yield but bear the least risk; they are the first to receive their monthly interest payments. At the other extreme of the risk/reward continuum are the triple-B holders, who enjoy the highest yield but bear the greatest risk. If some of the 1,000 homeowners fail to make their mortgage payment (not unlikely), the triple-B holders won't get their full interest, or perhaps will get none at all. If enough mortgage holders default, even the double-A or single-A tranche holders may not get paid.

THE CORRELATION THING

The structure of an MBB is sometimes compared with that of a multifloor apartment building in a flood. The basement units can practically count on getting drenched, and in a bad flood, the first or even second floors might flood as well. In an utter catastrophe (think Noah's ark), even the top floors could be inundated with water. But that's not very likely, of course. The holders of upper-tranche bonds, deemed "investment grade" for their comparatively low risk of default, could reasonably expect to always get their payments. After all, is it even conceivable that so many homeowners would be delinquent on mortgage payments or have their houses repossessed that single-A, double-A, or even triple-A investors have to worry? Nobody seemed to think so in 2003 and 2004, when investors ate up mortgage-backed securities the way Homer Simpson chomps doughnuts.

But there was a hidden problem, a big one, especially for the subprime mortgage-backed securities. These were written on pools of mortgages held by homeowners with comparatively weak credit histories—that is, people more likely to default on their loans than were other mortgagees. The problem went back to the rating agencies and a key assumption they made when rating subprime mortgage-backed bonds. They presumed (incorrectly, as it turned out) that the mortgages underlying the MBB offerings, even the subprimes, were sufficiently diversified, geographically and otherwise, that the overall default rate for a given pool would be consistent with historical default rates—something like 1 percent. Mathematically speaking, they assumed that the default rates of the individual subprime mortgages were statistically *uncorrelated*. When any of these mortgages defaulted, they reasoned, it would be for factors unique to the individual mortgage holder, or at least to the region, and not due to something affecting all mortgages. If Mr. Smith defaults because he gets fired from his job for cheating on his expense reports or whatever, his transgression is not going to make it any more likely for Mrs. Jones across the street to default on hers. And defaults on mortgages in Florida, for example, would happen for reasons that would not also affect mortgages in, say, Montana. The agencies didn't seem to think there was anything going on to put the entire housing market at unusual risk, something to cause a given mortgage pool to default at rates any higher than had been observed in the past.

Despite the confidence of the agencies, there were indeed factors that would affect default rates across the entire subprime mortgage market. Economists and pundits continue to debate what all did it, but one factor is the very reason for the growth of subprime mortgages in the first place: lending standards were dropping like mad. For reasons that go well beyond the scope of this discussion, it was easier than ever to obtain a mortgage in the late 1990s and early 2000s. Whereas once you might have had to put down a 10 or even 20 percent down payment on your house, you could in those years get a mortgage with effectively no down payment. You needn't provide as much proof of your ability to repay your loan as you had in the past, you could defer payment of principle with an "interest-only" (IO) mortgage, and you might even get a loan with no interest payment required at all! The lender would simply lend you more money each month to make your interest payment, thus increasing your outstanding principal over time, rather than decreasing it. It was crazy. More important, it was new. The market hadn't worked this way before, so historical default rates—on which the agencies based their ratings—no longer applied. Going back to the apartment-building-in-a-flood analogy, it was as if renters' insurance companies didn't realize that new buildings were constructed of bricks that crumbled when they got wet. When the basement flooded, the bricks could no longer support the upper floors, so the whole dang thing came down.

There was a rational explanation for what looks in hindsight like reckless subprime lending, and it had to do with yet another presumption: that housing prices would rise indefinitely, that the bubble would never burst. Were you to take out, say, a $100,000 mortgage on a $100,000 home that was certain to appreciate in value to something like $125,000 or $150,000 or whatever before it came time to pay off your mortgage, who would care if you still owed $100,000 or even more? You'd be able to pay it off with the proceeds when you sold or refinanced your house. No problem.

You can see where this is going, of course. And notice that derivatives aren't even in the story. Until now.

CREDIT DEFAULT SWAPS

The credit default swap (CDS) acts very much like collision insurance on your car, wherein you pay some annual premium for the peace of mind that if your car gets totaled, the insurance company will write you a nice big check. The CDS differs in two key ways. One, the peril of concern is not the totaling of your car but the default of a bond. Two, you need not own the bond or have anything whatsoever to do with it. It's like collision insurance not on your own car but on some other guy's. Why might you buy such a thing? Maybe you lent the guy the money to buy this car, and for some reason or another, he is now uninsured. You might take out your own policy on his car, just to make you whole should he wreck the car and default on his loan to you. That would be using the third-party collision policy for hedging, which as you recall is one of only two reasons most people use derivatives.

The other difference is speculation. Maybe you don't know the guy or have anything to do with his purchase of his nice new car, but you know he's a horrible driver with a history of wrecking cars, and you're pretty sure he's likely to total this one, too. You take out the collision insurance—with yourself as the beneficiary—as a bet. And that's what some people did with the CDS. They used it to speculate that certain bonds would default. Figure 12-4 illustrates how a credit default swap is very much like an insurance policy on a loan.

The CDS was invented in the 1990s for insuring not mortgage-backed bonds but traditional corporate bonds. Firms like J.P. Morgan, Deutsche Bank, and other Wall Street names you'd recognize did a brisk business using these inventive products for insuring moun-

FIGURE 12-4

Auto Insurance and Credit Default Swap (CDS)

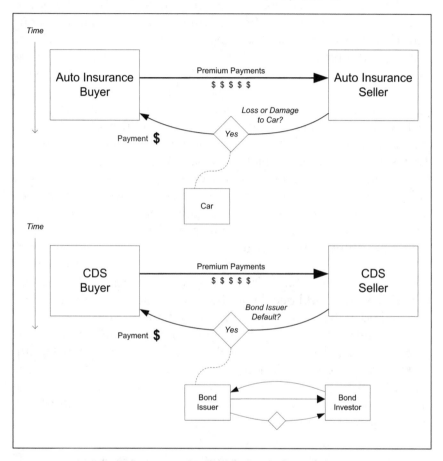

tains of commercial debt. And they seemed to do a fairly good job at it, too. Unlike bonds based on pools of high-risk mortgages, bonds from individual bond issuers didn't have the correlation problem.

So now imagine it's 2003 or 2004, and you are a speculator, shopping for bonds on which to buy credit default swaps—that is, bonds you want to bet will default. What would you look for? Why, you'd look for bonds most likely to default, of course. And not only that, you'd look for bonds that seemed to you more likely to default than the rating agencies thought they did, because those insurance policies—er, credit default swaps—would be cheaper, just as good drivers pay less for car insurance than do lousy ones. And back in 2003–2004, what bonds might seem to some speculators to fit that bill? That's right, subprime mortgage-backed bonds. The ones with the correlation problem.

You see, not everybody drank the Kool-Aid about the never-ending housing bubble or the supposed lack of correlation among subprime mortgage defaults. These contrarians had a hunch the subprime MBBs were misrated and, therefore, overpriced. (The yields were too low, remember, meaning the prices were too high.) They wanted to short those things—that is, make a bet that would pay off should the bond prices fall—and the CDS was the perfect tool for shorting bonds. So before long, you had firms like AIG selling credit default swaps on subprime mortgage-backed securities. They sold lots and lots and lots of these things, grinning all the way to the bank, thinking they were collecting bets that would never pay off. They were so confident they would never have to pay, in fact, that they didn't bother keeping the capital on hand to make good on the wagers. Insurance companies, which also face enormous potential liabilities, use reinsurance and other means of being sure they will be able to make good on claims—and insurance regulators make sure of it. But CDS writers are not considered insurance companies and could decide on their own, essentially, whether and how to hedge their exposures. They chose not to.

The next security to play a big (big) role in the saga that was 2008 was not a derivative at all. But its role was extremely significant; it was used in conjunction with derivatives and (as we'll see presently) was indeed synthetically *created* with derivatives. In short, you can't understand the 2008 meltdown without understanding this security, known as the CDO.

COLLATERALIZED DEBT OBLIGATIONS

The clever idea behind a *collateralized debt obligation* (CDO) goes basically like this: Consider a pool of subprime mortgages. Were you to package these comparatively high-risk loans into a mortgage-backed bond, intuitively you might expect such a security to warrant a triple-B rating. That translates to a lower price, meaning a lower commission (more or less) for the bond dealer. If only, wondered the dealers, they could be packaged in some way to fetch a higher price. Granted, each of the mortgages is at a comparatively high risk of default. But over time, will all of them default? No, of course not. Some of the mortgages will default, and others will not.

So let's do the tranching thing, as shown in Figure 12-5. Let's use this pool of triple-B mortgages to create a series of bonds, just as we did when we created the old-fashioned MBB (when we used more diversified pools of mortgages, not just triple-Bs, as we are with the CDO). We'll make some triple-As, whose holders will get first dibs on subprime mortgage payments, and some double-As, and so on.

And it worked. Bond dealers made triple-A (higher-priced) securities out of, essentially, triple-B (lower-priced) securities. In

FIGURE 12-5

Collateralized Debt Obligation (CDO)

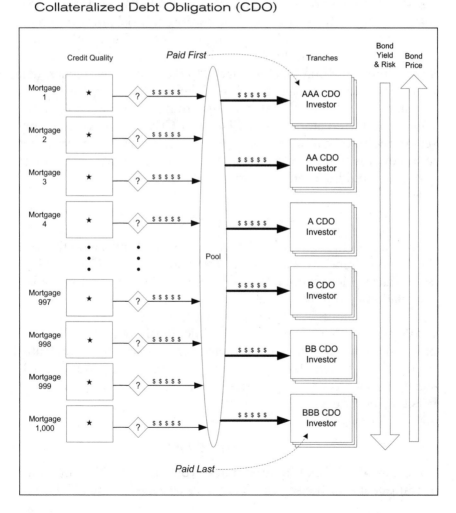

hindsight, the whole idea of using the CDO to transform triple-B securities into higher-priced triple-A securities seems like so much alchemy. But at the time, it seemed perfectly reasonable, assuming, again, that default rates among the underlying pool of mortgages were uncorrelated. However, that was a bad assumption. Going back to the apartment building analogy, it was as if nobody realized the walls supporting the building were now made of clay or some other material that softens when it gets wet, so the whole building would start sinking during a flood, bringing upper floors within reach of the water.

Oh, and what of the triple-B CDO securities? The bottom of the barrel, as it were? The mortgages underlying these things were the worst of the worst of the original pool of triple-Bs, mortgages most likely—very likely—to default. They were high risk, meaning high yield and low price. Could anything be done to fetch better prices for these dogs? Certainly! Just pool them up and pour the whole lot into the tranching machine again to create a second-generation CDO, or *CDO-squared*. It might seem beyond comprehension that investors would actually fall for these things, but you can't blame them. The formulators of the CDO and CDO-squared need only secure the imprimatur of one of the rating agencies, convincing it to bestow the blindly trusted triple-A stamp of approval, and most investors wouldn't even think to ask any more.

CDS on CDO

Think back to the short sellers of the subprime MBBs, who thought the triple-B tranches were overpriced and used the CDS to place a bet those prices would fall as mortgage default rates exceeded expectations. What would they think of triple-A CDOs made of the very same triple-Bs? Or the triple-A CDO-squared securities? They would think at least some of them ridiculously overpriced and be only too happy to speculate on their collapse using the CDS. Thus, we had CDS dealers like AIG writing policies on CDOs (and CDO-squareds), as shown in Figure 12-6, once again collecting wagers on bets they never expected to pay off.

Synthetic CDO

If the idea of the CDO-squared makes you crazy, you'll be fitted for a straitjacket over the security known as a *synthetic CDO*. The origi-

FIGURE 12-6

CDS on Collateralized Debt Obligation

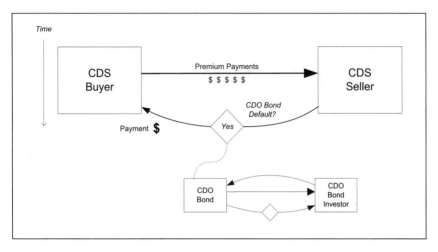

nal CDOs proved extraordinarily popular, selling as they did like sunscreen at the seashore. It was a sellers' market, and the sellers faced this problem: there were only so many subprime mortgages out there. That is, there were only so many actual homeowners making actual monthly payments to ultimately pass through to actual CDO investors—and hence there were only so many CDOs one could sell. Hmm. There must be, thought some very clever financial engineers, some way around this problem of limited supply. And indeed there was.

Consider the CDO investor. Like any bond investor, he or she makes an investment of principal in return for future interest payments, all with the implicit understanding the investor may never see that principal should the issuer default. If you're a CDO dealer, trying to attract more customers, wouldn't it be great if someone were willing to make payments to a CDO investor (who wouldn't know the difference or even care that payments weren't coming from an actual CDO), say, in return for the promise of receiving a big payment if some third-party bond issuer blows up? But wait, doesn't that describe the CDS buyer? Why, yes, it does. So before anyone could say Ben Bernanke three times fast, you had bond dealers pooling up not mortgages but CDS contracts—which, remember, nobody expected to actually ever pay off—to create not actual CDOs but synthetic CDOs, which the

FIGURE 12-7

Synthetic CDO

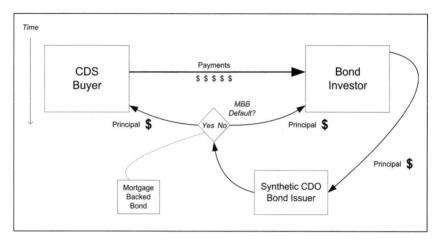

rating agencies would (rubber?) stamp with a bond rating to set the investor's mind at ease that all was kosher. Figure 12-7 shows the cash flows and parties involved in a synthetic CDO. Notice the bond (CDO) investor makes a principal payment, receives interest payments, and faces the risk of loss, just as if her or she were investing in a real CDO.

GASOLINE ON THE FIRE?

Economists are likely to debate for decades just what happened to bring on the disaster that was 2008. Nobody is likely to make a convincing argument it was all the fault of derivatives. After all, plenty of the comparatively plain-vanilla subprime mortgage bonds went bust all by themselves with nary a CDO or CDS in sight. And Fannie Mae and Freddie Mac—the ultimate lenders behind the lenders of the original mortgage money—in the end had to be nationalized to keep them in operation. They were not, directly at least, parties to the CDO and CDS transactions. But the widespread and (in hindsight) reckless use of the previously arcane credit default swap cost the U.S. taxpayer quite a lot of money. AIG, one of the biggest of CDS casinos, all by itself required $180 billion of public assistance, primarily to pay off the gamblers.

Unfortunately, the money for AIG was just a fraction of the total government bailout. If derivatives on subprime mortgages had never been invented, the relaxed lending standards and poorly rated mortgage-backed securities would still have led to quite a mess when the presumptions on which those ratings were based turned out to be false. But these derivatives were invented, they were sold in staggering numbers, and they did, without a doubt, only make matters worse.

Are Derivatives Any Good?

Derivatives exist because so does financial uncertainty. We don't know what the future will bring, and we certainly don't know what things will cost, or whether or not people and organizations will fulfill their financial obligations. Derivatives quantify uncertainty, thereby letting us put exposures into reasonably tangible packages that can be measured, managed, priced, and—most important—traded. That's their power. Derivatives allow the efficient transfer of risk from one party to another. When applied wisely, derivatives are a powerful financial tool for doing some amazing and unquestionably beneficial things. When applied not so wisely, derivatives can be the most costly troublemaker our economic universe has ever known.

For better or worse, we just can't seem to get enough of these "wild beasts of finance," to use Alfred Steinherr's moniker. The global market for financial derivatives is colossal and gets colossally larger every day. How big is it? Putting a monetary figure on this market is like measuring a cloud with a yardstick. Where do you put it? And when? Want to know that there are something like 100 million option contracts in effect? That the notional values of outstanding interest rate derivatives total in the hundreds of *trillions* of dollars—and are climbing all the time? It's a big place, this world of derivatives; trust me on this. And you'll just get a headache Googling for truly meaningful statistics.

DERIVATIVES AS ENABLERS

Most applications of derivatives, you'll be happy to know, are remarkably safe and nothing to get alarmed over. They are, if you will, good things. They just help folks do what they otherwise might not. A farmer may want to plant wheat but fear that the price of wheat will decline while it's growing, forcing the farmer to sell it for less than what it cost to grow. A commodities future, one of the oldest of all derivatives, lets the farmer lock in the price of wheat before the first seed hits the soil. A manufacturer may want to borrow money to build a plant but can only do so at a floating rate of interest, raising the possibility of financial insolvency should interest rates float too high. An interest rate swap lets the company convert that debt to a fixed rate, removing that risk. And on and on and on.

The whole of derivatives affects not just individual industries and institutions. It also acts as a network of financial fibers connecting very different corners of the economy with one another: A farmer sells wheat forward on the futures market to lock in a return from his planting investment. The miller buys wheat forward on the same futures market to lock in a future profit, and does a swap with a commercial bank to convert the debt from purchasing a machine to grind that wheat from a floating rate to a fixed rate. The bank uses long Eurodollar futures to hedge the swap. A hedge fund combines short Eurodollar futures and long U.S. Treasury bonds to arbitrage pricing discrepancies between those two instruments. A global pharmaceutical firm uses protective puts on Treasury bonds to hedge the bond portion on its pension fund, and buys Japanese yen forward on the foreign-exchange market to lock in the U.S. dollar price of a future purchase from a Japanese supplier. A French commercial real estate developer sells yen forward to lock in the recent appreciation of property she holds in Osaka. And so on.

DERIVATIVES AS DISABLERS

When things go wrong with derivatives, they tend to go wrong in a big way. If there had been an Academy Award for derivative-disaster spectacles—even before the global financial contagion of 2008, stoked in part by credit default swaps—there would have been no shortage of nominees each year. "And the Oscar goes to . . . Long-Term Capital Management!" Complexity and risk spell occasional disaster in many worlds, not just finance. Aeronautics and aviation come to mind, as does the practice of thoracic surgery and the manufacture of chemicals. Mistakes can be painful. Fortunately, we tend to learn a lot from mistakes, and sometimes—not always—we learn to avoid repeating them.

What have we learned from derivatives disasters? In 2008 we learned, painfully, the systemic risks associated with unbridled over-the-counter (OTC) trading of credit derivatives. The chief lesson from before 2008, which must not be ignored as time marches on, is that it's the commonsense stuff that gets us in trouble—stuff like not anticipating future cash flow requirements, giving managers too much power, and lending gamblers obscene amounts of money to fund their bets. And those aren't just hypotheticals. Those three mistakes were spectacularly demonstrated by three names destined to go down in the history of derivatives: Metallgesellschaft, Barings Bank, and Long-Term Capital Management.

In the early 1990s, MGRM, a division of the large industrial complex Metallgesellschaft, sold oil forward to OTC counterparties for terms going out as long as 10 years. At fixed prices. MGRM hedged its short forward contracts with stacks of long futures contracts, with terms often going out only a few months. And this extreme difference in terms is what got the company into trouble. As the futures did what futures do, their payoff neutralized any loss or gain from buying oil spot to make good on their forwards. Basic hedging. And every month, MGRM would put on new futures hedges for future obligations, as part of its "stack-and-roll" hedge.

The strategy was theoretically sound over the long run, but when oil prices dropped sharply, the company simply didn't have enough cash on hand to satisfy margin calls on its futures positions. Recall that long futures positions lose money when prices decline, and the MGRM positions were huge. The corresponding gains on the oil forwards just weren't sufficient for making up the difference. Before long, there was simply not enough cash to keep the thing going, so management shut it down. But the size of the firm's positions made doing so all at once very costly, as it involved numerous "unwinds" at a substantial loss. In the end, something like $1.5 billion went down the proverbial toilet.

In the mid-1990s, the venerable Barings Bank suffered the "rogue trader" syndrome. This is where a trader puts on speculation trades that exceed reasonable risk tolerances, trades that turn out to be bad bets. Plenty of places have suffered from rogue traders. But Barings suffered with particular pain because the trader, Nick Leeson, was also in essence his own manager—approving his own speculation on the Japanese stock market from his base in Singapore and hiding the losses from his managers. Normally, firms strictly separate their "front office" (where trading happens) from their "back office" (where settlements, accounting, and related functions take place).

According to government studies of the debacle, Leeson apparently employed a short straddle on the Nikkei 225 stock index. Recall that the payoff of a short straddle is like an inverted V, with unlimited losses possible should the underlier go above or below a certain level. When the Nikkei fell more sharply than Leeson expected, the position lost money. Lots of it. When he placed an equally aggressive bet that stocks would rise—in hopes of compensating for his straddle losses before anyone found out—things just got terribly worse. By the time the parent company found out what its wayward child was up to, the losses on the Nikkei trades exceeded the entire capital of the bank by something like a billion U.S. dollars. The 250-year-old bank was forced to declare bankruptcy. Leeson spent a few years in jail, after which he gave speeches on the dangers of rogue traders for a reported $100,000 a crack. Barings is gone for good.

In the late 1990s, the hedge fund Long-Term Capital Management (LTCM) was having a grand time, showering its investors with annual returns of close to 40 percent. The firm's principal strategy appears to have been arbitrage, using sophisticated analytical models to detect the subtlest of pricing discrepancies in the government bond markets. Some of those bonds were issued by Russia, which just happened to default on its bonds. Oops. Now, LTCM had hedged its long bond positions with short positions on the Russian currency the ruble, because in theory, those currency positions would increase in value when the long bond positions tanked. But the ruble tanked so hard that their currency counterparties basically shut down. And Russia itself suspended all trading in its currency.

Now, this ruble issue was a decidedly bad thing for LTCM, but what really made matters bad—not just for LTCM but for the system as a whole—was that LTCM had borrowed nearly all of its money to do this cool arbitrage. At one point, LTCM had a stake in the market of well over $100 billion. The firm's equity was something like *half* a billion dollars. This is an extraordinary leverage ratio and is not unlike buying a million-dollar house with a down payment of $5,000. So now you've got all these lenders with a great deal of skin in the game. And then you've got something called a "flight to liquidity" in the global fixed-income markets, such as the U.S. Treasury markets, where investors all seemed to be putting their money in response to the Russian bond crisis.

The intricacies of LTCM's position were such that it was not hedged against the negative effects of the flight to liquidity, so it found itself against the ropes with no hope of recovery. But the financial system couldn't just let this fighter die, because banks and other financial firms had lent it all that money, and besides, those banks and firms were also exposed to the ill effects of the liquidity crisis. And with all the interdependencies among players in the capital markets game, if every lender simply tried to call in its debts, you'd have defaults and bankruptcies rippling through the system like cracks in a shattering piece of glass.

So what happened? The Federal Reserve Bank of New York, which is for all intents and purposes an arm of the U.S. government, got a bunch of banks together in a conference room and convinced them to write checks totaling $3.5 billion. This "gift" was injected into the system to prevent a catastrophic meltdown but still did not cover everyone's losses. Nobody can say for sure, but banks took additional write-offs totaling another billion or so dollars of losses that year, so it's not a stretch to put the overall price tag of the LTCM folly at around $5 billion—not exactly chump change.

As demonstrated colorfully by the LTCM disaster, and then colossally by the credit crisis of 2008, the sheer web of interdependency spun by derivatives is perhaps the cause for greatest concern when it comes to these wily financial instruments. Checks and balances, whether from industry sensibility or government mandate, are clearly essential to keeping the bad things from overpowering the good things.

All About Interest

Think of interest as the price of money. You want to borrow a million bucks to expand your business? It'll cost you some interest. You want to lend some money to the U.S. government, by purchasing a bond, so it can build roads or wage wars? The government will pay you interest. For our purposes, interest is the money paid by the borrower of money to its lender. It doesn't always seem that way, because "paying for" money is different from paying for, say, cantaloupes. You don't generally pay for cantaloupes with cantaloupes, but you do pay for money with money. Also, you don't so much purchase money as rent it. The grocer doesn't expect to see his cantaloupe again, but bankers most certainly expect to be reunited one day with their money.

INTEREST RATES

The way we measure interest is, of course, with the interest rate. The interest rate specifies a cost of borrowing money for some unit of time. A one-bedroom Chicago apartment might go for $1,300 per month. A tanning booth might rent for $39 per hour. A million bucks from Citibank might go for $65,000 of interest per year. Of course, interest rates aren't expressed in dollar amounts but rather in percentages. So the price of a million from Citibank is expressed not as $65,000 per year but as 6.5 percent per year. This ability to express a cost as a percentage of the thing we buy turns out to be quite a convenience and is possible, of course, because we pay for money with money.

With interest rates, the unit of time is always one year. Well, not always, but trust me, you can go the rest of your life assuming every interest rate you ever hear is for one year, and you'll be just fine. Of course, we work all the time with units of time smaller or greater than one year—monthly payments, quarterly accruals, and so on—and later on we'll get into that. But the interest rate itself expresses an annual rate—that is, the rate for one "annum," or year.

And what does this mean exactly, this 6.5 percent per year, or six and one-half percentage points? The term is from the Latin *per centum*, or "per hundred," and is indicated by the percentage sign: %. So a rate of 6.5 percent is six and one-half dollars for every hundred dollars borrowed. How many hundreds are in a million? Ten thousand. Multiply this by 6.5, and there's your $65,000.

$$6.5 \text{ percent of } 1,000,000 = ?$$
$$6.5\% = 0.065 = 6.5 \text{ per } 100$$
$$1,000,000/100 = 10,000$$
$$10,000 \times 6.5 = 65,000$$
$$6.5 \text{ percent of } 1,000,000 = 65,000$$

When it comes to measuring interest, there's another unit to know: the basis point (BP, pronounced "bip"). It turns out a percentage point is way too big to be practical in a world where a billion-dollar deal is no big deal. In this world, we deal in hundredths of percentage points, and one-hundredth of 1 percent is what we call a basis point. One hundred basis points equals one percentage point, and vice versa. So when we speak of "25 basis points" we simply mean one-quarter of a percent, or 0.25 percent. Five basis points is 0.05 percent or one-twentieth of 1 percent. Here are some more examples:

$$1 \text{ basis point} = 0.01\% = 0.0001$$
$$25 \text{ basis points} = 0.25\% = 0.0025$$
$$100 \text{ basis points} = 1\% = 0.01$$
$$150 \text{ basis points} = 1.5\% = 0.015$$
$$1.5\% + 25 \text{ basis points} = 1.75\% = 0.0175$$

If you are familiar with U.S. coinage, it can help to think of 1 percent as a dollar and one basis point as a penny. Then when you see 25 basis points, you think of a quarter, and hearing "five bips" brings to mind a nickel, which you know without thinking is one-twentieth of a dollar.

$$100 \text{ basis points} = \text{"one dollar"}$$
$$25 \text{ basis points} = \text{"one quarter"}$$
$$10 \text{ basis points} = \text{"one dime"}$$
$$1 \text{ basis point} = \text{"one penny"}$$

However you do it, you need to be comfortable thinking in terms of basis points because this numerical sliver can itself be too big to be practical. So we speak about hundredths or even thousandths of basis points. This isn't so ridiculous when you're a large derivatives dealer with trillions of dollars' worth of contracts on your books.

$$1 \text{ basis point} \times \$100 = \$0.01$$
$$1 \text{ basis point} \times \$1 \text{ million} = \$100$$
$$1 \text{ basis point} \times \$1 \text{ billion} = \$100,000$$
$$1 \text{ basis point} \times \$1 \text{ trillion} = \$100 \text{ million}$$

FLOATING INTEREST, RATE INDEXES, AND LIBOR

Interest rates in practice are expressed as fixed or floating. A fixed rate is an interest rate that does not change over the life of a loan. If your bank lends you $100,000 for 10 years at 7 percent, with interest payments due monthly, neither you nor the bank can expect that rate to change over that 10 years (unless you renegotiate the loan).

In a floating-rate loan, the interest rate does change over the life of the loan. Say your bank lends you $100,000 for 10 years under the condition you will make monthly payments not at a fixed rate, but at a changing rate known as LIBOR. Pronounced "lie-bohr" or "lee-bohr," LIBOR is an example of a rate index. Indeed, in the land of rate indexes, LIBOR is king. A rate index is just a price index like the ones we introduced earlier, providing an average price from a survey of related things. Like other price indexes, a rate index can, and very often is, employed as a derivative underlier.

With respect to swaps and other interest rate derivatives, think of a rate index as an undisputed thermometer that monitors some aspect of an ever-changing environment and reports it as a number. A real thermometer monitors temperature; a rate index monitors interest rates. Like temperature, interest rates change continuously and unpredictably. If you borrow money at LIBOR, the exact amounts of your future payment obligations are unpredictable at the time you take out the loan. Nobody uses the word *unpredictable*, with all its negative connotations, so instead we use the euphemistic term *floating*. It's so much nicer on the ear.

LIBOR is short for London Inter-Bank Offer Rate. Every business day in London, at 11:00 ' ⌐ . local time, the British Bankers' Association (BBA) publishes a set of interest rates, "fixing" or "setting" LIBOR for the day for a number of different currencies. For loans denominated in U.S. dollars, the association publishes U.S. LIBOR rates. For loans denominated in pounds sterling, it publishes GBP LIBOR rates. And so on. In swap parlance, these daily events are also known as resets. Once fixed for the day, they do not change until the next fixing day, when they can indeed change. From day to day, the rates change unpredictably, but once fixed, there is no quibble over the daily proclamations of those helpful British bankers. Perfect ingredients of a rate index.

So, let's turn back to your $100,000 loan. If it "floats with LIBOR," each month when your interest payment is due (we ignore principal payments for now), the rate with which to calculate that payment is read from the LIBOR thermometer. If it's 6.02 percent one month, you owe roughly $501.67 (one-twelfth of $100,000 × 0.0602). If the next month it's 5.26 percent, you owe $438.33. And so on. Figure A-1 depicts a sample of actual one-month LIBOR rates taken at monthly intervals just to show how wildly rates can float from month to month.[1] And don't be confused by the terminology. These "one-month rates" are still expressed as annual rates. They just pertain to money borrowed for one month.

Rate indices such as LIBOR are profoundly useful in the stormy world of finance, as they are reliable, precise, and undisputed. While real thermometers may sometimes stop functioning, and different observers might quibble whether the mercury is at 70½ or 70¾, rate indexes for all practical purposes are unambiguous and undisputed.

In addition to LIBOR, another common index is based on the prime rate, a rate of interest offered by a bank to its most creditworthy customers. Every business day of the year, for example, Citibank

---

[1] For the curious, these are Eurodollar deposit rates sampled monthly by the U.S. Federal Reserve, starting in April 1995.

FIGURE A-1

One-Month LIBOR Rates

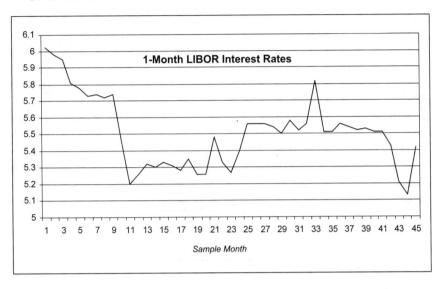

publishes its prime rate. And every day, you can obtain an average, or index, of such primes and base a loan on that rate. You can count on it being there, you know exactly what it is, and you don't have to wonder whether it's correct or not. Other indexes include commercial paper rates, indicating rates at which businesses will pay to borrow funds, and numerous indexes analogous to LIBOR for other financial centers besides London.

TERM STRUCTURE AND YIELD CURVES

For any given index on any given day, there is no single interest rate. An index is, in fact, like an entire set of thermometers. This is because interest rates vary by term or maturity, or the length of time money is borrowed. An annual LIBOR rate for a 3-month loan is almost always different from the annual LIBOR rate for a one-year loan. So we have 3-month LIBOR, 6-month LIBOR, 12-month LIBOR, and so on. This variation in interest rate by time to maturity is known as the term structure of interest rates. Having so many different rates for a single index can be rather unwieldy, but thankfully we have an indispensable device known as a *yield curve* for dealing with term structure. Figure A-2 shows what a yield curve looks like.

FIGURE A-2

LIBOR Spot Yield Curve

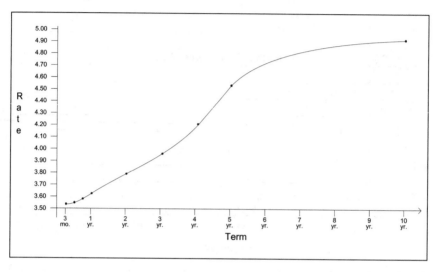

A yield curve illustrates term structure by depicting, for one index, different rates of interest—or yield—for different terms, all at a glance. This curve tells us that money borrowed for three years can be had for an annual rate of around 4.0 percent, while money borrowed for six years will cost you around 4.7 percent. So think of "yield" as another word for "interest rate." The word comes from the world of bonds, where bond issuers (borrowers) raise money by selling bonds to investors (lenders), who are thereafter known as bondholders. Issuers pay money to holders (money costs money, recall), and those payments constitute the return, or gain, or yield to the investor. Yields are expressed as some percentage of the amount invested. Sound familiar? A yield is just an interest rate.

Constructing a Spot Curve

The best way to understand a yield curve is to construct one. Now, there are two fundamental types of interest rates in the land of derivatives, spot rates and forward rates, and two corresponding types of curve, spot curves and forward curves. Spot interest rates apply to money borrowed now, and forward interest rates apply to money borrowed in the future. We'll cover forward rates and curves in the next section.

Right now, let's construct a spot curve to illustrate this whole yield curve thing. We start with a fictitious but plausible set of U.S. LIBOR rate fixings. Let's say it's 11:00 ' ⊥ . in London, and the BBA publishes the following rates for the following terms:

U.S. LIBOR Rate Fixings

3-month	3.53
6-month	3.54
9-month	3.59
1-year	3.69

Here we have four spot interest rates, or prices of money. You want to borrow today for three months? That'll be 3.53 percent per year, or 0.8819 percent for three months if we keep it simple (3 months = 3/12 of a year, and 3/12 = 1/4 = 0.25, and 3.5275 × 0.25 = 0.8819 percent). You want it today for six months? The rate goes up one basis point to 3.5375 percent, or 1.7688 percent for the half year. You want it today for a year? That rate is 3.69 percent.

To construct this yield curve, we simply plot these points on a simple graph where the x-axis (horizontal) represents the term, or time to maturity, of a theoretical loan starting today. The y-axis (vertical) represents the interest rate. So Figure A-3 shows our plot, with the points connected by straight lines.

Now, this is not much of a "curve," being so elbowed and incomplete, although it does convey some sense that interest rates increase with time to maturity. But it doesn't give a rate for, say, a five-year loan. After all, the longest LIBOR term is one year. A common way of handling this is to extend the curve with yields from various Eurodollar futures or U.S. Treasury securities, or both.

A Eurodollar futures contract is an exchange-traded derivative obligating the long party to borrow $1 million not today but on some future date, for a period of three months, at the prevailing three-month LIBOR rate as of that future date. Notice we're referring now to a future loan, so the rates involved are forward rates and not spot rates. The Eurodollar, especially front-term Eurodollars for borrowing three, six, and nine months down the road, are highly

FIGURE A-3

Beginnings of a LIBOR Spot Curve

liquid.[2] The prices at which they trade, then, can be seen as indicators of where people expect the BBA to publish LIBOR rates in the future. Because interest is just the price of money, the price of a Eurodollar is just an interest rate in disguise.

Where were we? That's right, looking for spot rates with which to extend our yield curve. Now the Eurodollars give us futures prices. And by applying a "futures-forward adjustment" involving math we won't delve into, we can deduce a forward price from a futures price.[3] And from such forward rates, we can deduce spot rates with which to extend our spot curve past the 12-month term available from the BBA.[4]

Following are some spot rates we might infer from the Eurodollars market:

---

[2] You'll see this lingo used all the time in the securities markets. "Front-term" or "front-month" contracts expire earlier than do "back-term" or "back-month" contracts, and they tend to be more liquid.

[3] Recall that a futures is just an exchange-traded forward whose value is affected by the daily marking to market, and with some math, we can back out that effect.

[4] Quick example: If the three-month spot is 2.50 percent and the three-month rate three months forward is 2.60 percent, the implied six-month spot rate must be the arithmetic average, or 2.55 percent. Any other rate would permit arbitrage.

Eurodollar Implied Spot Rates

3-month	3.53
6-month	3.54
. . .	
18-month	3.72
21-month	3.75
. . .	
45-month	4.03
48-month	4.07

Now we have perfectly defensible interest rates for loans going out four years.

Incidentally, liquid futures markets of all kinds are used this way all the time, whenever we need an indicator of expected future prices. Does it matter if the expectations come true? No. You cannot tell future prices from futures prices. But as long as we have an indicator of expected prices, and liquid markets for securing obligations based on those expectations, we're all set. And as you can imagine, front-term futures prices tend to be more reliable than those in the back terms, as futures prices converge to spot prices as we get closer to their maturity dates. It's like weather forecasting. A one-day forecast is more likely to come true than a one-week forecast, and a one-hour forecast is probably even more reliable.

Extending our curve with Eurodollar two-year, three-year, and four-year rates gives the growing curve in Figure A-4. To get spot rates for longer terms, we can turn to the market for U.S. Treasury securities. These are more liquid, so they are more reliable for price discovery than Eurodollars going out beyond four years. Treasuries consist of bills, notes, and bonds issued by the U.S. government for varying terms.[5] Treasury notes and bonds are loans to the U.S. Treasury, which makes interest or coupon payments semiannually (every six months) at a fixed coupon rate. As marketable securities,

---

[5] The distinction between these types of securities is primarily in maturity. Bills go out to a year and pay interest only at maturity; instruments like this are sometimes known as "zero-coupon" instruments or just "zeros." Notes go out to 10 years, bonds go beyond 10 years, and both notes and bonds make period coupon payments to their holders (i.e., lenders).

FIGURE A-4

Partial LIBOR Spot Curve Going out Four Years

once issued, they are heavily traded on secondary markets. This just means bondholders actively buy and sell (trade) them, and the price at which they trade determines their effective interest rate or yield, which can be wildly different from the coupon rate.

By the way, does it seem bizarre that a coupon rate and effective rate can be different? Here's how it happens: Say you buy a five-year Treasury with a face value of $100,000 (the amount you lend to Uncle Sam) and a coupon rate of 4.75 percent (the annual interest rate for semiannual interest payments). If you hold this bond to maturity, you can look forward to a stream of cash flows over the next five years based on the 4.75 percent rate. Now if you add up the present values of these cash flows, you will get $100,000, or face value.

Imagine that you buy one of these from the U.S. Treasury, and right away someone buys it from you on the secondary market for $101,200. Now your buyer can look forward to those cash flows based on the coupon rate—whose present value is just $100,000! He or she clearly paid a premium for your bond—i.e., more than the present value of its cash flows. It's as if the buyer bought a bond that pays a coupon of something less than 4.75 percent. In fact, I'll do the math for you and tell you the buyer effectively bought a bond that pays an annual rate of 4.53 percent. And this is how we deduce spot interest rates from Treasury prices.

And while we are spinning tangents, do you notice that the three-month Treasury rate of 3.38 percent is 15 basis points lower than the three-month LIBOR rate of 3.53 percent? This is a great example of a credit spread, which we'll speak more of later on. LIBOR rates are intended for commercial loans, whereas Treasuries are for loans to the U.S. Treasury. All other factors equal, a commercial loan is more likely to default than a U.S. Treasury loan. A lender demands a risk premium for this increased credit risk, which in this case is 15 basis points.

Now back to the matter at hand. Let's say U.S. Treasury yields look like this on the same day as our LIBOR rate fixings did:

U.S. Treasury Rates

3-month	3.38
6-month	3.37
1-year	3.44
2-year	3.76
5-year	4.53
10-year	4.92
20-year	5.53
30-year	5.44

When we add Treasury rates to the LIBOR curve for the 5-year and 10-year points, we get something like Figure A-5.

Our nascent curve now covers a longer set of maturities, but still it doesn't give an exact rate for a term between the given points, say for a three-year loan. You might think you can simply read up from the three-year point and stop when you hit the line, and this will indeed give you an approximation, but mathematicians will tell you there is a better way to make this curve more useful. It's called curve smoothing. To get an idea for curve smoothing, just imagine taking a pencil and eyeballing a smooth line that connects the dots and extends the lines beyond the first and last dots. It might look like the curve in Figure A-6.

Now we have a yield curve. And while it's a theoretically correct curve, it's a bit wavy to be useful. In practice, we like a

FIGURE A-5

Complete LIBOR Spot Curve Before Smoothing

FIGURE A-6

Complete LIBOR Spot Curve with Some Smoothing

FIGURE A-7

Complete LIBOR Spot Curve with More Smoothing

smoother curve and are even willing to adjust the sample points a bit to fit a nice smooth line, creating something like the solid line in Figure A-7.

You can, of course, adjust even further and end up with a line so smooth is it perfectly straight. But that's too smooth. How smooth is smooth enough? Here we will step off the bus, because to go further requires a generous helping of math. It turns out there are a number of formulas or algorithms for smoothing a curve, given a sample of points. Some are in the public domain, widely known and taught in school, and some are highly proprietary or secret to their creators. (In addition to curve smoothing, the choice of inputs is also proprietary. Do we use the one-year LIBOR or one-year U.S. Treasury rate? Do we take rates from the spot market or futures market? And so on.) These algorithms and choices are secret because things like this—drawing better yield curves and developing better algorithms—are the sort of thing that helps you make money in the world of derivatives. For our purposes, we'll stick to the curve shown in Figure A-8.

FIGURE A-8

LIBOR Spot Yield Curve

The Forward Rate and Forward Curve

A spot rate is an interest rate for money borrowed now. It's the rate (price) available right now on the spot market for money and is the type of rate depicted in our spot curve in Figure A-8. If you ask your bank for a six-month loan commencing immediately, the rate the banker will quote you is a spot rate. A forward rate is an interest rate for money borrowed for some future period of time. If you ask your bank for a six-month loan commencing not today but one year from now, the banker will quote a forward rate. This is a rate (price) at which the bank agrees today (guarantees) to lend you money in one year's time. Sound familiar? It should! The forward rate is just the delivery price of a forward contract whose underlier is borrowed money. (Such contracts are known as forward rate agreements, as were introduced in Chapter 2, "The Forward Contract.")

A forward curve looks just like a spot curve, but the rates depicted are for a loan commencing some time hence. And different lag periods get their own forward curves. So on any given day for any given index, you will have a spot curve, a 3-month forward curve (for loans of varying maturities commencing three months later), a 6-month forward curve, 12-month curve, and so on. Here's the main thing: forward rates are derived from spot rates. And forward curves, therefore, are derived from spot curves. For any given spot curve, there is only one possible 3-month forward curve, one possible 6-month forward curve, and so on. So the first step in constructing a forward curve is always the construction of a spot curve. You can't make toast without bread, and you can't make a forward curve without a spot curve.

Forward Rates from Spot Rates

Say you want to borrow $10,000 six months from now for a period of three months. The six-month spot rate is 3.5 percent, and the nine-month spot rate is 3.55 percent. What is the three-month forward rate for a loan commencing in six months, or 6×9 ("six by nine") rate? It's 3.6 percent.

How come? Imagine two hypothetical scenarios. In scenario A, you borrow for nine months at 3.55 percent, paying interest at the end of the loan period. In scenario B, you borrow for six months at 3.5 percent and then take out a new, three-month loan at the then-current three-month spot rate.

Both scenarios should cost the same because they both give you the same thing: a nine-month loan of $10,000. This means the three-month spot rate in six months—the 6×9 rate—is the one that makes both scenarios cost the same. In other words, it's the rate that makes the present value (PV) of one scenario's interest payments equal to the PV of the other scenario's interest payments. (Any other rate would allow arbitrage, which you'll recall is simultaneous trading to make a riskless profit from pricing discrepancies, and the correct price for anything in the land of derivatives is the one, and only one, that prevents arbitrage.) The rate that does that is 3.6 percent. Here's the math:

Scenario A: Nine-Month Loan Today

Notional:	$10,000.00
Nine-month spot rate:	0.0355 percent
Day fraction:	$9/12 = 0.75$
Payment rate:	$0.355 \times 0.75 = 0.026625$
Interest payment:	$10,000 \times 0.026625 = 266.25$
Months till payment:	9
Discount factor:	$(1/1.0355)^{0.75} = 0.97416$

Interest payment PV: $266.25 \times 0.97416 = 259.37$
Scenario A total interest PV: $259.37

Scenario B: Six-Month Loan Today
Notional: $10,000.00
Six-month spot rate: 0.0350 percent
Day fraction: $6/12 = 0.5$
Payment rate: $0.350 \times 0.5 = 0.0175$
Interest payment: $10,000 \times 0.0175 = 175.00$
Months till payment: 6
Discount factor: $(1/1.035)^{0.5} = 0.9829$
Interest payment PV: $175.00 \times 0.9829 = 172.02$

Three-Month Loan in Six Months
Notional: $10,000.00
Three-month forward rate: 0.0359
Day fraction: $3/12 = 0.25$
Payment rate: $0.359 \times 0.25 = 0.008967$
Interest payment: $10,000 \times 0.008967 = 89.67$
Months till payment: 9
Discount factor: $(1/0.10355)^{0.75} = 0.9742$
Interest payment PV: $89.67 \times 0.9742 = 87.36$
Scenario B total interest PV: $\$172.02 + \$87.36 = \$259.37$

Figure A-9 shows what a complete three-month forward curve might look like, given using spot rates from our spot curve and a bit of smoothing.

Here's another factoid for you: the forward curve is above the spot curve at all points. This is always the case for upward-sloping spot curves. When spot curves slope downward (it happens), the forward curve is below spot. That's all academic, of course. The main thing for us is that from a curve like this, we can obtain three-month forward rates for three-month loans commencing at any point out 10 years. This comes in very handy when we value a swap.

FIGURE A-9

LIBOR Forward and Spot Yield Curves Superimposed

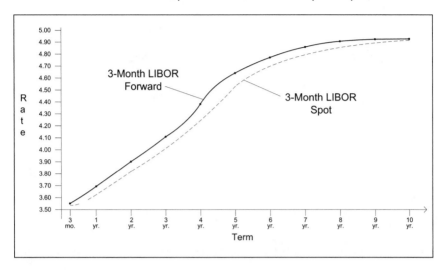

APPENDIX B

Swap Conventions

In addition to conventions introduced in the swaps chapters and Appendix A, "All About Interest," there's yet another batch of concepts applicable to swaps and virtually all interest rate derivatives used in practice. Some of these are mathematical, and some are just conventions that have arisen over the years.

COMPOUNDING

We examined *compounding* in Chapter 8, "Pricing Forwards and Futures." Swap interest rates can be specified as compounding or noncompounding. Recall that when a loan is based on a compounding rate of interest, interest is paid not only on the principal (the amount borrowed) but also on accrued interest. If you owe me interest but don't pay it to me, then it's just the same as if I'm lending you more money—money that will cost you more interest. And if you don't pay me that interest, it will cost you more interest, and so on, until you finally fork over the dough. That's compounding, which can be applied to either a fixed- or floating-rate loan.

AVERAGING

The concept of rate averaging applies to floating-rate obligations. Here, when it comes time to make a payment, the rate applied is not the current reading of the index thermometer but the average of some number of previous readings.

An example illustrates it best. Say we observe the following rate fixings for six-month LIBOR:

Monday:	3.60
Tuesday:	3.58
Wednesday:	3.59
Thursday:	3.60
Friday:	3.57

Now say it's Friday and time to calculate a payment. For a non-averaging obligation, we choose the Friday fixing, or 3.57 percent. For an obligation based on a five-day average rate, we calculate the average of all five rate fixings, or 3.59 percent, and use that.[1]

The 5-day period is just an example. You can have an obligation based on a 30-day average, six-month average, whatever.

AMORTIZATION

Amortization occurs when a loan, either fixed or floating, has a principal that changes over the life of a loan. All interest rate derivatives have a *principal*, also known as the *notional* in the context of interest rate derivatives, against which an interest rate is periodically applied (as on payment dates) for the purpose of calculating some amount of interest. Perhaps you've borrowed $10 million, and each year must make a 6 percent interest-only payment. The $10 million is your notional, the amount by which the 6 percent rate is multiplied to calculate your $60,000 payment. If your loan is nonamortizing, the notional remains constant over the life of the loan, and every payment is calculated from it. If your loan is amortizing, the notional changes, or amortizes. All amortizing obligations include a schedule of notional amounts, predefined at the outset of a trade. This amortization schedule may follow some neat pattern, or it may be downright wacky, as long as both parties agree to it up front.

The most common forms of amortization are additive, straight-line, multiplicative, and mortgage-style amortization.

Additive Amortization

The simplest amortization involves adding to (or subtracting from) the previous level some fixed amount. Say you begin with $10 million and decrease the notional by $1 million each period. That's additive amortization; you're just "adding" a negative number.

Period 1: $10,000,000
Period 2: $10,000,000 − $1,000,000 = $9,000,000
Period 3: $9,000,000 − $1,000,000 = $8,000,000
Period 4: $8,000,000 − $1,000,000 = $7,000,000
Etc.

---

[1] 3.60 + 3.58 + 3.59 + 3.60 + 3.57 = 17.94, and 17.94/5 = 3.59.

Straight-Line Amortization

Straight-line amortization is a special case of additive amortization where the notional steps down by the same amount each period, and the final notional amount is the stepping amount. Say you amortize $1 million over four periods; you would reduce the notional by $250,000 each period.

Period 1: $1,000,000
Period 2: $750,000
Period 3: $500,000
Period 4: $250,000

Multiplicative Amortization

With multiplicative amortization, instead of adding to the previous amount, we multiply it by some amount. That amount is typically (but not always) some fractional amount between 0 and 1. A multiplicative amortization schedule starting at $1 million and decreasing by 12 percent each period starts off like this:

Period 1: $1,000,000
Period 2: $1,000,000 − ($1,000,000 × 0.12) = $880,000
Period 3: $880,000 − ($880,000 × 0.12) = $774,400
Etc.

Mortgage-Style

A mortgage-style amortization schedule will be familiar if you've ever borrowed money to purchase real estate. Each payment consists of some notional plus interest, such that each payment is the same and all notional is repaid by the end of the loan. A four-period amortization schedule, starting at $100 million and using a 7 percent mortgage rate, with annual payments, might look like the example in Table B-1.

Note that mortgages are typically paid in arrears, which simply means you pay for the money after you have it for some period of time. So the interest is based on the remaining notional at the beginning of the period. In the example in Table B-1, then, the first-period interest is 7 percent of the full $100 million notional, or the notional as of the beginning of the first period. The second-period interest is 7 percent of $100 million less the notional paid off with the first payment ($22,522,811.67). And so on.

TABLE B-1

Mortgage-Style Amortization of $100 Million over 4 Years

	Notional (N)	Interest (I)	Payment (N 1 I)
Period 1	$22,522,811.67	$7,000,000.00	$29,522,811.67
Period 2	24,099,408.48	5,423,403.18	29,522,811.67
Period 3	25,786,367.08	3,736,444.59	29,522,811.67
Period 4	27,591,412.77	1,931,398.89	29,522,811.67
Total	100,000,000.00		

CALENDARS

The calendar used for interpreting a contract's terms might seem so basic it's not worth covering, but the simple and meaningful fact is this: people don't work every day of the year. We take off weekends and holidays, known as nonbusiness days, leaving the rest as workdays or business days. And for reasons soon to be revealed, it is crucial for transaction counterparties to agree on which days are business days and which are not. Is Groundhog Day a business day? Boxing Day? John Lennon's birthday?

Fortunately, there are a set of predefined calendars to make this task easier. Each calendar is named for a city—New York, London, Tokyo, etc.—and each is basically a list of weekdays not considered a business day in that locale. (Saturdays and Sundays, I am happy to report, appear to be nonbusiness days the world over.) The calendar definitions are for all intents and purposes universally accepted, so we never have to quibble over individual holidays, just the calendar. Figure B-1, for example, shows one year's September holidays in New York and Tokyo.

So for any given transaction, we simply specify one or more of these calendars up front. More than one? Sure. It's not uncommon for a transaction to specify as its calendar some combination of calendars—say, New York and Tokyo. And a contract might specify the New York calendar for one aspect of a trade and Tokyo for the other.

Using our previous examples, if a trade is based on a New York calendar, then September 18 is a business day. But if the trade is based on a Tokyo calendar, then September 18 is not a business

FIGURE B-1

Example of September Holidays: New York and Tokyo

	September									September					
	Su	Mo	Tu	We	Th	Fr	Sa			Su	Mo	Tu	We	Th	Fr	Sa

New York

Sep 4 : Labor Day

Su	Mo	Tu	We	Th	Fr	Sa
					1	2
3	4	5	6	7	8	9
10	11	12	13	14	15	16
17	18	19	20	21	22	23
24	25	26	27	28	29	30

Tokyo

Sep 18 : Respect for the Aged Day

Su	Mo	Tu	We	Th	Fr	Sa
					1	2
3	4	5	6	7	8	9
10	11	12	13	14	15	16
17	18	19	20	21	22	23
24	25	26	27	28	29	30

day. If the trade's calendar is New York + Tokyo, then September 18 again is not a business day; for multicalendar trades, a nonbusiness day anywhere is a nonbusiness day for the sake of the trade.

Business Day Conventions

A trade's calendar tells us which dates over the life of that trade constitute business days and which do not. So what if some meaningful date—say, the date on which a payment is due—falls on a weekend or holiday? Does someone come into the office? The two parties in a trade can decide to handle this situation however they want. But as with calendars, they will no doubt wish to select from a number of standard business day conventions at the outset of a trade. These are simply rules that specify what to do when a meaningful date falls on a nonbusiness day. The most common of these are pretty easy to grasp:

- **Following:** Go forward in time till you get to a business day, and use that one.
- **Previous:** Go back in time till you get to a business day, and use that one.
- **Modified following:** Go forward in time till you get to a business day, and use that one—unless that day should take you into the next month, in which case go backward in time till you get to a business day, and use that one.
- **No adjustment:** Someone is coming into work. Use the date as-is.

Day Count Conventions

Interest rates are almost always expressed as annual rates—that is, the cost of borrowing money for exactly one year. When you see a rate "5.325 percent," you just know it applies to one year. Same with "1.25 percent" or "10 percent." When it comes time to calculate an actual amount of interest, however, the period we are concerned with is almost never one year exactly. Instead, we want to calculate a payment due for some accrual period such as "three months commencing April 1" or "September 3 through October 5" or "85 days starting May 17." What rate do we apply?

It turns out there's more than one way to reasonably arrive at an applicable rate for a given period of time. And to bring some clarity to this gray area, there are five techniques, or algorithms, known as day count conventions. Some of these are more tedious than others, but all are well understood, and that's all that matters. Every trade specifies one of these at the outset of a trade, to be applied when necessary to calculate interest accruals.

The whole thing boils down to fractions. If your rate of interest is 6 percent per year and you want to calculate interest for a period less than a year, clearly you need to apply only a fraction of that 6 percent. That fraction is known as a day fraction. This ubiquitous computational ingredient tells us how much of an annual interest rate to apply when calculating interest for some period of time. If the period of time is less than one year (typical), the fraction is less than 1, if exactly one year, the fraction is equal to 1, and if greater than one year (it happens), the day count fraction is greater than 1. As a math problem, it looks like this:

$$\text{Interest} = (\text{Annual Rate} \times \text{Day Fraction}) \times \text{Notional}$$

Ignoring the real conventions for a second, imagine you want to calculate 6 percent interest on a million dollars for exactly one year. Our day fraction is, of course, 1:

$$\text{Interest} = (0.06 \times 1) \times \$1,000,000 = \$60,000$$

Now if we want to calculate interest for one-half of a year, our day fraction is clearly ½, and we just do this:

$$\text{Interest} = (0.06 \times \tfrac{1}{2}) \times \$1,000,000 = \$30,000$$

The day count conventions specify what to put in the numerator (the top part) and denominator (the bottom part) of a day count fraction. Several conventions are floating around out there (some of them quite convoluted!), but the following are a few of the common ones and how they work.

Actual/365

For the actual/365 convention, we basically divide the actual length of the accrual period by 365 to get our day fraction.[2] So for the numerator, we need the number of days—business and non-business—in the period for which we want to calculate interest. Say the period starts September 15 and ends December 14 in 2006. Looking at a 2006 calendar, we see there are 90 actual days in that period, including the end date but not the start date. So 90 goes into the numerator. The denominator under this convention is 365. So under the actual/365 convention, the day count fraction for calculating the applicable rate of interest for the period September 15, 2006, through December 14, 2006, is 90/365. Multiplying this fraction by 6 percent gives us the accrual rate. For a notional amount of $1 million, then, the payment in dollars works out to be $14,794.52.

Accrual start:	September 15, 2006
Accrual end:	December 14, 2006
Actual days:	90
Day fraction:	90/365
Annual rate:	6 percent
Accrual rate:	$0.06 \times 90/365$
Accrual:	$\$1,000,000 \times 0.06 \times 90/365 = \$14,794.52$

Actual/360

For actual/360, we use a similar routine, but we put 360 in the denominator instead of 365. For a notional amount of $1 million and annual rate of 6 percent, the payment in dollars works out to be $15,000 on the nose.

---

[2] The convention I describe here is known technically in some quarters as "actual/365 (fixed)" and is not to be confused with a different actual/365, which is also known as "actual/actual." Now you see why I'm giving only a few examples.

Accrual start:	September 15, 2006
Accrual end:	December 14, 2006
Actual days:	90
Day fraction:	90/360
Annual rate:	6 percent
Accrual rate:	$0.06 \times 90/360$
Accrual:	$1,000,000 \times 0.06 \times 90/360 = \$15,000$

30/360

To apply the 30/360 convention, also known as the *bond basis* convention, we take the difference between the start and end date as the numerator but in a funny way. Rather than looking at a calendar and counting days, we instead assume every year has 12 months of 30 days each, for 360 days total (which we use for the denominator). To arrive at the number of days in the period, we take the ending year less starting year times 360, ending month less starting month times 30, and ending day minus starting day times one. Using a DD/MM/YYYY format, which helps illustrate this thing, the payment for the period starting 09/15/2006 and ending 12/14/2006 is $14,833.33.

Accrual start:	9/15/2006
Accrual end:	12/14/2006
Year difference:	$(2006 - 2006) \times 360 = 0$
Month difference:	$(12 - 9) \times 30 = 90$
Day difference:	$(14 - 15) \times 1 = -1$
Total difference:	89 days
Day fraction:	89/360
Annual rate:	6 percent
Accrual rate:	$0.06 \times 89/360$
Accrual:	$1,000,000 \times 0.06 \times 89/360 = \$14,833.33$

SWAP ATTRIBUTE SUMMARY

This section offers a few words on most of the features of a plain-vanilla swap, starting with features that apply to a trade in its entirety, then zooming in on features of individual legs.

Trade-Level Features

Several attributes typically apply to the trade overall—that is, both legs of the swap:

- **Notional:** What is the amount of money, or principal, on which interest will be calculated? Recall that this amount typically does not actually change hands in a plain vanilla. It is a reference amount for interest calculation.
- **Effective date:** When does the swap go into effect? More precisely, on what day does interest start to gather up in reserve in anticipation of a payment?
- **Maturity date:** When does the swap end? What is the last day on which interest accrues?
- **Discount curve:** For present-value calculations (say, to calculate the current market value of the swap), what interest rates will we choose? And because interest rates vary by term, and a yield curve conveys a whole set of rates at once, what yield curve shall we reference for this swap? Note that the discount curve need not be the same as the pricing curve.[3]

Accrual Features

At the outset of a swap, we must specify precisely how interest will gather or accrue over the life of the trade. These attributes can, and typically do, pertain to both legs of the trade. Here are some of the major ones:

- **Compounding:** Will interest accrue only on principal (non-compounding), or will it also accrue on interest earned but not yet paid (compounding)? If it does compound, at what frequency will it do so? Monthly, daily, continuously?
- **Averaging:** When it comes time to choose an interest rate from an index in order, say, to calculate a payment, do we choose a rate fixing from a single day (nonaveraging)? Or

---

[3] The fact that a swap has both a pricing curve and discount curve illustrates one of the ways interest rate derivatives are so interesting (so to speak). Interest rates are used in two very different ways: first to provide a spot price of the underlier, and second for the purpose of discounting cash flows.

do we calculate the average of some number of daily rate fixings (averaging)? If it is averaging, how far back to we go when collecting rate fixings to average? Five days, one month, one year?

- **Amortizing:** Will the notional, or swap principal, remain unchanged over the life of the trade (nonamortizing), or will it change (amortizing)? If amortizing, how exactly will it change from period to period? Straight-line, mortgage-style, custom?

Leg-Level Features

Leg-level features are typically specified separately for each leg of a trade, and they often differ between legs:

- **Tenor:** At what frequency will cash flows occur? Three-month tenors, in which cash flows or coupons occur every three months, are quite common.
- **Coupon date:** On which day of the month are cash flows exchanged? In other words, on which day of the month does one coupon period end and another begin? And in what month will the first coupon occur?
- **Stubs:** In many cases, the effective date of a trade differs from the coupon date. Or the period of time between the effective date and first coupon date does not equal the tenor of the trade. In either case, we are left with *stub* periods, or periods of time less than the tenor. We can handle these in one of two ways. We can treat this like a regular coupon and just calculate interest on some number of days less than a regular period. We call these "short stubs." Or we can add the stub to the first regular coupon and accrue on some number of days greater than a regular coupon. We call these "long stubs." Note, too, that stubs can occur at the end of a trade, where again we can treat them as either long or short.
- **Day basis:** To apply an annual interest rate to an accrual period whose length is less than or greater than one year, we need a *day fraction* for converting the rate. Which day basis convention shall we use? Common selections here are actual/365, actual/360, 30/360, and others.

- **Calendar:** Of all the days between the effective date and maturity date of our swap, which shall we consider business days? Do we agree on one calendar, such as New York? Or a blended calendar, such as New York + London?
- **Adjustment:** If a meaningful date such as a coupon payment date should fall on a nonbusiness day, should we use that date in our interest calculation? Or should we select a nearby date according to one of the business day adjustment conventions such as previous or modified following?

Fixed-Leg Features

There's really only one attribute unique to the fixed leg, but it's an important one:

- **Fixed rate:** What is the rate of interest, never to change over the life of the swap, for the calculation of cash flows on the fixed leg? If we had to choose just one attribute of a swap, this would be the single most important one, known also as the *swap rate*. Analogous to the delivery price in a forward, it is often the last attribute calculated, chosen so that the initial value of the swap is zero to both parties.

Floating-Leg Features

The following features pertain to the cash flows calculated with a changing rate of interest:

- **Rate index:** What is the source of a yield curve for the calculation of accruals on coupon dates? This yield curve is known as the pricing curve (to distinguish it from the discount curve, which may or may not reference the same index); the most common rate index for swap pricing curves is LIBOR.
- **Reset offset:** For an accrual period commencing on some given day, which business day's rate fixing should we use? For example, if an accrual period commences on a Thursday, do we use the LIBOR fixing from Tuesday? This attribute is expressed as a simple integer indicating a number of days preceding the start of the accrual period, and for LIBOR is typically two days.

- **Reset calendar:** When the reset offset is something other than 0, and if we find ourselves needing to move some number of days away from the accrual start date, which of those days should we consider business days? What calendar should we follow?
- **Reset adjustment:** If we land on a nonbusiness day when choosing a rate-fixing date in accordance with the reset offset and reset calendar, what should we do? Which convention do we follow? Previous? Modified following?

Now, keep in mind that swaps are over-the-counter instruments and the two swap parties can add whatever additional features they can agree on, tossing ISDA definitions out the window if they'd like, making them just as complex and weird as you can imagine. But this section sums up the definitions used by the vast majority of swap users.

More Binomial Option Pricing

In this appendix, we'll extend the basic concepts we introduced in Chapter 10, "Pricing Options." We'll walk through the nitty-gritty of pricing an option using a multistep binomial tree, present formulas for option pricing with a binomial tree, and demonstrate the important concept of risk-neutral pricing using the binomial tree.

A MULTISTEP TREE

In Figure C-1, we've constructed a two-step binomial tree using the same basic setup as our one-step tree in Chapter 10. Now we start on the right side by determining the option value at each of the end nodes. That's easy. It's just max(0, $S - K$) applied with three different values of S (i.e., the stock price of ZED).

FIGURE C-1

Two-Step Binomial Tree

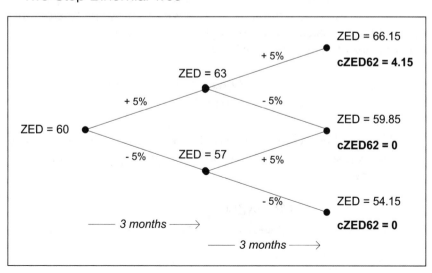

Now we work our way to the left and calculate the value of cZED62 at each of the two nodes in the middle. Look at the node where ZED equals $63. We have here a value for the underlier and the value of the option under two different future prices—just what we need to solve an option price with a one-step tree. First we calculate delta:

$$\Delta 66.15 - 4.15 = \Delta 59.85 - 0$$
$$\Delta 66.15 - \Delta 59.85 = 4.15$$
$$\Delta(66.15 - 59.85) = 4.15$$
$$\Delta = 0.6587$$

Next we need the portfolio value in three months, when ZED is trading for $66.15 or $59.85. We need only consider one case, but let's do both anyway:

$$P_{t=3mo} = \Delta 66.15 - 4.15$$
$$= (0.6587)66.15 - 4.15$$
$$= 39.42$$
$$P_{t=3mo} = \Delta 59.85$$
$$= (0.6587)59.85$$
$$= 39.42$$

Recall what we need next? The present value of the portfolio value. Same math as before, but notice we multiply the rate by one-quarter (0.25) instead of one-half (0.5) because our period is now one-quarter of a year (three months):

$$P_0 = 39.42e^{-(0.04)(0.25)}$$
$$= 39.03$$

Now we have values for two of three components of our portfolio and can solve for the third. Don't forget the price of ZED is $63 at this node:

$$RP = \Delta ZED - cZED62$$
$$39.03 = 0.6587(63) - cZED62$$

$$\text{cZED62} = 41.50 - 39.03$$
$$\text{cZED62} = 2.47$$

Now we need an option value for the node where ZED equals $57. First we calculate delta:

$$\Delta 59.85 - 0 = \Delta 54.55 - 0$$
$$\Delta 59.85 - \Delta 54.55 = 0$$
$$\Delta(59.85 - 54.55) = 0$$
$$\Delta = 0$$

Then we need the portfolio value in three months, when ZED is trading for either $59.85 or $54.55:

$$P_{t=3\text{mo}} = \Delta 59.85 - 0$$
$$= (0)59.85 - 0$$
$$= 0$$
$$P_{t=3\text{mo}} = \Delta 54.55 - 0$$
$$= (0)54.55$$
$$= 0$$

The portfolio in either case is worth 0. And the present value of 0 is, of course, 0:

$$P_0 = 0e^{-(0.04)(0.25)}$$
$$= 0$$

Again we have values for two of three components of our portfolio and can solve for the third:

$$\text{RP} = \Delta \text{ZED} - \text{cZED62}$$
$$0 = 0(57) - \text{cZED62}$$
$$\text{cZED62} = 0 - 0$$
$$\text{cZED62} = 0$$

The value of the option at this node is 0. Our tree now is shown in Figure C-2.

We're left now with a single one-step tree. The math should be familiar now, so we'll jump right to the solution. The completed tree looks like Figure C-3.

This tells us the option price of $1.47 is correct no matter which of the four possible price paths is actually taken by the underlier.

FIGURE C-2

Nearly Complete Tree

FIGURE C-3

Complete Tree

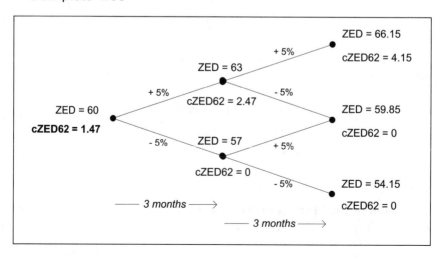

Any other price would allow arbitrage. This price is clearly different from the $2.53 we calculated with a one-step tree. But we like it better—that is, we think it's closer to the real value—because the price path model is (ever so slightly) better using a two-step tree than a one-stepper.

Now, a 3-period tree provides 8 possible paths, so we'll like a price from one of those trees even more. A 4-period tree allows for 16 possible paths, and so on. You can see where I'm going. The algebra works, no matter how big the tree. And by using a tree with sufficiently short and numerous branches, we can model a very large number of possible price paths. And the number of paths grows very quickly (it's just 2 raised to the number of steps). So a 20-period tree allows for over a million paths, and a 30-period tree more than a billion. Think of it this way: Nobody can predict the actual future price path of an underlying asset between now and some time in the future. But if we construct a model with a billion possible price paths, odds start getting pretty good that the actual price path will be one of, or very close to one of, those billion. So an option price that works for any of those billion price paths is a mighty good one.

GENERAL BINOMIAL FORMULAS

First, let's summarize in a key the symbols we've seen so far. Algebra is all about representing things with symbols, right?

S = stock price

K = strike price

C = call option value to the long party

u = 1 + stock return after an up move

d = 1 + stock return after a down move

S_u = stock price after an up move = $S \times u$

S_d = stock price after a down move = $S \times d$

C_u = call value after an up move = $\max(0, S_u - K)$

C_d = call value after a down move = $\max(0, S_d - K)$

$\Delta = (C_u - C_d)/(S_u - S_d)$

ΔS = delta shares of stock = $(C_u - C_d)/(u - d)$

r = risk-free interest rate

t = time between steps in years

e = Euler's number = 2.7182 . . .

B = borrowed money in synthetic option position

$\qquad$ = $(dC_u - uC_d)/[e^{rt}(u - d)]$

And to this mix, we need to add the symbol p for pseudoprobability of an up move, or uptick. Now *pseudo* just means "sorta" or "not really, but it'll work." As we'll see when we explore risk neutrality in this appendix, we're working now in a world without risk. It doesn't matter whether stock prices go up or down, so we don't need real probability, just as we don't need a real interest rate. But for the math to work, we do need an interest rate for discounting, for which we use the risk-free rate. And we also need a probability, for which we use this p:

p = pseudoprobability of an up move = $(e^{rt} - d)/(u - d)$

$1 - p$ = pseudoprobability of a down move = $(u - e^{rt})/(u - d)$

Now recall how we expressed the value of a call option using the components of a synthetic option or leveraged stock position:

$$cZED62 = \Delta ZED - B$$

or:

$$C = \Delta S - B$$

It turns out we can apply yet some more algebra and convert this expression into the rather simple Formula C.1 for the value of a call option. You ready? Refer back to the symbol key, take it slowly, and this might not seem so bad at all:

$C = \Delta S - B$

$\quad = (C_u - C_d)/[(u - d)] - (dC_u - uC_d)/[e^{rt}(u - d)]$

$\quad = (C_u - C_d)e^{rt}(u - d)/(u - d)e^{rt}(u - d) -$
$\qquad (dC_u - uC_d)(u - d)/(u - d)e^{rt}(u - d)$

$\quad = [(C_u - C_d)e^{rt}(u - d) - (dC_u - uC_d)(u - d)]/(u - d)e^{rt}(u - d)$

$$= [(C_u - C_d)e^{rt} - (dC_u - uC_d)]/e^{rt}(u - d)$$
$$= [e^{rt}C_u - e^{rt}C_d + uC_d - dC_u]/e^{rt}(u - d)$$
$$= [e^{rt}C_u - dC_u + uC_d - e^{rt}C_d]/e^{rt}(u - d)$$
$$= [(e^{rt} - d)C_u]/[e^{rt}(u - d)] + [(u - e^{rt})C_d]/[e^{rt}(u - d)]$$
$$= e^{-rt}[(e^{rt} - d)/(u - d)]C_u + e^{-rt}[(u - e^{rt})/(u - d)]C_d$$
$$= e^{-rt}pC_u + e^{-rt}(1 - p)C_d$$
$$= e^{-rt}[pC_u + (1 - p)C_d]$$

Thus, the call value from a one-step binomial tree is

$$C = e^{-rt}[pC_u + (1 - p)C_d] \qquad \text{(Formula C.1)}$$

The formula for puts—Formula C.2—is darn near identical:

$$P = \text{put option value to the long party}$$
$$P_u = \text{put value after an up move} = \max(0, K - S_u)$$
$$P_d = \text{put value after a down move} = \max(0, K - S_d)$$
$$P = e^{-rt}[pP_u + (1 - p)P_d] \qquad \text{(Formula C.2)}$$

For a two-step tree, we have another end node (which you can reach by two different paths, recall) to consider. Take a look at Figure C-4.

To price each of C_u and C_d, we re-express the formula using the appropriate node names:

$$C_u = e^{-rt}[pC_{uu} + (1 - p)C_{ud}]$$
$$C_d = e^{-rt}[pC_{ud} + (1 - p)C_{dd}]$$

And we already know that

$$C = e^{-rt}[pC_u + (1 - p)C_d]$$

By merging these three formulas—that is, by replacing C_u and C_d in the one-step formula with their respective formulas, we arrive at a single Formula C.3 for the price of a call using a two-step binomial tree:

FIGURE C-4

Two-Step Tree

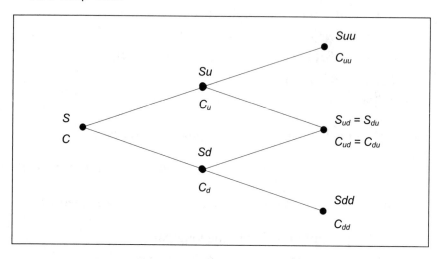

$$C = e^{-rt}[pC_u + (1 - p)C_d]$$
$$= e^{-rt}[pe^{-rt}(pC_{uu} + (1 - p)C_{ud}) + (1 - p)e^{-rt}(pC_{ud} + (1 - p)C_{dd})]$$
$$= e^{-rt}[pe^{-rt}pC_{uu} + pe^{-rt}(1 - p)C_{ud} + (1 - p)e^{-rt}pC_{ud} +$$
$$(1 - p)e^{-rt}(1 - p)C_{dd}]$$
$$= e^{-rt}[e^{-rt}(ppC_{uu} + p(1 - p)C_{ud} + (1 - p)pC_{ud} +$$
$$(1 - p)(1 - p)C_{dd})]$$
$$= e^{-rt}[e^{-rt}(p^2C_{uu} + 2p(1 - p)C_{ud} + (1 - p)^2C_{dd})]$$
$$C = e^{-2rt}(p^2C_{uu} + 2p(1 - p)C_{ud} + (1 - p)^2C_{dd}) \qquad \text{(Formula C.3)}$$

So what is the call option formula using an n-step tree where n is any positive integer? We'll not derive the formula (i.e., show you how we get it), but we will take a look at it, once I introduce more symbols:

$$n = \text{number of steps to a node}$$
$$j = \text{number of up moves to a node}$$
$$n - j = \text{number of down moves to a node}$$
$$a = \text{minimum number of up moves before option}$$
$$\text{is in the money}$$

And here are some math functions we'll use along the way:

Symbol	Definition	Example
$n!$	n factorial	$5! = 5 \times 4 \times 3 \times 2 \times 1 = 120$
	$n! = n(n - 1)(n - 2) \ldots (2)(1)$	
$\sum\limits_{x=1}^{n}$	Summation of $x_1, x_2, x_3, \ldots x_n$	

Now here is the expression for determining the number of paths from the starting node to some node $C_{u^j d^{(n - j)}}$, that is, a node n steps away where you went up j times and down $n - j$ times:

$$\frac{n!}{j!(n - j)!}$$

And the value of a call option, from an n-step binomial tree, is given by Formula C.4:

$$C = e^{-rt} \sum_{j = a}^{n} \left(\frac{n!}{j!(n - j)!} \right) p^j (1 - p)^{n - j} [u^j d^{(n - j)} s] -$$

$$e^{-rt} \sum_{j = a}^{n} \left(\frac{n!}{j!(n - j)!} \right) p^j (1 - p)^{n - j} K \qquad \text{(Formula C.4)}$$

THE RISK NEUTRALITY THING

The appearance of the "pseudoprobability of an uptick" factor in our valuation formulas illustrates one of the basic ideas behind how we price derivatives, and it's a very, very important one: the value of an option is its expected payoff in a risk-neutral world, discounted at the risk-free rate. (This is true for all derivatives, by the way, not just options.) A risk-neutral world is one in which investors are neither risk-averse nor risk-inclined. Unlike investors in the real world, investors here require no compensation for risk.

An expected value is just a future value times the probability of it occurring. Say you put a $100 wager on red at a roulette wheel for the chance to win double your bet if the wheel stops on a red number. Say half the numbers are red, so there's a 50 percent chance of your winning $200. The expected future value of your "investment" is $100. Yippee.[1]

The risk-neutrality thing applies both to binomial option pricing and to Black-Scholes. If this risk-neutrality thing is correct, we should be able to (1) use the risk-free rate to calculate a future value of the underlying stock in a risk-neutral world, (2) deduce a probability factor from that future stock value, (3) use this probability to calculate an expected value of the option, given its strike price, and (4) discount this option value using the risk-free rate—to get the same option value we got in a world not risk-neutral using no-arbitrage arguments.

Let's see if we can do that with the binomial tree. Recall the setup from the one-step binomial tree example, depicted in Figure C-5. The stock ZED trades for $60 and will go up or down by 10 percent in six months, to $66 or $54. A 62-strike call option will be worth $4 if it goes up and 0 if it goes down.

What's the value of the option? The expected value of the stock is its future value using the risk-free rate of 6 percent. From that, we can back out a probability like so:

$$66p + 54(1 - p) = 60e^{(0.06)(0.5)}$$
$$12p = 61.8273 - 54$$
$$p = 0.6523$$

FIGURE C-5

One-Step Tree

We can assert now that there is a probability of 0.6523 that the call option will be worth $4 in six months, and a probability of 0.3477 that it will be worth 0. We know enough now to calculate the expected value of the option:

$$(0.6523 \times 4) + (0.3477 \times 0) = \$2.6091$$

Discounting using the risk-free rate, we get the risk-neutral valuation:

$$2.6091e^{-(0.06)(0.5)} = 2.5320$$

The value of the call option using risk-neutral valuation is $2.53, the same result we got using no-arbitrage arguments.

BIBLIOGRAPHY

Baird, Allen Jan. 1993. *Option Market Making: Trading and Risk Analysis for the Financial and Commodity Option Markets.* Wiley.

Bernstein, Peter L. 1992. *Capital Ideas: The Improbable Origins of Modern Wall Street.* Macmillan / The Free Press.

Bodie, Zvi, Alex Kane, and Alan J. Marcus. 1996. *Investments.* 3rd ed. Irwin.

Boyle, Phelim, and Fiedhlim Boyle. 2001. *Derivatives: The Tools That Changed Finance.* Risk Waters Group.

Caouette, John B., Edward I. Altman, and Paul Narayanan. 1998. *Managing Credit Risk: The Next Great Financial Challenge.* Wiley.

Clewlow, Les, and Chris Strickland. 1998. *Implementing Derivatives Models.* Wiley.

Cox, John C., and Mark Rubenstein. 1985. *Options Markets.* Prentice-Hall.

Culp, Christopher L., and Merton H. Miller. 1995. "Metallgesellschaft and the Economics of Synthetic Storage." *Journal of Applied Corporate Finance* (Winter).

Gonick, Larry, and Woollcott Smith. 1993. *The Cartoon Guide to Statistics.* HarperCollins.

Hull, John C. 1997. *Options, Futures and Other Derivatives.* 3rd ed. Prentice Hall.

———. 2009. "The Credit Crunch of 2007: What Went Wrong? Why? What Lessons Can Be Learned?" Draft Paper. http://www.rotman.utoronto.ca/~hull/DownloadablePublications/CreditCrunch.pdf.

Hull, John, and Alan White. 2000. "Valuing Credit Default Swaps I: No Counterparty Default Risk." University of Toronto.

Jarrow, Robert, and Stuart Turnbull. 1999. *Derivative Securities: The Complete Investor's Guide.* Thomson Learning.

Jorion, Philippe. 2001. *Financial Risk Manager Handbook: 2001–2002.* Wiley.

Kolb, Robert W., and James A. Overdahl. 2003. *Financial Derivatives.* 3rd ed. Wiley Finance.

Kuprianov, Anatoli. 1995. "Derivatives Debacles: Case Studies of Large Losses in Derivatives Markets." *Federal Reserve Bank of Richmond Economic Quarterly* 81/4 (Fall).

Lewis, Michael. 2010. *The Big Short: Inside the Doomsday Machine.* Norton.

Lownstein, Roger. 2010. *The End of Wall Street.* Penguin.

Lynagh, Stephen, and Sanjiv R. Das. 1997. "Enron Corp. Credit Sensitive Notes." Harvard Business School. Case Study 9-297-099.

McDonald, Robert L. 2003. *Derivatives Markets.* Addison Wesley / Pearson Education.

Morris, Charles R. 2008. *The Two Trillion Dollar Meltdown: Easy Money, High Rollers, and the Great Credit Crash.* Public Affairs.

Natenberg, Sheldon. 1994. *Option Volatility and Pricing: Advanced Trading Strategies and Techniques.* McGraw-Hill.

Neftci, Salih N. 1996. *An Introduction to the Mathematics of Financial Derivatives.* Academic Press.

Newbold, Paul. 1995. *Statistics for Business and Economics.* 4th ed. Prentice-Hall.

Schwartz, Robert J., and Clifford W. Smith Jr., eds. 1997. *Derivatives Handbook: Risk Management and Control.* Wiley.

Steinherr, Alfred. 1998. *Derivatives: The Wild Beast of Finance.* Wiley.

INDEX

Michael Durbin is a former professional bowler inducted into the PBA Hall of Fame in 1984 but is not, alas, the author of this book, which is too bad, because a few tips on avoiding gutter balls would have certainly livened things up. The Michael Durbin who actually did write this book is a sometimes author, adjunct professor, and financial systems development consultant who has spent the bulk of his career thus far managing the design and development of software systems for the pricing and trading of financial derivatives.

That work began on the MOATS[1] team at the old First Chicago Capital Markets, where he discovered his possession of the rare gene that makes one actually enjoy working with interest rate mathematics and fixed-income derivatives, before moving down the street and up the Sears Tower to Bank of America's massive swaps desk, where he helped morph the giant and overly complicated IRP system into the giant and overly complicated Advantage system. In 2003, enticed by the prospect of branching into options and eating lunches catered by Wolfgang Puck,[2] he moved to a new job a few blocks up Franklin Street at the Citadel Investment Group, where he managed projects that led to the creation of a high-frequency options-trading system reportedly poised to take over the world any day now.

In 2005 he moved his family to Chapel Hill, North Carolina, to direct the development of an automated options market-making and proprietary trading operation for the Blue Capital Group—managing developers, securing trading rights and colocation space, dealing with compliance, etc.—and to develop a taste for vinegar-based barbecue sauce. While hanging out in the mild and enviable climes of the Carolina Piedmont, he also had the great

---

[1] Mother Of All Trading Systems, managed by the one-of-a-kind Kurt Phillips-Zabel.

[2] This is true. Three meals a day plus snacks anytime, and a Häagen-Dazs ice cream sundae cart they would literally drive to the desk of any employee unable to walk from overeating.

opportunity to teach derivatives as an adjunct professor at the business schools of both Duke University and the University of North Carolina–Chapel Hill, where only once or twice he showed up for class wearing the wrong shade of blue. There is more about Michael Durbin (the author, not the bowler) at michaelpdurbin.com.